Troublesome Border

A PROFMEX Monograph

This book uses conflict as a unifying theme to examine historical and contemporary relationships in the U.S.-Mexico borderlands. Well into the twentieth century, Mexico and the United States faced many troublesome issues at the border that often erupted into armed confrontation. Settling the final boundary between the two countries in itself caused long-term contentiousness, leaving a legacy of bitterness on both sides, but particularly in Mexico. Unauthorized armed incursions from the United States into Mexico for the purpose of fomenting revolution and detaching land from the latter country likewise created serious friction. The border partitioned a distinguishable geographic and cultural region inhabited by Indians and Mexicans, creating untold predicaments for both groups. Indian raids across the border became a source of international strife until the 1880s. For Mexicans who remained south of the boundary as well as for those who became Mexican Americans by virtue of their incorporation into the United States, the border shaped frontier life-styles that differed markedly from those of the mainstream societies in each nation. After discussing each of these themes, the author provides an overview of current-day border issues. The book concludes with general comments that place the U.S.-Mexico border experience in perspective.

Oscar J. Martínez

Troublesome Border

The University of Arizona Press
Tucson

THE UNIVERSITY OF ARIZONA PRESS

Copyright © 1988
The Arizona Board of Regents
All Rights Reserved

This book was set in 10/12 Baskerville.
Manufactured in the U.S.A.

Library of Congress Cataloging-in-Publication Data

Martínez, Oscar J. (Oscar Jáquez), 1943–
Troublesome Border.

(Profmex monograph series)
Bibliography: p.
Includes index.
1. Mexican-American Border Region—History.
2. Mexican-American Border Region.   I. Title.   II. Series.
F786.M42 1988   979   87-34294
ISBN 0-8165-1033-4 (alk. paper)

British Library Cataloguing in Publication data are available.

To Jamie, Gabriel, Daniel, David, and Andres

CONTENTS

Maps

PREFACE

This book is about conflict in the U.S.-Mexico border region. My intent is not to present a comprehensive history of that subject but rather to examine selected topics that illuminate past and contemporary relationships in the borderlands. I have chosen conflict as the unifying theme for the somewhat diverse chapters presented here because so much of the interaction between the two countries and among the different ethnic groups in the area has been characterized by contentiousness. I do not wish to suggest, however, that conflict has governed the lives of border people. Far from that, peaceful relations have prevailed over the course of history. Yet strife has been a persistent fact of life in the region, and my interest is in identifying its roots and in tracing some of the ways it has manifested itself over time.

The idea for this book occurred to me some years ago when I was preparing to teach a course on the history of the U.S.-Mexico border at the University of Texas at El Paso. As I searched the literature for background information, I became aware of the myriad controversies that existed at the frontier. I found numerous works on conflict and many other border topics, but few attempts had been made to synthesize or to interpret events and processes. Recently some studies have appeared that offer historical overviews of the region, but the emphases are different from what is found here.[1] My purpose is to examine border history from various perspectives and to trace problems that confront border society today. Thus this is a topical history, rather than a traditional chronological treatment. If offers an alternative, nontraditional way to examine some of the complexities of border history.

Part of the volume was written during 1981–82, while I was a fellow at the Center for Advanced Study in the Behavioral Sciences (CASBS) at Stanford, California. I gratefully acknowledge the financial support provided by the CASBS, the National Research Council, the Andrew W. Mellon Foundation, and the National Endowment for the Humanities. I am especially grateful to the staff at the CASBS for providing editorial, library, secretarial, and word-processing assistance, but most of all for making my stay at Stanford exceedingly pleasant and memorable. It would take a page to list those at the CASBS who extended kindness and help to me and my family; to all, *muchísmas gracias*. Anne Holder, Larry McConville, and James W. Wilkie provided valuable editorial suggestions, which have improved the work in numerous ways. Finally, I thank the staff of the Center for Inter-American and Border Studies at the University of Texas at El Paso, including Carmen García, Mary Mendoza, Nancy Gavaldón, Rose Torres, and Isabel Robles, for assistance in preparing the manuscript for publication.

Troublesome Border

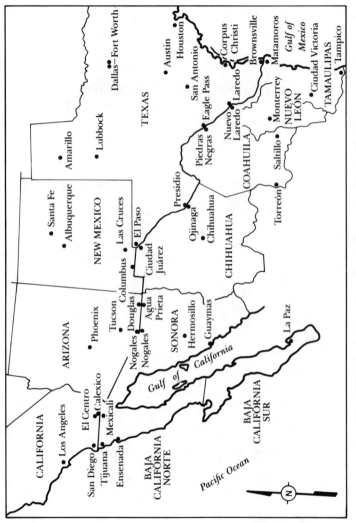

The U.S.-Mexico border region. Drawn by Linda Marston.

Introduction

A recently published book characterized the U.S.-Mexico border as a region that "has never known a placid year since it emerged from the Mexican War of 1848," and a "real trouble zone" in contemporary society.[1] That perception is widely shared among Americans, who have long associated the border strip between the Texas Gulf and the Pacific with international disputes, banditry, racial strife, uncontrolled illegal migration, large-scale smuggling of drugs, corrupt behavior of officials, and a haven for unassimilated and separatist-prone people (Mexican Americans, or Chicanos).[2] Preoccupation with the border situation reached a new high in the 1970s and 1980s, as repeated stories in the U.S. national print media and network television well indicate. The level of apprehension over undocumented migration, by far the most controversial border issue, is perhaps best illustrated by the following remark made by President Ronald Reagan: "The simple truth is that we've lost control of our own borders and no nation can do that and survive."[3]

Americans are largely unaware that Mexicans also view their northern border with concern, and at times even alarm. Historically, the northern zone has been seen as having economic interests, customs, and traditions vastly different from other parts of Mexico. Border communities, such as Ciudad Juárez and Tijuana, have long been subjected to heavy criticism from Mexico City and other interior areas for their close ties to the United States, a country viewed with apprehension and suspicion by the Mexican citizenry. Frontier Mexicans have been accused of succumbing to *agringamiento* (Americanization) and of focusing too much of their energies on foreign-oriented economic activities. Border tourism in particular has come under attack for allegedly cultivating a permissive moral climate in order to lure American dollars. In recent years, officials at all levels of government have become concerned over the potential for social unrest at the border owing to widespread social problems like poverty and unemployment in the urban centers adjacent to the boundary. Indeed, since the outbreak of the national economic crisis in Mexico in 1982, street demonstrations over a variety of social issues have escalated at the frontier.[4] Moreover, in the electoral arena, residents of Chihuahua City and Ciudad Juárez in 1983 strongly manifested their displeasure with the ruling party, the Partido Revolucionario Institucional (PRI), by electing candidates of the opposition party, the Partido Acción Nacional (PAN), as mayors of the two cities. In 1985, the people of Juárez shocked the PRI again by electing three PAN members to the federal Congress. To the powerful PRI, these unprecedented losses at the ballot box conjured images of another *norteño* (northern) rebellion[5]; by 1986 the ruling party had taken political control of Chihuahua again through massive electoral fraud.

Thus, whether viewed from the north or south, the border is perceived as a trouble spot. Yet what often appears to both Americans and Mexicans as a breakdown of institutions, social systems, and legal structures at the Rio Grande is in many respects the normal functioning of the border. By nature, border zones, especially those that are far removed from the core, spawn independence, rebellion, cultural deviation, disorder, and even lawlessness. The U.S.-Mexico border fits within that universal scheme.

The history of countless nations illustrates how borderland regions frequently depart from the norms of interior zones and how they develop institutional patterns and interests quite separate from those of the centers of power. Isolation, weak institutions, lax administration, and a different economic orientation prompt people on the periphery to develop homemade approaches to their problems and unconventional means of carrying on mutually beneficial relationships across an international boundary.[6] People on the U.S.-Mexico border view the boundary, and the function it is supposed to serve, in terms fundamentally different from those of their compatriots in interior regions. If national laws appear unjust or are viewed as impractical in a border context, it becomes culturally acceptable to work around them or ignore them altogether. Lacking an educated understanding of the unique conditions at the periphery, the mainstream society is constantly irritated at the deviant behavior found at the border and is perpetually concerned about the problems the zone generates for the nation-state. Indeed, the historical record confirms that the border has been a persevering headache for the both countries, although the degree of aggravation over the years has depended on the nature of the issues under dispute (Table I.1.).

Table I.1
Selected Border Conflict Issues, with Periods of Intensity and
Relative Importance at National, Regional, and Local Levels
(Conflict levels: 1 = low, 2 = moderate, 3 = occasionally intense, 4 = intense

Conflict Issue	Period of Intensity	National		Regional		Local	
		USA	Mex.	USA	Mex.	USA	Mex.
Territorial integrity							
Boundary delimitation[a]	1821–54	4	4	4	4	2	2
Boundary maintenance[b]	1884–1963	2	4			2–3	2–3
Filibustering	1820s–1900s	2	4	2	4	2	2–3
Indian depredations	1840s–1880s	4	4	4	4	4	4
Irredentism[c]	1915–16	2–4	1	4	1	4	1
Economic integrity							
Trade protectionism	1848–Present	1	2	1	1	2–3	2–3
Mexican free zones	1848–1905; 1937–Present	2	2	1	2	2–3	1
Smuggling	1848–Present	2–3	2	1–2	1	1	1
Sociocultural issues							
Banditry	1848–1920	2–3	2–3	4	4	4	4
Racial strife	1848–Present	1–2	2	2–4	1	2–4	1–2
Land claims[d]	1836–1900s	1–2	1–2	2–4	1	2–4	1–2
Migration	1900–Present	4	2	4	1–2	2–4	1–3
Environmental issues							
Water allocation	1890–Present	2	3	1	1	2–3	2–3
Water contamination	1950s–Present	2–3	3	1	1	2–3	3
Air pollution	1960s–Present	2	2	1	1	3	2
Sewage spills	1970s–Present	2	1	2	1	4	3
Boundary flow							
Transportation	1970s–Present	1	1	1	1	2–3	2–3
Fences, towers, etc.	1930s–Present	1–2	2–3	1	1	2–3	2–4
Bridge incidents	1920s–Present	1–2	1–2	1–3	1–3	2–4	2–4

[a] Process by which the boundary was established, that is, conflict over territoriality.
[b] Process of maintaining the physical stability of the boundary, for example, control of the shifting Rio Grande.
[c] Attempt by some frontier Mexicans to promote rebellion in south Texas against established Anglo authority for the purpose of establishing a new political order.
[d] On the U.S. side, land claims involved Chicanos/Hispanos' attempts to assert or reclaim rights to Spanish and Mexican land grants, especially in New Mexico.

Essential to understanding the many conflicts that the United States and Mexico have experienced at their common border is an awareness of the process by which the boundary was determined and the many difficulties that both countries have encountered in preserving the integrity of the dividing line. This theme is the focus of Chapters 1 and 2. In the history of the relations between the two nations, no other issue has caused so much controversy, bitterness, and outright confrontation. Border delimitation is, of course, an age-old problem in the relations between neighboring states. For centuries nations have competed and fought over territorial possessions, and in cases where strong countries abut weak ones, the latter commonly have had to yield lands to ambitious or aggressive neighbors. History demonstrates that few boundaries have been created as a result of peaceful negotiations; power politics, military pressures, and warfare have been the determining factors in most cases.[7] Besides governmental attempts to enlarge the national domain by force, in many cases zealous citizens have, on their own, undertaken unlawful incursions intended to detach possessions of neighboring countries. Such was the experience of the United States and Mexico.

An issue related to the delimitation and maintenance of borders is the impact that those processes have on people who reside in what becomes the "borderlands." In the broadest sense, the U.S.-Mexico boundary partitioned a distinguishable geographic and cultural region inhabited by Indians and Mexicans. The consequences of that momentous development constitute the focus of Chapters 3, 4, and 5. Fundamentally the experience of these groups parallels that of other peoples in other parts of the world whose homelands have been partitioned by the redrawing of borders. Power politics, the driving force of border delimitation, has always had little regard for preexisting cultural entities that lie in territories targeted for partitioning. Throughout history the imposition of arbitrary boundaries has forced millions of people to migrate or to switch political loyalties, learn new languages, and function in alien cultural environments. Instances of natural ethnographical situations seriously disrupted by artificial borders abound in the African continent, and examples of culturally distinct populations absorbed against their will into alien sovereign-states through the process of territorial expansionism may be found almost anywhere in the world.[8] In the case of the Indians of northern Mexico and the U.S. Southwest, the infiltration of foreigners into their homelands began with the arrival of Spaniards in the sixteenth century. The establishment of the permanent international border in the mid-nineteenth century brought increased pressures from waves of Anglo-American and Mexican immigrants, but just as important, it imposed restrictions on the mobility of those Indians who lived in the vicinity of the line of demarcation. Unaccustomed to such restraints, certain tribes ignored the boundary altogether, triggering many local problems and seriously upsetting relations between the United States and Mexico.

For the Mexican-origin population, the new border brought a set of dilemmas and predicaments typical of groups who reside on the periphery of nation-states and who are subjected to international forces beyond their control. Mexican Americans, or Chicanos (those living permanently north of the border), and Mexicans (those living south of the border) felt deeply the impact of the boundary in the formation of lifestyles, attitudes, and cultural orientations. Although the border separated Mexican Americans politically from Mexico, physical proximity kept them tied to their roots culturally and socially. Those continuing links to the motherland shaped to a significant degree their marginality within American society. Their compatriots across the Rio Grande or on Mexican soil found themselves insulated from American political domination but not from economic and cultural influences; that reality, coupled with sheer geographic remoteness from the core of the nation, assured that the *norteños* and *fronterizos* (borderlanders) would develop societal patterns distinct from the rest of Mexico. Thus the presence of the border played a fundamental role in converting border Chicanos and Mexicans into entities that stood apart from the mainstream societies of each nation.

Those who negotiated the boundary in the 1840s could hardly have anticipated the human consequences of their decision. The Mexican government did attempt to maintain the integrity of the Rio Grande region by proposing that the line of demarcation be drawn to the north of that stream such that a buffer zone would shield the remaining Mexican frontier from further American advances. But it was the U.S. government that dictated the terms of the division of the northern Mexican territories, and the American negotiators, consumed by a spirit of aggressive expansionism, did not take into consideration how the local populations would fare. The American approach to determining the border with Mexico contrasted sharply with policies followed during the period of the formation of internal U.S. state and territorial boundaries, when the human factor received eminent consideration. During those earlier determinations, population centers were seen as nuclear areas, or cores, from which to calculate where boundaries would be drawn in outward directions at appropriate distances. Guided by the principle that boundaries should only separate people who were already living apart, boundary makers conscientiously avoided lines that would split naturally congregated populations. The drawing of state and territorial borders that resulted from the famous Compromise of 1850 well illustrates the weight assigned to the interests of people.[9] Unfortunately, Indians and Mexicans native to the U.S.-Mexico border area did not receive such considerations.

Chapter 6 examines border issues that are of contemporary concern to both nations, with emphasis on ecological problems, environmental pollution, and human conflict spawned by the intense binational interaction in the region. Fundamentally it is the boundary itself that acts as the agent of friction, given that it obstructs the normal movement of people and products. Because of the interference with the natural order of things, conflictive situations develop continuously. A related complication arises from the fact that the border communities have become increasingly crowded in recent decades, spawning intense competition for space and resources between the adjoining populations. Fortunately, these tension-generating circumstances at the frontier are well enough understood by local people, especially decision makers, and many conflicts are diffused through the use of time-tested informal mechanisms that often circumvent national laws. However, major problems that have an affect on interior zones are much harder to resolve informally because of overwhelming pressures that emanate from the core areas. International migration is such an issue. Federal officals, in their quest to "control" the border by stopping "invasions" of foreigners, dictate policies and make laws frequently detrimental to the welfare of the border communities. The constant struggle between local needs and national "interests" represents a basic element in the complex periphery-core heritage of the border frontier.

Viewed in the context of U.S.-Mexico relations, the border has occupied a preeminent place in countless disagreements and agreements entered into by the two countries. It is not an exaggeration to say that border issues have overshadowed all other binational concerns since the two neighbors began to negotiate with each other as independent nations. Over time, four distinct phases are apparent in the role played by the border in that bilateral relationship. The first phase began with the initial contact between Spain and England in contested territories of North America and ended with the signing of the Adams-Onís Treaty in 1819, which demarcated the line between the United States and New Spain. Those years produced an infiltration of Englishmen and Americans into Spanish territory, filibustering, and aggressive U.S. diplomacy calculated to alter the boundary. In the second phase, Mexico, after its successful drive for independence from Spain, assumed the challenge of containing the aggressive American advance on the northern frontier, but to no avail. Between the 1820s and early 1850s, the borderlands witnessed the Texas rebellion; the War of 1846–

48; and the signing of the border-altering Guadalupe Hidalgo and Gadsden treaties (1848 and 1853, respectively), both of which were highly favorable to the United States. The third phase, lasting from 1853 to 1920, saw chronic transboundary encounters that almost produced international warfare on numerous occasions. Intense nationalistic feelings arising out of continous violations of the integrity of the border combined with racial strife north of the Rio Grande to create an explosive climate in the border communities. Perhaps the most difficult era was the 1910s, when the Mexican Revolution raged throughout northern Mexico and spilled across the boundary. The fourth phase began in 1920 and continues to the present. By the end of the Revolution, friction over border violence ceased to be a major concern between the two countries. Armed invasions of each other's territory ended, significantly reducing nationalistic feelings that had reached fever proportions in the 1910s. Henceforth the two governments sought to solve their problems, many of which actually arose from disagreements unrelated to the border, through diplomatic negotiation rather than through direct confrontation. The new approach reflected profound changes that had transpired in the border region and in each nation's core by the first quarter of the twentieth century, including the end of U.S. territorial expansionism, reduced isolation of the frontier, the onset of modernization, a rise in population in the periphery, the founding of new border cities, the beginning of political stability in modern Mexico, and an improved framework for solving international conflicts.

CHAPTER 1

Whither the Boundary?

Fixing the limits of territorial jurisdiction between neighboring countries can be a complicated process that may involve conflict. A line that is not precisely and permanently determined at an early stage of contact may prove a source of contention for generations. Examples abound of nations that have engaged in prolonged and frustrated border negotiations, culminating in many cases in acrimonious diplomacy or outright warfare. The case of the United States and Mexico fits this pattern, although the problems associated with boundary delimitation and territorial sovereignty are largely historical rather than contemporary.

The lengthy story of the establishment of the U.S.-Mexico boundary began when Spain, France, and England competed for possessions in North America. Upon achieving independence, Mexico and the United States inherited the territorial disputes of their former colonial masters. Yet Anglo-Americans added a crucial ingredient to the process—national expansionism spurred by the ideology of "Manifest Destiny"—that triggered bitter and long-lasting struggles. Once set, the boundary's location significantly shaped the destiny of each nation. But many problems remained to be worked out because of the legacy of strife associated with the creation of that boundary and because the line itself had built-in imperfections. Numerous refinements of the border became necessary, and even in the second half of the twentieth century, Mexicans and Americans continued to address technical difficulties pertaining to boundary location.

EUROPEAN DISPUTATION AND
THE LOUISIANA CONTROVERSY

Penetration of North America by the European powers began in the early sixteenth century, when Spaniards explored lands from Florida to California and then established permanent colonies in a wide arc that became known as the "Spanish Borderlands." In the seventeenth century, the French began their expansion into the continent via the St. Lawrence River Valley to the Great Lakes region, the Ohio River Valley, and the Mississippi River Valley. The English, having established colonies on the Atlantic Coast, gradually moved west and south. Once contact was made on the frontier, the European powers maneuvered to establish territorial claims on the basis of prior explorations, occupation and alliances with Indians.

France constantly tested Spanish claims during the first half of the eighteenth century, particularly in Texas. The Spanish-French rivalry ended in 1763, when the Treaty of Paris removed the French from continental North America, allowing Spain to acquire Louisiana and to move its eastern boundary to the Mississippi River. But as France stepped out, England stepped in, threatening Spanish territory along the northern Mississippi and on the northern Pacific coast. Spain faced the monumental task of defending a vast frontier, but it responded by blazing new trails, establishing new settlements, and befriending Indians who could serve as a buffer against the English. When the United States won its political freedom, it continued the British tradition of contesting Spain's claims by probing deeply into the western lands.[1] The danger posed to Spain by the new nation is exemplified by the following statement, which appeared in an American publication in 1786:

Two thousand brave Americans . . ., animated with resentment against those troublesome neighbors [the Spaniards], and having in object the conquest of the richest country in the world, would complete in a few weeks, from their arrival at the Natchez, the reduction of West Florida and Louisiana, in spite of all the Spanish efforts to resist us. Another army of about the same number of men . . . would carry the war into the very heart of Mexico.[2]

The aggression advocated in that statement was more widely supported in the mid-nineteenth century, when the United States indeed "would carry the war into the very heart of Mexico."

In the late eighteenth century, competition for the Indian trade and for territorial control kept the Upper Mississippi and Upper Missouri valleys in constant turmoil. A pattern soon developed whereby Spaniards would move forward to repel the English/American penetration but would eventually be forced to fall back, resulting in gradual effective recession of the Spanish frontier.[3] As the nineteenth century began, the situation became more confused as Louisiana exchanged hands and Americans became confirmed expansionists. In 1800 Charles IV of Spain, in return for certain Italian lands, ceded Louisiana to Napoleon under a treaty that failed to specify the precise extent of the Louisiana territory. Three years later, Napoleon, unable to occupy his new acquisition and fearing that it might fall into English hands, sold Louisiana to the United States. This transaction followed precedent by leaving territorial limits very unclear, thus assuring a prolonged conflict between Americans and Spaniards.

Once the treaty of cession from France was signed, President Thomas Jefferson expressed the view that Louisiana included all western lands to the Rio Grande. Under this interpretation, old Spanish settlements such as San Antonio and Santa Fe had suddenly become American cities! To substantiate his claim on Texas, Jefferson cited French settlement of the Gulf coast in the seventeenth century and the trade monopoly given by Louis XIV to one of his subjects in 1712 over territory extending as far as New Mexico. Spain, armed with maps and other historical evidence, countered that France's presence had been ephemeral and that those areas had long been colonized, settled, and administered as Spanish territory.[4] When appeals and negotiation failed to advance the U.S. position, Jefferson pushed his claims by sending exploring parties beyond the Mississippi. The Lewis and Clark expedition of 1804 was particularly important in giving impetus to American hunger for more western land. In Lower Louisiana, a border conflict nearly triggered hostilities, but these were avoided through the signing of the Neutral Ground Agreement, which applied to the area between the Arroyo Hondo and the Sabine River. In West Florida, U.S. intrusions and seizure of land kept Spaniards constantly on the defensive. Anxiety was also high in New Mexico, where Americans repeatedly penetrated the marginal local defenses.[5]

For many years the United States persisted in its efforts to convince Spain to give up Texas, offering alternative borders from the Sabine to the Rio Grande. The dispute over the Louisiana border was finally settled in 1819, when Secretary of State John Quincy Adams and

Spanish minister Luis de Onís concluded a treaty that fixed the border between the United States and Spain along an irregular line beginning at the Sabine, proceeding north to the forty-second parallel, and from there to the Pacific. Spain acknowledged American ownership of East Florida and gave up claims on the Pacific north of the forty-second parallel. The Spaniards, however, refused to accede to Adam's demand that Texas be placed under U.S. jurisdiction. The treaty of 1819, which was ratified in 1821, concluded another phase of Spain's long struggle to hold onto its colonies.[6] Once again Spain's borderlands had been compressed, but American expansionists were still not satisfied. Feeling that the United States should not have given up Texas, to which Americans were "entitled" by "prior ownership," many would press for the "reannexation" of that province in subsequent years.

U.S. EXPANSION INTO MEXICO

With independence achieved in 1821, Mexico inherited from Spain the challenge of safeguarding the vast northern frontier. More population was needed to strengthen the defenses of California and Texas particularly. Following policies begun by Spain, Mexico in the 1820s allowed the entry into Texas of large numbers of American immigrants in order to further populate that sparsely settled province. Anxious to settle in the fertile Texas lands, those Americans expediently swore allegiance to Mexican laws, religion, and customs. Within a short time, Mexico would realize what a volatile situation it had unwittingly created within its own borders. Powerful forces would come together on the periphery and lead to armed conflict and loss of vast territories to the United States.

The isolation of Texas, New Mexico, and California from the rest of the nation, coupled with the inability of the central government to effectively govern and attend to the needs of norteños, fostered regionalist tendencies and even separatist movements.[7] That situation played into the hands of U.S. expansionists who coveted those provinces. Once the philosophy of Manifest Destiny took firm hold in the American mind, the outcome seemed clear: sooner or later the United States would detach Mexico's northern territories.

Mexico's apprehensions about threats to its northern frontier surfaced during initial contacts with American officials. From earlier Spanish reports, Mexicans knew that Americans desired to expand their borders to the west and south. Luis de Onís had warned as early as 1812 that the American government was prepared to use intrigue and to foment trouble in order to absorb Texas, Nuevo Santander,

Coahuila, New Mexico, part of Nueva Viscaya, and Sonora.[8] Another Spanish diplomat had stated in 1820 that Americans believed they were destined to extend their dominion "to the Isthmus of Panama, and . . . over all the regions of the new world." Mexican envoys to Washington quickly got a taste of the American territorial ambition reported earlier by the Spaniards. "Americans will be our own sworn enemies," stated a Mexican diplomat in 1822, "and foreseeing this we ought to treat them as such from the present day." In 1823 another Mexican official noted that the American desire for Texas was so strong that U.S. troops might soon be ordered there.[9]

Rather than attempting to acquire Texas by force, however, the United States in the 1820s and 1830s adopted a policy of seeking to persuade Mexico to sell that province along with adjacent territories, but Mexico proved unreceptive. Joel Poinsett, who would become the first U.S. minister to Mexico, first met as a private citizen in 1822 with a representative of Agustín de Iturbide's government to discuss the U.S. desire to alter the border created by the Adams-Onís treaty. When he became minister in 1825, Poinsett expressed the American interest in fixing the border so that New Mexico, California, and parts of Nuevo León, Coahuila, Sonora, and Baja California would be transferred to the United States. An unskilled diplomat, Poinsett simply aroused Mexican suspicions and made no headway. Two years later, under instructions from President John Quincy Adams, Poinsett offered to buy Texas. In 1829, one year after both countries had signed a treaty affirming the boundary established by the Adams-Onís Treaty of 1819, President Van Buren instructed Poinsett to renew the offer for Texas. Poinsett was to suggest options for a new border and was to offer up to $5 million for the line most advantageous to the United States.[10] Before he could act, however, Poinsett was relieved of his post, and for the next six years Anthony Butler represented the United States in Mexico. Butler, politically inept and an unprincipled expansionist, tried various means of acquiring Texas, including threats and the attempted bribery of high officials. By 1835 Mexico City had arranged for his recall.[11]

The use of dollar diplomacy to detach Texas from Mexico became moot in 1836, when Anglo-Texans, assisted by American funds and volunteers as well as some Mexican Texans, staged a successful insurrection against a Mexican government weakened by political instability and economic disarray. Americans widely assumed that the United States would soon annex the independent Republic of Texas, but sectional rivalry delayed that event until 1845. When the annexation occurred, Mexico interpreted it as a serious and hostile act by the United States, for it still considered Texas part of its national domain.

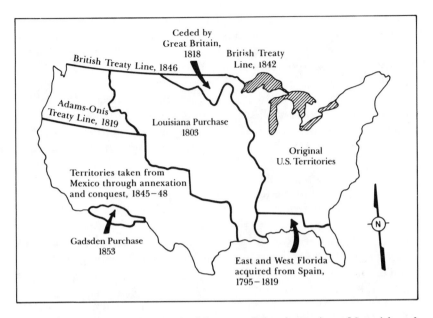

Territorial expansion of the United States and the absorption of Spanish and Mexican territories, 1795–1853. Drawn by Linda Marston.

By late 1845, relations between the two countries had seriously deteriorated. Not only had the United States taken Texas; it was also adamantly claiming that that province extended to the Rio Grande. In December, U.S. envoy John C. Slidell traveled to Mexico to discuss the boundary and to negotiate other matters, in particular pending damage claims submitted by Americans who had suffered losses in Mexico during periods of political instability.[12] The timing, however, was not favorable for such delicate bargaining. The Mexican government refused to receive Slidell, and President James Polk interpreted this refusal as an insult to the United States. By early 1846, Polk ordered U.S. troops to proceed to the Rio Grande, thereby setting the stage for direct confrontation. Mexico had tolerated American military control of territory north of the Nueces River while the status of Texas remained uncertain, but the advance across that stream constituted a flagrant act of aggression because Mexicans viewed Texas as extending no farther than the Nueces. On April 24, a skirmish between U.S. and Mexican troops resulted in the death of some Americans, and Polk immediately declared war on the grounds that Mexicans had "shed American blood upon American soil." Polk sidestepped the issue of American provocation: after all, U.S. troops had penetrated disputed territory. What is

more, even before the skirmish occurred, the United States had block-
aded the Rio Grande. For the next two years, the two countries fought
a war that ended with the occupation of Mexico and the signing of the
Treaty of Guadalupe Hidalgo in February 1848, by which Mexico
ceded half of its territory to the United States.[13]

The incident seized on by Polk as justification for declaring war illustrates the determination of American expansionists to sustain the claim
that the territory of the United States extended to the Rio Grande. The
declaration of the Texans in 1836 that their new republic extended that
far and the agreement signed that same year by President Antonio
López de Santa Anna while a prisoner at San Jacinto, which recognized
Texan jurisdiction to the Rio Grande, lent plausibility to that claim. To
expansionists, it hardly mattered that the Texas declaration constituted
a unilateral action, or that the Mexican Congress, the only treaty-
making entity under Mexico's constitution, repudiated the Santa Anna
agreement.[14] Polk chose to ignore the vast documentation that undermined his claim to the Rio Grande boundary, relying instead on the
weak and biased research of contemporary expansionists. Spain had
clearly defined the Nueces River as the southern border of Texas, and
Mexico had never given Texas jurisdiction over the strip between the
Nueces and the Rio Grande. Over the years, responsibility for the
Nueces strip rested with the state of Tamaulipas. Mexicans clearly had
physical possession of the disputed territory, with settlements well established on the north bank of the Rio Grande.[15] Most maps and atlases
published during the period, including European ones, showed Texas
extending no farther than the Nueces. Even Stephen F. Austin, the
"father of Texas," recognized that border in three maps he prepared
in the 1820s, and national leaders such as John Quincy Adams and
Andrew Jackson concurred.[16]

Many Americans who were knowledgeable about the border issue
condemned Polk for starting the war and then labeling Mexico as the
provocateur.[17] Members of Congress, editors, intellectuals, and other
influential Americans viewed Polk as a liar and as the instigator of national aggression calculated to end in the absorption of land belonging
to a weak neighbor. John C. Calhoun, who refused to vote on the war
bill, felt that Polk had created hysteria and had used stampede tactics
to obtain support. Calhoun believed that less than 10 percent of Congress would have voted with Polk if they had had time to examine the
documents closely. Abraham Lincoln felt Polk waged "a war of conquest." If expansionists had not coveted Mexico's northern provinces,
the dispute would have been settled "in an amicable manner," said Lincoln.[18] Once the war was in progress, however, many of the critics supported it, on the principle of "country first, right or wrong."

Dissent notwithstanding, the United States took the war deep into

Mexico, forcing its neighbor to negotiate a drastic change in the border. The draft treaty carried by U.S. State Department representative Nicholas Trist called for the acquisition of New Mexico, Upper California, and Lower California,[19] and for the establishment of American rights across the Isthmus of Tehuántepec. If Mexico agreed to these terms, $30 million would be paid; if not, lesser sums would be offered for less territory. By then Mexico was resigned to the loss of large amounts of northern land but struggled for the best terms possible under the circumstances. Thus Mexico rejected the Tehuántepec provision and insisted that in any transfer of territory in its northwest, a Mexican land connection between Lower California and Sonora be maintained. Mexico also proposed the creation of a neutral buffer zone between the Nueces and the Rio Grande, hoping thus to keep Americans at a distance and to exert better control of smuggling. Trist agreed to the buffer strip and to a line along the thirty-third parallel, which would have placed San Diego, California, in Mexican territory. Unhappy with those terms, Trist's superiors in Washington not only rejected the compromise but ordered Trist home. Disobeying orders, Trist remained in Mexico and continued negotiations, though he lacked the authority to do so. By December 1847, Mexico had withdrawn the buffer idea, instead proposing that a line be drawn one league north of the Rio Grande, but still insisting on the land connection that would keep San Diego in Mexican territory. Further talks followed as the pressure mounted on Mexico. Finally it agreed to the Rio Grande as the eastern half of the border and to a line across the desert from Paso del Norte (present-day Ciudad Juárez) to the Pacific as the western half, placing San Diego in U.S. hands.[20]

Exulting in the strong bargaining position of the United States, many expansionists criticized their government for seeking only a portion of Mexico. Instead, they argued, all of Mexico should be seized. Providence had willed the fall of Mexico, and higher duty demanded that Americans rescue the Mexicans from their "depraved" and "backward" state. Thus adherents of this view, affected by Manifest Destiny and the psychology of war and impatient with the prolonged negotiations, launched a crusade that seriously threatened the future existence of Mexico as a nation. Support for the "all Mexico" idea spread quickly among members of Polk's cabinet, in both chambers of Congress, in the military, in the press, and among other influential sectors of American society.[21] No doubt this ominous development motivated the Mexicans to "seize the opportunity" to part with their northern territories before Washington dismembered their country altogether. In February 1848, the negotiators signed a peace treaty, and Trist quickly forwarded it to Polk.

The unexpected arrival of that document, known as the Treaty of

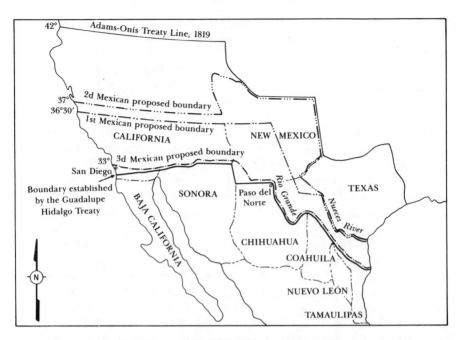

Mexican boundary proposals during the Treaty of Guadalupe Hidalgo boundary negotiations, 1847. Based on Prescott, *Boundaries and Frontiers*, 81. Drawn
by Linda Marston.

Guadalupe Hidalgo, abruptly halted the "all Mexico" drive. Despite
Trist's dubious status, Polk accepted the treaty since it fulfilled his original territorial desires, and U.S. domestic political considerations dictated a termination of the war. By then, serious resistance to the campaign to absorb Mexico had developed among Polk's political opponents, including people concerned about slavery, proponents of peace,
and race-conscious elements who had apprehensions about admitting
nonwhites to the Union. Southerners especially expressed anxiety over
the prospect of extending U.S. citizenship to dark-skinned Mexicans,
whom they deemed inferior and incapable of self-government. For
example, in his bitter denunciations of the "all Mexico" movement,
John C. Calhoun frequently buttressed his position with racial argu-
ments.[22]

Many historians are convinced that if negotiations had dragged on
much longer, the "all Mexico" movement would have prevailed. Fate
took an unexpected turn, however, and Mexico continued to exist.[23]
Nevertheless, American expansionism up to 1848 had cost Mexico half
of its territory, including Texas, New Mexico, Arizona, California,

Nevada, and Utah, and portions of Wyoming, Colorado, and Oklahoma. In part to mitigate the appearance of outright landgrabbing,
the United States paid Mexico $15 million for this vast domain and as-
sumed old claims of its citizens against Mexico, valued at just over $3
million. Never before or since has the United States negotiated a treaty
that yielded so much and cost so little. The border question, however,
was far from settled.

Article V of the Guadalupe Hidalgo Treaty provided for the surveying and marking of the boundary by two separate commissions, repre-
senting the interests of each nation. Following their appointment in
1850, the Mexican and American commissioners managed to lay out
the western portion of the boundary, but controversy erupted when
they attempted to establish the dividing line between New Mexico and
Chihuahua. The treaty described the boundary of southern New Mexico only as a line that ran "north of the town called Paso," without speci-
fying distance.[24] Lacking precise information concerning the exact location of Paso del Norte, a crucial landmark, and unable to find an accurate map, the treaty negotiators had used an erroneous one, which
placed that town 34 miles north and 130 miles east of its true location.

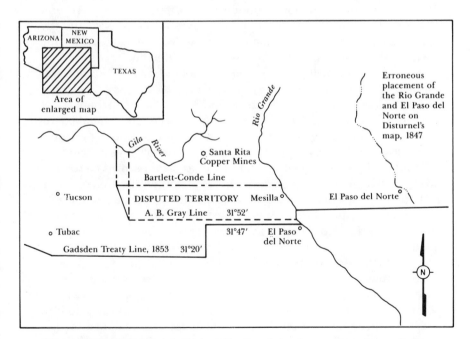

Settlement of the New Mexico–Chihuahua boundary controversy, 1848–53.
Drawn by Linda Marston.

It was up to the commissioners to decide exactly where the line should be drawn. The Mexicans proposed a line from the Rio Grande to the Gila River that would leave the Santa Rita del Cobre mines and the fertile Mesilla Valley in Mexico; the Americans countered with a line that would not only place that valuable real estate in the United States but would assure a much-desired pathway for a proposed railroad route to the Pacific. Commissioners Pedro García-Conde and John Russell Bartlett compromised by agreeing on a boundary that would leave the Mesilla Valley in Mexico but place the Santa Rita mines in the United States and include enough territory for the railroad route. Expansionists in Washington rejected that agreement, however, arguing that the best railroad path had been surrendered. Several members of the U.S. Boundary Commission, including the principal surveyor, refused to give their approval as well. The issue became embroiled in Washington politics, with the result that the Conde-Bartlett pact was declared null and void. Moreover, by late 1852 the U.S. Boundary Commission itself was disbanded, although a new one was created the following year to survey the Rio Grande from Paso del Norte to the Gulf.

The presence of settlers in the disputed territory made resolution of the New Mexico–Chihuahua boundary even more difficult. Around 1850, approximately two thousand people from New Mexico and the El Paso area who wished to remain subjects of Mexico had founded the town of Mesilla in what they believed was Chihuahua territory. New Mexico Governor William Carr Lane, however, claimed Mesilla was within American jurisdiction and even insisted in 1852 that those settlers had petitioned for U.S. citizenship. When Lane sought to assert U.S. control over Mesilla, Governor Angel Trías of Chihuahua responded by mobilizing Mexican troops at the frontier. Both governors issued strong warnings regarding the possible use of force to bring justice on behalf of each nation's interests. Once again armed confrontation over disputed land seemed imminent between the United States and Mexico, but a determination to resolve the matter through negotiation eventually prevailed. Lane, whose impetuous actions had contributed significantly to bringing about the crisis, unintentionally helped matters by resigning the New Mexico governorship for reasons unrelated to the border controversy.

Confrontation at the New Mexico–Chihuahua frontier gave way to hard bargaining in Mexico City with the arrival in 1853 of newly appointed U.S. Minister James Gadsden. This envoy had instructions to reach a settlement on the border question, to seek abrogation of Article XI of the Treaty of Guadalupe Hidalgo (which bound the United States to prevent Indian raids into Mexico), to seek restoration of normal commercial relations between the two countries, and to establish American transit rights through the Isthmus of Tehuántepec.[25] Seeing the troubled state of affairs in Mexico, Gadsden grasped the opportunity to pressure the Mexican government into parting with more of its northern territories. His maneuvers recalled those of offensive predecessors who had previously attempted to alter the border. In a letter to the Department of State, Gadsden asked whether money could be made available if circumstances favored the immediate acquisition of Sonora and Chihuahua and more territory later. Gadsden wished to establish a more "perfect" and "durable" border that would start at the Gulf of Mexico a short distance south of the Rio Grande and extend westward to the Pacific to include Baja California within the United States. In conversations with President Antonio López de Santa Anna, he proposed a line that would follow mountains and deserts, noting that to make that possible Mexico would need to sell two or more of its frontier states.[26]

Apparently Gadsden undertook the preceding initiatives on his own, but in October he received secret instructions from Washington to propose to Mexico six alternative boundaries, along with differing sums of money for purchase of land. The Franklin Pierce administration favored the option that called for the annexation of Coahuila, Chihuahua, Sonora, and Baja California in exchange for $50 million. The other proposals included less territory and of course carried smaller price tags, but in all cases the United States sought at a minimum the acquisition of favorable terrain for a railroad route to the Pacific and a port on the Gulf of California.[27] Before presenting these proposals formally to the Mexicans, Gadsden revealed his aggressive expansionist tendencies in a letter to Foreign Minister Manuel Díaz de Bonilla. Gadsden had learned that Mexico was seeking an alliance with European powers in case of conflict with the United States, and he warned Díaz de Bonilla that any European meddling would only hasten the inevitable absorption of a sizable part of northern Mexico into the United States. It would be wiser for Mexico, advised Gadsden, to avoid that possibility by consummating the sale of the additional territory.[28] This attempt at intimidation illustrates the contempt for Mexico then widely felt in the United States. Washington knew it had the upper hand. Santa Anna needed funds desperately to prop up his teetering regime, and Gadsden conveniently stepped in to offer the dictator a financial deal.

But the Mexican negotiators proved tougher than Gadsden had anticipated. They resisted the American plan for the cession of several

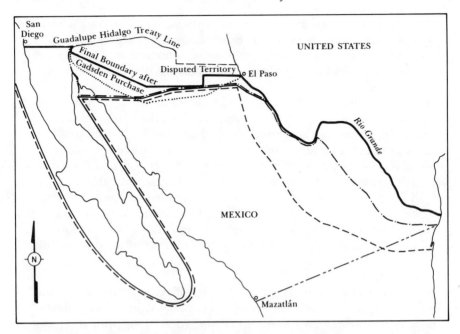

American boundary proposals during the Gadsden Treaty negotiation and ratification process, 1853. Under instructions, James Gadsden presented the following options to Mexican negotiators:

– – – Line most desired by President Pierce. Proposed cash payment to Mexico: $50 million.

– · – Second line most desired by President Pierce. Proposed cash payment: $35 million.

——— Third line designated by President Pierce. Proposed cash payment: $30 million.

········ Line agreed upon by Gadsden and Mexican negotiators.

– – — Line proposed by Senator Gwin before ratification of Gadsden Treaty.

Based on Garber, *Gadsden Treaty*, 90–93; and Zorrilla, *Historia de las relaciones* 1:352–53. Drawn by Linda Marston.

northern states, conceding only the minimum amount of land required for the desired railroad route. After considerable hard bargaining, the two sides signed a treaty in December 1853, known as the Gadsden Treaty. Its major features included (1) payment of $15 million to Mexico in exchange for the Mesilla strip, (2) U.S. assumption of American claims against Mexico (amounting to about $5 million), (3) abrogation of Article XI of the Treaty of Guadalupe Hidalgo, (4) affirmation of U.S. navigation rights in the Gulf of California and on the Colorado and Brazos rivers, and (5) the promise of mutual cooperation to suppress filibustering expeditions.[29] The terms were hardly unfavorable to the United States, yet many Americans had come to expect greater concessions from Mexico. Opposition to the treaty burst forth among members of the Pierce administration, the Senate, and prominent private interests.

In a heated Senate debate that lasted three months, the document underwent considerable alteration. Ironically, on the border question the final document provided for the acquisition of less territory than the agreement negotiated by Gadsden. Several Senators did attempt to drive the border deeper into Mexico, but each time their amendments failed. Finally Senator James M. Mason of Virginia offered the decisive compromise on the boundary, but even then the treaty failed on the first vote of the full Senate. Passage came only when the treaty was amended to give the United States transit and other privileges across the Isthmus of Tehuántepec, including the right to intervene on behalf of American investors.[30] The Mexican government received the revised document with considerable displeasure, but it was in no position to reject it. Nonacceptance could bring war with the United States. Besides, Santa Anna was predisposed to go along because he needed funds immediately to fight an insurrection in the state of Guerrero. Thus Mexico reluctantly accepted the new U.S. Senate–imposed terms, which included (1) payment of $10 million for the ceded land instead of the $15 million agreed upon originally, (2) removal of the clause concerning American assumption of claims against Mexico, and (3) elimination of the provision that bound the United States to formally cooperate in suppressing filibustering expeditions into Mexican territory.

Santa Anna's acceptance of the Gadsden Treaty provided his enemies with additional ammunition to use against him, and within a year Santa Anna was overthrown and eliminated from Mexican politics. Once again Mexico faced painful introspection as it tried to determine the causes of the loss of additional territory. Another distasteful agreement had been forced on the nation to accommodate foreign designs and the intrigues of its own opportunistic leaders. Fears remained that the country would be further dismembered, for the U.S. government continued to seek more border "adjustments," while many Americans joined adventurers from other lands in filibustering expeditions against Mexico's northern provinces. The actions of the filibusters, which gave Mexico many headaches but did not result in the loss of land, are treated in Chapter 2.

U.S. ATTEMPTS TO PURCHASE
ADDITIONAL MEXICAN LANDS

The United States made additional efforts to acquire Mexican territory during the 1850s. Following the established pattern, such attempts came particularly when the United States perceived a weakness in the Mexican regime in power, such as a need for official external recognition, a need for funds, or both.

In 1857 President James B. Buchanan instructed U.S. Minister to Mexico John Forsyth to propose to the Ignacio Comonfort government a plan for the transfer of parts of Chihuahua and Sonora and the entire Baja California peninsula to the United States. The purpose of this acquisition would be to allow private interests to build a railroad from the Rio Grande to the Sonora coast. Forsyth resurrected the old notion of the need for a more "natural" border between the two nations "to preserve the cordial relations that exist." The American approach to maintaining good relations, observes Mexican historian Luis G. Zorrilla, meant that "for harmony to exist between the two neighbors it was necessary that one kept feeding the other, each time between shorter intervals." The Mexican government rejected Forsyth's offer. In early 1858 Forsyth tried to obtain the desired change in the border, along with additional concessions in the Isthmus of Tehuántepec from the Felix Zuloaga administration, but the Mexican answer was still no. Undeterred and obsessed with the issue, Forsyth at one point told the Ministry of Foreign Relations that sooner or later, through the inscrutable designs of the Creator, his country would obtain the territory that had been denied him. Forsyth urged his government to take vigorous measures, including the seizing of Sonora, since "American blood [had been] spilled near its line," and demanding of Mexico that it "give us what we ask for in return for the manifest benefits we propose to confer upon you for it, or we will take it." A short time later the Mexican government asked Washington to remove Forsyth from Mexico; he had become persona non grata.[31]

Having failed to convince Mexico to accede to U.S. designs and exasperated over personal injury suffered by Americans in Mexico, Buchanan then proposed to the U.S. Congress the creation of a protectorate in Chihuahua and Sonora under the guise of defending both Americans and Mexicans against Indian depredations and general lawlessness. The idea of occupying Mexico "for her own good" and for the protection of American interests had been raised in early 1858 by then–U.S. Senator Sam Houston, who introduced a resolution in Congress calling for the creation of a committee to determine "whether or not it is expedient for the government of the United States to declare and maintain a protectorate over the so called republic of Mexico." Buchanan's plan failed to win congressional support owing to partisan and sectional considerations, aversion to granting too much power to the executive, and the perceived greater receptivity to American aims when Benito Juárez rose to power. Houston, however, continued to promote direct intervention independent of Washington once he returned to Texas and assumed the governorship. According to Walter Prescott Webb, Houston planned to engage the services of warring Indians and even some Mexicans, including Tamaulipas leader and sometimes social bandit Juan "Cheno" Cortina, adding a bizarre twist to the scheme. Only a lack of funds kept Houston from acting on his plan, says Webb.[32]

The United States saw its next opportunity to wrest concessions when the exiled Benito Juárez government struggled to survive in

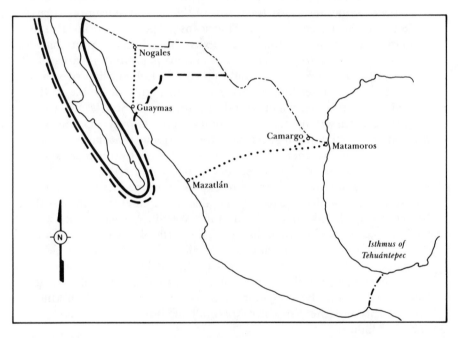

U.S. Proposals to alter the boundary and to secure transit privileges in northern Mexico and in the Isthmus of Tehuántepec, 1857 and 1859.

≡≡≡ Offers presented to Mexico by the Buchanan administration to bring about a change in the border, 1857.

••••• Routes over which the United States would have transit privileges, as provided by the negotiated (but never ratified) McLane-Ocampo Treaty, 1859.

—·— Isthmus of Techuántepec route, over which the United States had obtained transit privileges as part of the Gadsden Treaty. Further rights were sought through the McLane-Ocampo Treaty.

Based on Zorrilla, *Historia de las relaciones* 1:368–69, 376–78, 393–94. Drawn by Linda Marston.

Veracruz during the devastating War of the Reform. Juárez stood to benefit from American recognition because he desperately needed loans and other external assistance. After a special U.S. agent reported favorably on the Juárez regime, Buchanan named Robert McLane as minister to Mexico and authorized him to recognize Juárez. These preliminaries and formalities completed, McLane began negotiations for a treaty that would encompass cession of Baja California, more concession in Tehuántepec, transit rights in Sonora, intervention rights in the transit areas, and resolution of claims against Mexico. Opposition within the Juárez government to altering the border prevented the cession of any territory, but McLane managed to win some extraordinary concessions nonetheless. By the terms of the McLane-Ocampo Treaty of 1859, Mexico agreed to grant Americans perpetual transit rights in Tehuántepec and across northern Mexico, including the prerogative to use military force to protect persons and property in those areas. In turn, the Juárez government would receive $4 million, half of which would be used for settling claims. Although highly favorable to the United States, the treaty met with defeat in the U.S. Senate. Since the treaty was discussed in executive session, it is not known precisely why the Senate rejected it, but apparently the possibility that slavery would be extended into northern Mexico motivated many to vote against it.[33]

In the 1860s, Confederate leaders turned toward Mexico in their quest for new territory in which to expand slavery. Their interest in absorbing part or all of Mexico is revealed in statements made shortly before the outbreak of the Civil War. "We must have Sonora and Chihuahua," wrote one prominent military official. "With Sonora and Chihuahua we gain Southern [Lower] California, and by a railroad to Guaymas render our state of Texas the great highway of nations." When those dreams failed to materialize, southerners sought to establish colonies with the cooperation of the French, who then ruled Mexico through the Emperor Maximillian, but such schemes also ended in failure.[34]

Although many Americans would continue to entertain hopes of further acquisitions of Mexican lands, following the Civil War the U.S. government's compulsion to seek negotiated "adjustments" of the border faded. Henceforth border disputes centered on maintaining the integrity of the established boundary. Technical questions over the exact location of the border, particularly confusion caused by shifts in the Rio Grande, would replace the old concern over which part of Mexico would next be annexed by the United States. There would still be controversy, but the character and level of animosity would differ significantly from that of earlier periods when the specter of land loss poisoned the relations between the two countries.

REFINEMENT OF THE BORDER

Although American expansionists used the notion of a "natural" boundary as a pretext for acquisition of Mexican territory, the failure to find an imposing physical barrier to divide the two countries guaranteed pronounced ambiguity regarding the chosen line. The Rio Grande in particular was certain to sow confusion and discord because of the river's unpredictability. Article V of the Treaty of Guadalupe Hidalgo specified that the boundary would follow the middle of that river; where more than one channel existed, the deepest one would prevail. It is difficult enough to identify "the middle" of any river; in the case of the Rio Grande, the problem was compounded by the river's tendency to overrun its banks and open up new meandering channels, frequently leaving detached tracts of land to the north or south of the original border. At times these shifts displaced only a few acres of rather inconsequential land, but on other occasions the affected terrain had considerable value because of its fertility or location at or near populated areas. Conflict over border placement was thus predictable, but by reason of the region's isolation and early sparse population, the problems that emerged after the signing of the Treaty of Guadalupe Hidalgo in 1848 and the Gadsden Treaty in 1853 did not assume importance until much later.

The most significant dispute arising from the shifting Rio Grande involved a tract of land in El Paso–Ciudad Juárez known as the Chamizal, named for the desert grass *chamizo*, which grew there. In the 1850s and 1860s, a series of floods caused the river to move southward, leaving some Mexican land on the north bank. Testimony from residents taken later indicated that torrential rains in 1864 had caused most of the river movement. The United States, assuming the boundary had changed with the shifting of the river, exercised jurisdiction over the tract, prompting Mexico to question the legality of that action in 1867. In the years that followed, Mexico made repeated attempts to resolve the problem, but American preoccupation with domestic issues and Washington's nonrecognition of certain Mexican regimes delayed discussion of the issue.[35]

In 1884, consideration of jurisdictional rights over Morteritos Island at the Texas-Tamaulipas border led to a treaty whereby both nations agreed that the boundary would change if a gradual shift in the river took place but would remain intact when "the force of the current" cut a new bed or produced a new channel.[36] To implement the new rule and to address other matters related to border placement, an ad hoc International Border Commission was created in 1889. The commission was made a permanent body in 1900, after it became evident that border concerns would surface with regularity.[37] The commission tackled a series of ticklish problems in the next few years, but the Chamizal was not one of them. Mexico felt the 1884 agreement did not apply in that case because the correct boundary at El Paso–Ciudad Juárez was the one determined in the original Rio Grande survey in 1852. With a solution indefinitely postponed, the Chamizal would become more perplexing as the years passed.

Meanwhile, the commission discovered discrepancies in that portion of the border established by the Gadsden Treaty. The monuments that marked the line had been placed incorrectly, resulting in a land loss for Mexico of approximately 210,000 acres. The terrain in question included some agricultural land and mineral resources, prompting Mexico to insist on several occasions on rectification of the line. But the United States refused to go along, maintaining that both nations had previously agreed to the permanence of the Gadsden Treaty line; besides, argued the Americans, the disputed tract lay in an isolated, uninhabitable, and generally useless region, and thus would not justify the expense of moving the monuments. Mexico reluctantly resigned itself to another distasteful U.S. policy decision.[38]

During the 1890s, the International Border Commission spent considerable time identifying small parcels of land, called *bancos*, which the meandering Rio Grande had detached from each country in the Texas-Tamaulipas border. A study indentified fifty-eight bancos from Camargo–Rio Grande City to the Gulf. The two sides found a practical solution to the problem of exercising legal jurisdiction over these tracts, signing a convention in 1905 that modified the 1884 treaty to allow for rectification of the border simultaneously with an exchange of bancos. To expeditiously eliminate the bancos, the revised treaty purposely assumed that all changes in the course of the river that had created bancos had been caused by slow erosion, even if that had not been the case; therefore, consistent with the principle of the 1884 pact, the boundary would change as well. All bancos on the right bank went to Mexico, all those on the left went to the United States. The original boundary would prevail only in those cases where the size of the tract exceeded 250 hectares, or where the tract had a population of over two hundred persons. Local residents could retain their original nationality or become citizens of the nation exercising jurisdiction over their locality.[39] In 1910, an additional thirty-one bancos were formally reassigned on the same basis, and through 1970, the total number of boundary changes that followed the precedent established in 1905 amounted to 247 and involved the exchange of thousands of acres.[40]

The commission's inability to resolve the Chamizal dispute and a related though less-significant controversy in the Ojinaga-Presidio area marred somewhat the accord reached on the bancos and other issues at the turn of the century. The Chamizal overshadowed other differences because of its location in a prominent binational urban setting. As El Paso–Ciudad Juárez grew in size and importance, the land in question increased in value, thus causing both the material and the symbolic stakes to rise. Mexico submitted its first formal claim to the Chamizal in 1895, but despite subsequent meetings and lengthy correspondence, nothing concrete materialized until 1910. That year both countries signed a "Convention of Arbitration," which referred the dispute to an Arbitration Commission comprised of a U.S. representative, a Mexican representative, and a neutral Canadian jurist. The basic question addressed by this body involved determining whether the change in the course of the river had been due to slow and gradual erosion or to sudden and violent movement or avulsion. Mexico and Canada concluded that avulsion had caused the shift, and therefore the boundary should revert to the 1864 position, when that movement took place. The Arbitration Commission proceeded to grant Mexico title to the land south of the 1864 channel and the United States title to the land north of that channel. The United States refused to abide by the decision, however, despite the fact that it had agreed in Article III of the convention that the commission's decision, "whether rendered unanimously or by majority vote of the Commissioners shall be final and conclusive upon both governments, and without appeal."[41]

The United States based its rejection of the commission's decision on the following grounds: (1) the guidelines of the arbitration agreement did not empower the commission to divide the disputed land; (2) the commission identified a process of channel change, namely rapid erosion, that was not covered by the 1884 treaty; and (3) the 1864 channel could not be identified with precision. Clearly the United States had made a painstaking search for technicalities to justify rejection of the decision. Mexico deeply resented that action, but its only recourse was to protest and continue to press for recognition of its claim.[42]

In the decades that followed, various administrations discussed the issue. In 1932 talks over the need to rectify the meandering Rio Grande in the El Paso–Ciudad Juárez area presented an opportunity to resolve the dispute, but continuing differences in interpretations led to the Chamizal's exclusion from the Treaty of Rectification, signed in 1933. As a result of that treaty, a small but important portion of the Rio Grande was straightened and stabilized through the construction of river levees. Attendant to the rectification was an exchange of equal portions of land between the two countries.[43]

The Chamizal problem came up for discussion again in the 1940s

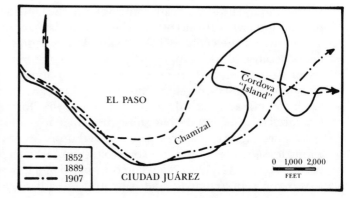

Movement of the Rio Grande in El Paso–Juárez, 1852–1907, and the location of the Chamizal and Cordova tracts. Based on Mueller, *Restless River*, 66. Drawn by Linda Marston.

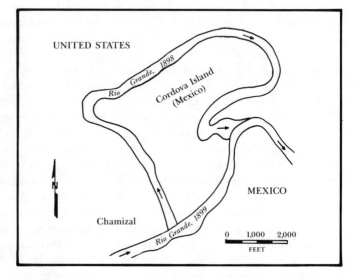

Cordova "Island" was created in 1899 with the digging of an artificial cutoff intended to reduce flooding and to increase efficiency in water flow. Based on Mueller, *Restless River*, 74. Drawn by Linda Marston.

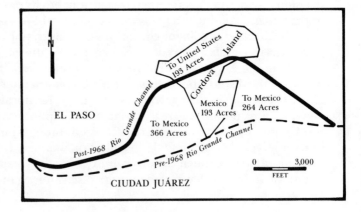

Chamizal settlement. The Chamizal Treaty of 1963 resulted in the relocation of the Rio Grande and the exchange of lands between Mexico and the United States. Based on Mueller, *Restless River*, 102. Drawn by Linda Marston.

and 1950s, but no progress was made. Finally, during the administration of John F. Kennedy, the matter was settled. Having that diplomatic sore spot lurking in the background was inconsistent with Kennedy's policy of improving relations with Latin America through the newly established "Alliance for Progress." Kennedy considered the decision of the United States not to accept the 1911 Arbitration Commission's findings a mistake, and in 1963 he signed a treaty that essentially gave effect to that panel's decision. By 1968 both countries opened a new concrete-lined river channel and completed an exchange of lands. Mexico received 630 acres and the United States 193 acres. A century of misunderstanding and bitterness over a parcel of land had ended.

Seven years after the signing of the Chamizal pact, both countries entered into a comprehensive agreement to resolve pending and future problems connected with changes in the Rio Grande and the Colorado River. Situations had arisen that could not be adequately addressed under existing treaties and conventions, suggesting a need to develop more-specific criteria for identifying and handling border shifts. Thus the Treaty of 1970 introduced more detailed and rigorous guidelines, superseding agreements contained in previous accords. Additionally, the new treaty (1) resolved the pending Ojinaga-Presidio dispute over a parcel of land in favor of Mexico; (2) transferred the Horcón and Morteritos tracts near Brownsville to Mexico in exchange for an equal amount of land transferred to the United States near Reynosa, Tamaulipas; (3) assigned eleven river bancos to Mexico and eight to the United States; and (4) set a permanent maritime boundary from the mouth of the Rio Grande twelve miles into the Gulf of Mexico. Thus this important document settled existing differences and wisely provided the mechanisms for dealing with future problems.[44]

The preceding paragraphs summarize the difficulties faced by Mexico and the United States in preseving a stable dividing line. Yet border maintenance has not been the only area of concern at the river boundaries. Another problem that has caused bitter controversy is the distribution and use of the waters of the Rio Grande, the Colorado River, and the Tijuana River.[45] Conflict began in the 1870s, when irrigation reached the U.S. borderlands and American farmers appropriated increasing amounts of Rio Grande water. Decades of binational negotiation resulted in two treaties that established terms for the division of waters, one in 1906 and another in 1944. Yet both documents contained serious flaws. The 1906 pact divided the water of the upper Rio Grande (from its source to Fort Quitman), but left the apportionment of the waters of the lower Rio Grande, the Colorado, and the Tijuana unresolved. These omissions triggered a generation of agitation. Matters calmed down somewhat in 1944 with the ratification of the second treaty, but the new pact (covering the waters of the Rio Grande below

Fort Quitman and the Colorado and Tijuana rivers) not only overesti-
mated stream flow but contained ambiguous provisions regarding
drought and water quality, thus leaving both Mexican and American
farmers dissatisified over the amount and type of water available for
their irrigation projects. These and other problems severely restricted
the treaty's effectiveness and revived international friction. The excessive salt content of the Colorado River water flowing into Mexico,
which after 1961 began causing serious damage to thousands of acres
of Mexican land, became a particularly troublesome issue. The two
countries did not resolve this problem until 1973, when a new binational pact provided for the reduction of salinity through the construction of a desalting plant by the United States, the cooperative re-
habilitation and improvement of the damaged land, and the waiver of
previous Mexican claims.[46]

SUMMARY AND CONCLUSION

The experience of Mexico and the United States in establishing and
maintaining their common boundary reveals how complex that process can be between neighboring countries. In setting the location of
the border, developments were influenced significantly by the disparity
in the two countries' strength. Try as it might, the weaker party could
not repel the expansionist advances of its neighbor, who considered
the addition of western territories an aspect of its "Manifest Destiny."
Mexico, a nation long burdened by neocolonial structures and conflicts, inherited a tradition of a receding northern frontier, while the
United States, an emerging world power, first followed the English
practice of contesting the possessions of others and then unfolded its
own formula for overcoming resistance: the use of dollar diplomacy
backed by the threat of force. Through purchase, annexation, and conquest, the United States acquired Florida, Louisiana, Texas, New
Mexico, Arizona, Nevada, California, and Utah and parts of Wyoming,
Colorado, and Oklahoma, all at the expense of Spain and Mexico. With
the natural resources, superb ports, and other riches thus acquired, the
United States assured itself a future of economic and military promi-
nence. Conversely, having lost some of its most valuable assets, Mexico
could look forward to diminished wealth, a scarcity of agricultural
land, and limited economic growth. Thus the location of the boundary
truly helped shape the destiny of each nation.

Boundary troubles also left a legacy of hatred, bitterness, and suspicion between the two neighbors. Mexicans deeply resented the pressure tactics and crude behavior of some American representatives who

were obsessed with "adjusting" the boundary. The offensive behavior of Joel R. Poinsett, Anthony Butler, James Gadsden, John Forsyth, and others grew out of feelings of superiority and contempt for Mexicans. Washington was especially intolerant of the political instability that reigned in Mexico because it complicated and slowed down diplomatic negotiations. Well cemented during the years of intense conflict, the American disdain toward their southern neighbors continued for many decades and gave rise to countless misunderstandings.

Mexico was especially frustrated by the behavior of Washington legislators, particularly members of the Senate, who constantly amended painstakingly negotiated settlements, usually to the further detriment of Mexico. The Mexicans found irritating the repeated American attempts to change extant treaties in order to accommodate the insatiable appetite for land, to gain new concessions, or to win release from existing obligations the United States did not want to meet. One of the most distressing experiences came at the critical moment of the negotiations over the all-important Treaty of Guadalupe Hidalgo, when Mexicans found themselves dangerously close to losing their nationhood. Little wonder that Mexicans came to lament their geographic position, "so far from God, so close to the United States," and hardly surprising that many felt that between Mexico and the United States "the best thing is the desert."

History makes it clear why the Rio Grande became half the boundary, but given the subsequent cost to each nation and to the people who have made the area their home, a high price was paid for that choice. Scholars familiar with the workings of international boundaries agree that rivers often make poor boundaries. Fertile river valleys attract people; boundaries serve to divide them. Rivers of subhumid zones such as the Rio Grande are often erratic, giving rise to border maintenance problems. Contention over the Chamizal, water disputes, and other issues associated with the Rio Grande, the Colorado River, and the Tijuana River helped to keep alive for several generations the painful historical reality of how the boundary came to be. Americans easily could, and often did, forget the events of 1848 and 1853, but Mexicans understandably found it much more difficult to do so. The late nineteenth and early twentieth century disagreements over the exact location of the border heightened the Mexicans' recollection of the earlier tragic years. Unquestionably the memory of the border "adjustments" figured prominently in the attitudes, perceptions, and policies adopted by Mexico toward the United States for generations, and indeed influence events to this day.

CHAPTER 2

Marked Frontier

The expansionism practiced by nineteenth century American governments tells only part of the story of "Manifest Destiny." Invasions of Spanish and Mexican territories by independent adventurers constitute a parallel process that gave impetus to official attempts to push the boundary westward and southward. Organized outside the law on American soil and directed at neighbors who had peaceful relations with the United States, such attacks became known as "filibustering." The exploits of William Walker and other filibusters of the 1850s are familiar to students of U.S.-Mexican relations, but less well known are the activities of self-appointed "liberators," revolutionary agents, and would-be colonizers of earlier and later epochs.

This chapter highlights major filibustering and pseudofilibustering incidents that occurred from the early nineteenth century through the first quarter of the twentieth century. The persistence of conspiratorial activity and unauthorized expeditions for such an extended period illustrates the intensity of that aggressive streak in American society to detach lands belonging to neighboring nations. Cuba, Central America, and Mexico were three areas "marked" for conquest by ambitious men who ignored tenets of national sovereignty to further dreams of personal aggrandizement. Northern Mexico, a receding frontier, long remained isolated and unprotected, thus inviting foreign infiltration and attack. So many plots and incursions took place that a comprehensive account here is impossible; thus narration of major episodes only will be given in the text, with some additional information in the notes.

FILIBUSTERING, 1800–1848

American frontiersmen increased the pace of infiltration of Spanish territory once the United States achieved its independence from England. Settlers drifted into East and West Florida, traders and trappers penetrated Texas and New Mexico, and sea merchants docked along the California coast. The U.S. government became very interested in getting information about these territories from its wandering citizens, and reports dribbled into Washington. Given Spain's preoccupation with foreign threats to its borderlands, a large number of the American infiltrators were arrested, jailed, or had property confiscated. Often, capricious Spanish frontier officials applied the law harshly, reinforcing the long-standing American antipathy toward Spaniards and their hold on desirable lands in the continent. That discontent led to widespread disregard for Spanish regulations and to an attitude among the more-aggressive frontier elements that Spanish territory was fair game for privateering and filibustering. Whether schemes succeeded or failed depended on many factors, including the political climate south of the border and the military strength of the perpetrators. To illustrate the different motives and tendencies of the earliest filibusters, brief descriptions of the adventures of Philip Nolan, Zebulon Montgomery Pike, Bernardo Gutiérrez de Lara, Augustus W. Magee, and James Long are given in this section.

Nolan and Pike may be thought of as "precursors" of filibustering, who fulfilled the important task of gathering intelligence for their country. In 1797 Nolan submitted a report to Thomas Jefferson through General James Wilkinson, commander of western forces, that contained observations on northeast Texas accumulated during Nolan's travels. Three years later Nolan undertook an expedition into Texas ostensibly to round up and sell horses, but his prolonged stay and penetration as far as the Brazos River aroused the suspicion of the Spaniards, who killed him and imprisoned his men. During the planning phase of the Texas adventure, Nolan had maintained communication with General Wilkinson, leading to speculation that Wilkinson supported Nolan's scheme or influenced him in some way. For years Wilkinson was associated with various shady operations, some of which involved violation of Spanish territorial sovereignty, but the extent of his participation in filibustering is difficult to determine because he carefully avoided overt ties to the activities of the conspirators.

Pike's mysterious trek into Spanish lands took place in 1806. Wilkinson had ordered Pike to escort Osage and Pawnee Indians to their homeland and to explore parts of the Arkansas and Red rivers, but Pike kept going westward and eventually crossed the border into Spanish territory. Interestingly, Wilkinson's son accompanied Pike's party for part of the trip. Although aware that Spanish officials from New Mexico and Texas had been alerted to his wanderings, Pike advanced through the Rockies into the upper Rio Grande region. From there a member of the party who was familiar with the area traveled to Santa Fe, ostensibly to settle a business matter with a French trader, but instructions from Pike reveal that he had a spying mission as well. When troops commanded by Bartolomé Fernández met the intruders, Pike feigned embarrassment, explaining that he thought he was on the Red River. Unconvinced, the Spaniards arrested Pike's party and took them to Chihuahua City by way of Santa Fe. Pike cleverly made friends with the Spanish authorities, and they eventually permitted him to return to the United States via Texas. Contrary to Wilkinson's advice to be cautious about revealing details of his trip, Pike wrote a report from memory that stimulated widespread interest in the territories he had visited.[1]

The Bernardo Gutiérrez de Lara–Augustus W. Magee expedition into Texas in 1813 exemplifies the subversion by foreigners of a genuine effort to aid Mexico's independence movement against Spain, with the outsiders' motive being the takeover of Texas. Gutiérrez de Lara, a Mexican, began his odyssey in the United States in 1811 as an agent of Miguel Hidalgo y Costilla, seeking aid from the American government to further the rebellion against Spain. He found receptivity in Washington, but the terms offered by the Monroe administration, essentially American occupation and control of Texas, were unacceptable. Hence Gutiérrez de Lara sought private assistance in New Orleans, a city that bustled with exiles, adventurers, mercenaries, and privateers of all shades. With the help of the American consul William Shaler, he organized a force of several hundred Mexicans, Americans, and men of various other nationalities. Augustus W. Magee resigned as a colonel in the American army to become the co-leader of the expedition, but his participation was cut short when he died in a battle at Goliad in 1812, whereupon his command passed to Samuel Kemper. The rebels seized San Antonio in April 1813, and a joint Kemper–Gutiérrez de Lara declaration of independence for Texas followed. According to Mexican historian Luis G. Zorrilla, mastermind William Shaler then decided to replace Gutiérrez de Lara because the latter's loyalty to Mexico presented an obstacle to American intentions of taking Texas. José Álvarez de Toledo, a Dominican adventurer who dreamed of forming a federation of free states in the Caribbean, replaced Gutiérrez de Lara. But the internal intrigues and dissensions took their toll, and following defeats at the hands of the Spanish army, the movement collapsed in late 1813.[2]

The desire among some frontier Americans to "liberate" Texas on their own and convert it into an independent nation is illustrated by the incursions of James Long and his followers. Long, married to the niece of General Wilkinson, had become acquainted with intrigues along the border. Like many other Americans, he adamantly objected to the signing of the Adams-Onís treaty, by which the United States had acknowledged Spanish possession of Texas. After holding a protest meeting, Long led fifty to seventy-five residents of Natchez, Mississippi, to Texas, where the invaders proclaimed that province a "free republic" in June 1819. Jean Lafitte, the famous pirate, turned down Long's invitation to join the movement, but veteran rebel Bernardo Gutiérrez de Lara responded in the affirmative, giving hope to Long that Mexicans in Texas would welcome the "liberating" forces. Within a few months, however, Spanish troops drove the intruders out of Nacogdoches. Long refused to give up, however, and organized another incursion with the pretext of seeking to help Mexico gain its independence from Spain. On their way to Goliad, Long's forces received word that Mexico had at last defeated the Spaniards and independence had become a reality. That eliminated the justification for their presence in Texas, but when asked by the Mexicans to leave, they refused. Finally, they surrendered at Goliad; Long was imprisoned and later shot in Mexico City in 1822.[3]

Long and the other American filibusters of the 1810s were aided significantly by the failure of the U.S. government to enforce its neutrality laws. Despite repeated Spanish protestations, Washington refused to take effective measures to curb the activities of the filibusters, allowing them to organize and launch incursions from U.S. territory. Americans overwhelmingly supported the cause of the Latin Americans against the Spanish Crown during the wars of independence; thus little enthusiasm existed in the United States for helping Spain retain its New World possessions. On the other hand, Washington avoided giving independence fighters any overt assistance for fear of risking direct conflict with the Spaniards. The chosen policy was to proclaim neutrality but do little to hinder those using American ports and land to plan expeditions into Spanish territory, which pleased the anti-Spanish elements and played well into the hands of ambitious expansionists and adventurers.[4]

Following Mexican independence in 1821, conditions changed on the northern frontier. Overt filibustering activity declined largely because liberal immigration policies enacted in Mexico City allowed thousands of Americans to settle in Texas. But the steady, pronounced immigration, both legal and illegal, soon overwhelmed the native *tejanos* and undermined Mexico's hold on the province. A preview of future troubles with the restless newcomers unfolded in December 1826, when thirty Texans seized a fort in Nacogdoches and proclaimed the "Republic of Fredonia." But that rebellion proved to be short lived, for within two months the Mexican militia drove the rebels across the border into the United States. Less than a decade later, however, the foreigners hatched the well-known independence movement that led not only to the creation of the Republic of Texas but inspired secessionism elsewhere and spawned imperialistic designs on additional Mexican territories.

One separatist movement in 1839–40 along Mexico's northeastern frontier sought to establish a "Republic of the Rio Grande," to be composed of Texas, Nuevo León, Tamaulipas, Coahuila, Durango, and New Mexico. General Antonio Canales, the commmander of the operation, moved freely across the international boundary, raising funds and recruiting followers. The rebels started with a thousand men under arms, including a company of Texans. They were able to capture Victoria, the capital of Tamaulípas, along with various Mexican border towns; they also came close to taking Matamoros, Monterrey, and Saltillo. The high point for the Rio Grande insurgents came in January 1840, when delegates from throughout the region proclaimed a government, drafted a constitution, and selected Laredo as their capital. Local Mexicans who despised the centralist regime in Mexico City hailed the new republic with cheers and the ringing of bells. But the dream of a mighty borderlands nation vanished as tactical mistakes on the battlefield and internal dissension triggered confusion and desertions. By the fall of 1840, the movement had been stopped by federal troops. The Mexican rebel forces scattered and the Texas volunteers dejectedly returned home.[5]

Shortly after the collapse of the Rio Grande Republic, the Texans sent an expedition into New Mexico ostensibly to promote trade, but the real intention was to attach that province to Texas. Howard Lamar, the Texas president, claimed all lands north and east of the Rio Grande as part of the Texas domain, basing his position on the old argument that the Rio Grande constituted the true boundary of Texas, an interpretation rejected by the New Mexicans. When the nearly three hundred armed Texas "merchants" arrived in New Mexico in mid-1841, they were promptly arrested and taken to Mexico City for imprisonment. Mistreatment of the Texans engendered increased hatred toward Mexicans. Some prisoners managed to escape, and within a year the Mexican government released the rest. For many years thereafter, distrust and bitterness characterized relations between New Mexicans and Texans.[6]

By the mid-1840s, the annexation of Mexico's northern frontier had become the cornerstone of American "Manifest Destiny." President James W. Polk is well known as the central figure among the expansionists who forced Mexico to agree, by treaty, to give up part of its territory following the War of 1846–48. Prior to that conflict, Polk's efforts to bring about the desired land transfer included the use of secret agents in Texas and California, some of whom attempted to provoke armed conflict with Mexico. In May 1845, just prior to the annexation of Texas to the United States, Commodore Robert F. Stockton arrived in Galveston with a squadron of U.S. naval vessels, prepared to start a war on the Texas-Mexico border. A wealthy man, Stockton planned to finance an army of at least two thousand men who would invade Matamoros under the leadership of Major General Sidney Sherman, the chief officer of the militia of Texas. That act would trigger conflict between Texas and Mexico and obligate the United States, which was in the process of annexing Texas, to extend "protection" to its new subjects. U.S. participation in the war would ensure victory and lead to the acquisition of Mexican territory, including the much-desired province of California. The plan did not materialize, however, because Anson Jones, then president of Texas, flatly refused to "manufacture a war for the United States." Evidence suggests strongly that Polk knew about and approved the Stockton intrigue, but the link to Washington remains a subject of debate among historians.[7]

Stockton's scheme was actually a variation of a plan advocated in late 1844 by Duff Green, a prominent Democrat and the U.S. consul at Galveston, during the last days of the John Tyler administration. Apparently acting on his own initiative, Green wanted to organize Plains Indians under a Texas-chartered corporation for the purpose of invading northern Mexico. Thus when the time arrived to annex Texas to the United States, additional, newly conquered Mexican territory could be absorbed as well. In his zeal to enlist the support of the Texans, Green acted in an aggressive and offensive manner, even attempting to bribe Anson Jones and other officials. That behavior earned him notoriety and doomed his plan.[8]

Although Texas was the undisputed center of conspiracies against Mexico, similar intrigues unfolded in California. Six months before the outbreak of war between the United States and Mexico, American consul Thomas O. Larkin secretly assumed the role of Polk's "confidential agent," charged with promoting the peaceful secession of California and subsequent voluntary adherence to the United States. But Larkin's mission was upstaged by the "Bear Flag" Rebellion that broke out in the early summer of 1846. The central figure in that insurrection was John C. Fremont, the famous western explorer, military officer, and presidential candidate. Fremont had led a "surveying" party into California in December 1845, but in March 1846, Mexican authorities, suspicious of his motives, forced him to leave. As Fremont and his fellow "scientists" traveled toward Oregon, an agent of Polk and Larkin delivered a secret message to them, whereupon they quickly turned southward. Many historians believe that Fremont received instructions from Polk to assist in the impending U.S. conquest of California, but lack of conclusive documentation makes it difficult to know if that was the case.[9] Under official orders or acting on his own, upon his return to California Fremont took charge of an armed movement started by American settlers in June 1846. At Sonoma the rebels proclaimed the "California Republic," with a "bear flag" as their standard. Fighting native Californians along the way, the rebels marched to San Francisco, where Fremont commanded the newly organized California Batallion of American Volunteers. On July 7, however, Fremont's "republic" dissolved as Commodore John D. Sloat officially invaded California on behalf of the United States as part of the war with Mexico.

The aggression of the United States against its southern neighbor in the 1840s yielded lands that Americans had coveted for years, accomplishing and validating what frontier expansionists outside of Texas had been unable to do. The relative ease with which the United States detached Mexico's frontier provinces encouraged countless adventurers to think that independent invasions would stand a good chance of succeeding; their hopes for support among their countrymen rose with the repeated pronouncements by prominent Americans for further territorial acquisitions, even after the signing of the Treaty of Guadalupe Hidalgo in 1848.

FILIBUSTERS OF THE LATTER NINETEENTH CENTURY

The years immediately following the U.S.-Mexico War have been called the "Golden Age" of filibustering.[10] Men seeking fortune or power cast their eyes on the resource-rich and thinly populated northern tier of Mexican states. War veterans, forty-niners, and miscellaneous travelers during the late 1840s and early 1850s had portrayed that region in colorful, exotic, and economically attractive terms. Great opportunities existed just beyond the new border; further, Americans felt that local Mexicans would easily be won over to the idea of alignment with Yankees because they would be "liberated" from political tyrants and protected from the disorder that prevailed on the frontier. Indeed, banditry, smuggling, and Indian depredations had kept the residents of Tamaulipas, Nuevo León, Coahuila, Chihuahua, and Sonora in a state of turmoil for many years.[11]

Northern Mexicans found the Indian danger the most troublesome and vexing problem because it contributed to the abandonment of existing settlements and discouraged prospective colonists from the interior from moving northward. The California Gold Rush acted as a further drain on the limited population in Sonora, as evidenced by the departure of over ten thousand *sonorenses* (residents of Sonora) despite official attempts to dissuade them. Even soldiers deserted their garrisons, leaving the region badly exposed to Indian attacks. Adding to the dilemma was the inability or unwillingness on the part of the United States to police the border in accordance with the Treaty of Guadalupe Hidalgo. Thus, those settlers who remained in Sonora and other neglected areas did so at considerable personal risk.[12]

The Mexican government found it exceedingly difficult to provide the northern frontier with added protection because it was hampered by incessant internal strife and lack of revenues. Nevertheless, national leaders offered various proposals between 1848 and 1852 that provided for the establishment of military-civilian colonies throughout northern Mexico. A particularly detailed plan presented by Sonora leader Mariano Paredes in 1850 called for granting many benefits to new settlers and for developing comprehensive commercial activity in undeveloped zones. Paredes hoped that Sonora would become strong enough "to serve as a barrier to the avaricious neighbor that lies in wait and does not hide his ambition for the fertile and extensive terrain that he visits daily and which he knows contains equal or more precious metals than those mined in Upper California; this neighbor will wait quietly until he thinks the day is at hand, and on that day he will turn into a monster, attracting opportunists from all parts of the world."[13] Paredes and others urged that Mexico seek European immigrants to populate the frontier. One highly respected senator stated that Mexico needed a population of 25 million, with large numbers concentrated in the north.[14]

Despite official endorsement of the colonization proposals, the effort did not get very far. Only a few of the contemplated colonies were established and within a short period most of these disintegrated. The failure is explained by poor planning, lack of resources, delays, and hesitation on the part of colonists to move to the boundary area. With its defenses weakened and its population thinned by outmigration, northern Mexico became an attractive target for Americans and others who thought little of violating the neighboring nation's territorial integrity.[15]

The filibustering phenomenon, which is the focus of this chapter, needs to be distinguished from the smaller but far-more-frequent incursions that were prompted by such motives as personal revenge, punishment of Indians, recovery of runaway slaves, theft, and smuggling. The commission sent by the Mexican government to investigate conditions along the northeast border in the 1870s documented constant small-scale attacks on Mexican citizens, towns, and farms from 1848 forward.[16] (Of course, such forays took place in the opposite direction as well, as evidenced by the investigations of American congressional committees.[17] But it was Mexico alone that had to contend with the other far-more-dangerous intrusions, those large-scale, well-financed expeditions meant to detach parts of the national domain.)

Along the Texas-Mexico border in the early 1850s, economic considerations provided a pretext for American merchants to become heavily involved in an invasion of Tamaulipas that had overtones of a secessionist movement. The Texans resented stiff enforcement of Mexican tariff regulations, which cut into their profitable smuggling operations. Mexican border businessmen likewise desired less government restrictions on trade. In 1849 a faction backed by business interests proclaimed the independence of the "Republic of Sierra Madre," but that insurrection degenerated into an assault on the Matamoros customshouse and attempted recovery of confiscated contraband at Mier. The second phase of the Sierra Madre episode occurred the following year when Texas sympathizer José María Carvajal led a revolt against the Mexican government. With financial support and volunteers from both sides of the border, Carvajal attacked Camargo and Matamoros, but eventually he withdrew north of the Rio Grande. An easing of the Mexican tariff regulations stabilized the situation temporarily, but by early 1852, Carvajal attacked Camargo again, this time with a force that included four hundred Anglo-Texans. The participation of so many foreigners in the rebellion prompted Mexicans to call Carvajal a traitor and a "sellout" to *gringo* gold. Carvajal's "army of liberation" subsequently occupied Mexican territory in 1852, 1853, and 1855, but the successes were always temporary and the idea of setting up a new "republic" was soon forgotten.[18]

While Carvajal and his Texas allies sought to "free" portions of Mexico's northeast, Frenchmen and Americans from throughout the

United States used California as a base of operations to launch invasions of Sonora and Baja California. Thousands migrated from France into California in the late 1840s and early 1850s after revolution and economic depression devastated that country. Of course the gold rush served as a magnet for many European as well as Latin American immigrants, who flooded California during the period. Before long the French learned of conditions south of the border and their spirit of adventurism burst forth. Aware of Mexico's desperate need to populate its frontier, the French and other groups sought the approval of the Mexican government to establish colonies in the sparsely populated zones.[19] It soon became apparent, however, that the "colonizers" had other motives.

Gaston Raousset de Boulbon, a nobleman and soldier of fortune, is perhaps the best known of the French invaders of Mexico's northern frontier. In 1852 he organized 150 of his compatriots into a company whose purpose would be to establish a mining colony in Sonora. Underwritten by Swiss bankers and actually approved by Mexican officials, the French colonists set sail for Guaymas, but there local officials delayed their movement inland. After encountering continuing obstructions, they proclaimed open rebellion and captured Hermosillo. Raousset unsuccessfully sought the support of the local people by posing as the champion of an independent Sonora. As Mexican hostility rose and as dysentery spread among the invaders, they decided to accept an offer to evacuate Hermosillo in exchange for unobstructed passage out of the country.

When Raousset reached California, San Franciscans gave him a hero's welcome, and that encouraged him to plan an even bigger venture. At first the Mexican government became alarmed at Raousset's new preparations to retake Sonora. But the wily Antonio López de Santa Anna, who was then president, concluded that the French might be used as a buffer against the more-dangerous American expansionists, especially William Walker, the "king" of the filibusters, who was then organizing his famous expedition into Baja California. With raised hopes, Raousset traveled to Mexico City, but he failed to get an official contract to establish his colony. Worse, he managed to anger Santa Anna and had to flee back to the United States, where he once again plotted a return to Mexico. His next scheme called for the establishment of a new country that would include Sonora, Chihuahua, Durango, and Sinaloa, but by then support was hard to come by because competitor Walker had become very popular in California. In 1854 Raousset received signals from Santa Anna's government that a colony under his leadership would now be welcome, and once again he made his way to Mexico, this time with 350 men. Not surprisingly, he succumbed to old imperialistic ambitions, seeking to convince Mexican military leaders in Sonora to join him in a rebellion against Santa Anna. Luck ran out as Raousset's forces tried to storm Guaymas: they were defeated and captured. Eventually most of the Frenchmen were pardoned but Raousset was shot by a firing squad. His demise brought an end to the era of French filibustering into Mexico.[20]

As mentioned, the most notorious of all the filibusters was William Walker, the lawyer from Tennessee who had gone to California in search of fortune. After Mexicans denied him permission to establish an American colony in Sonora, Walker used a brig that belonged to the American consul at Guaymas to conquer Baja California in 1853. He landed at La Paz with fifty-three men, imprisoned the governor, allowed his mercenaries to loot the town, and established the "Republic of Lower California." The invaders then sailed up the coast to Ensenada, where Walker organized a government with himself as president. Local delegates reluctantly swore allegiance to Walker when they were summoned to a convention. Soon, however, the foreigners were driven from the area, whereupon they set out to conquer Sonora, which had previously been "annexed" to Walker's "republic." After a brief and fruitless stay in Sonora, they returned to Ensenada, only to encounter fierce resistance from Mexican troops, civilian volunteers, and even bandits. Weakened and disrupted, the filibusters fled across the boundary, where they surrendered to the U.S. Army. American authorities tried Walker for violating neutrality laws, but a sympathetic jury acquitted him. That ruling gave Walker the freedom to undertake a more-successful conquest of Nicaragua in 1855. His brand of imperialism touched other parts of Central America, but eventually he perished before a firing squad in Honduras.[21]

Another important filibuster of the period was Henry A. Crabb, who in 1857 led one hundred men into Sonora, intending to link up with local insurgents actively trying to overthrow the governor of that state. Crabb had understood that the eventual goal of the Mexican rebels was to seek annexation of any conquered territory to the United States and that his help would be welcome. Crabb's "Arizona Colonization Company" included influential Californians and former prominent American politicians. By the time the Yankees arrived in Sonora the rebels had taken power, but instead of providing a welcome, the Sonorans repelled the foreigners. After a ten-day battle, nearly seventy Americans surrendered; only a boy of fourteen survived the firing squad.[22]

As with previous generations of adventurers who preyed on Mexico, Crabb and the other "Golden Age" filibusters enjoyed considerable freedom to organize their expeditions on American soil. Mexico repeatedly accused the U.S. government of failing to live up to its neutrality law, which provided "that if any person shall, within the territory or jurisdiction of the United States, begin or set on foot, or provide or prepare for, any military expedition or enterprise, to be carried on from thence against the territory or dominion of any foreign prince or state, colony, district, or people with whom the United States are at peace, every such person so offending, shall be declared guilty of a high misdemeanor and shall be fined not exceeding three thousand dollars, and imprisoned not more than three years."[23]

American officials did take measures, albeit weak ones, to prevent filibustering, including issuing warning statements, alerting military commanders, seizing boats, conducting arrests, and bringing alleged offenders to trial. These actions, however, proved insufficient and ineffective, allowing filibustering activity to flourish. Mexicans felt that Washington's lackadaisical attitude was due to tacit approval of the incursions, given the prospect that any territory taken from Mexico might eventually be annexed to the United States.[24] Historian J. Fred Rippy concludes, however, that Washington was *unable*, not *unwilling*, to restrain lawless adventurers. He argues that American officials made sincere efforts to deal with the problem, but they faced obstacles that made it difficult to prosecute offenders. First, the language in the law was too imprecise; second, the law provided for apprehending suspects *after* commission of the crime, not before, thus making it difficult to arrest individuals only thought to be planning incursions; and third, the filibusters had the sympathy and support of the public. Federal prosecutors found convictions hard to come by in those areas where juries sided with the filibusters. For example, a jury in South Texas declared twelve members of the Carvajal expeditions innocent, and a California jury acquitted William Walker and dropped charges against his followers. It is true that three high-level accomplices of Walker were found guilty, but they were never punished for their crime.[25]

In 1853, the filibustering issue complicated the negotiations undertaken by James Gadsden to resolve the dispute over the southern boundary of New Mexico. The Mexicans would not accept a pact that did not obligate the United States to stop the unlawful incursions and the document finally negotiated by Gadsden did provide for the U.S. Navy to pursue filibusters who eluded civil and land military forces. The U.S. Senate, however, eliminated the article from the treaty.[26]

By the late 1850s, the filibustering spirit still remained strong in the United States, but actual incursions declined. Some ambitious undertakings never got beyond the planning stage or they fizzled out as soon as they began. Sam Houston's bold plan of 1859 to use thousands of Texas Rangers and Indians to establish a protectorate in northern Mexico failed to materialize, apparently for lack of funds.[27] Former

California Senator William McKendrie Gwin's scheme in the early 1860s to become the "Duke of Sonora" by leading a mining and commercial colony of disgruntled southerners drew a mixed reaction from the French (who then ruled Mexico through Emperor Maximilian) and definite antagonism from the people of Sonora. Meetings in Paris with Napoleon and other high officials had raised Gwin's expectations, but his lobbying efforts in Mexico failed to get concrete results.[28] Many Confederates did succeed in getting French approval for setting up farming communities south of the border, and for a time their enterprises prospered. However, the ever-present native hostility toward foreign colonization, the disruptions caused by the fighting between Mexican patriots and the French imperialists, and the opposition of the U.S. State Department undermined the work of the southern exiles. When Benito Juárez deposed Emperor Maximilian in 1867, foreigners desirous of beginning colonies in Mexico no longer had the French connection available to further their plans, and the Confederate colonies dissolved.[29]

After the Civil War in the United States, adherents to the ideology of Manifest Destiny continued to believe that further changes in the U.S.-Mexican boundary would surely take place. In the 1870s, border raiding became such a troublesome issue that U.S.-Mexican diplomatic relations reached the boiling point, encouraging some to capitalize on the friction to annex Mexican territory. For example, Texas Ranger L. H. McNelly and army officer Dewitt C. Kells conspired in 1875 to precipitate a war by creating a border incident. Their plan called for the gunboat USS *Rio Bravo*, then scheduled to patrol the Rio Grande river, to "return" fire from Mexico that would actually originate with Texas Rangers who would shoot from the Mexican bank after clandestinely crossing the river. The shooting would give the appearance of Mexican aggression, spark retaliation, and quickly escalate into a large-scale conflict. Mexico would lose, thus allowing Texas to extend its boundaries to the eastern Sierra Madre. However, American officials discovered the plot before any planned exchange of fire took place and replaced Kells as commander of the *Rio Bravo*. That removed an important element in the provocation scheme, but trouble ensued when Captain McNelly's rangers crossed into Mexico to "recover" stolen cattle, triggering a clash with Mexican ranchers and rural police at Las Cuevas. The subsequent arrival of U.S. troops on Mexican soil to aid McNelly's men threatened to escalate the hostilities, but the invaders soon withdrew to Texas. Fortunately, calm prevailed in Mexico City and in Washington during the altercation, diffusing a potentially explosive situation begun by ambitious Texans who had the support of some U.S. military officers, albeit not the American government.[30]

Two aborted filibustering schemes hatched in Southern California in the late nineteenth century illustrate the role of the American press in exposing and stopping such activities. An important factor that precipitated international adventurism at this time was the termination of the Southern California land boom and the wishes of some Americans to extend it beyond the border. Interest in Baja California among restless elements hoping to acquire land increased when the International Company, a U.S. concern with considerable holdings in Mexico, regularly advertised available tracts on the peninsula.[31] In 1888, Los Angeles resident Colonel J. K. Mulkey organized the Order of the Golden Field, a secret society with branches in Texas and Arizona. The group intended to plant American filibusters in Baja California posing as ordinary workers, farmers, and miners, who in time would foment revolution and proclaim the peninsula the "Republic of Northern Mexico." Mulkey unwisely talked about the plan with a reporter from the *San Francisco Chronicle* who pretended to be a potential member of the society. Armed with documents from American and Mexican officials who purportedly favored the scheme, Mulkey asserted that twenty thousand troops would be available for service. "When the time comes," he boasted, "the order will be so powerful that there can be no successful opposition. It will simply be the story of Texas over again."[32] But Mulkey never got the opportunity to initiate another Texas-style movement, for the information he revealed doomed the enterprise. To protect himself, the colonel later claimed he had purposely given a false account because he distrusted the reporter, but suspicions about the order's true intentions remained.

Two years after Mulkey's fiasco, a more ambitious plan to detach Baja California from Mexico was organized by a group of American businessmen and ex–military officers with backing by the Mexican Land and Colonization Company, an English syndicate. Anticipating a successful insurrection, the conspirators named a council of fifteen men to rule the peninsula following a declaration of independence. Most of the offices in the revolutionary government, which ranged from president to postal general, would go to Americans, but two or three cooperative and "deserving" Mexicans would also be rewarded as a way of enlisting the support of the native population. Just before the uprisings were to take place at Tijuana and Alamo, the *San Diego Union* broke the story and the whole affair collapsed. Conspirator Captain J. F. James saw that setback as temporary only, however, insisting that the desires of the people of Baja California for freedom made revolution inevitable. Indeed, several Mexicans opposed to the Porfirio Díaz government had met with the American plotters, presumably to join their efforts, but the feelings of the people of the peninsula at large are unknown. General John C. Fremont, the old "bear flag" filibuster of an earlier age, called the aborted scheme "a mad one and thoroughly improbable. It has its origin in the wish of certain people to see the peninsula of Lower California annexed to the United States. They believe that annexation would mean a rise in the value of land and personal emolument is at the bottom of the whole thing."[33] As usual, denials followed, with some people taking the matter lightly; others, including the publishers of the *San Diego Union* and the *San Diego Review*, felt enough evidence was available to sustain the theory that a real and elaborate plan to "liberate" Baja California had certainly existed.

THE LAST FILIBUSTERS

As the twentieth century began, most of northern Mexico found itself in the midst of an economic boom. Porfirio Díaz's emphasis on political order and promotion of foreign investment accounted for much of the growth. Expansion of mining, agriculture, ranching, and trade were stimulated by closer external ties brought about by the establishment of a railroad network in the border region. The southwestern United States experienced even greater prosperity, and great demand existed there for Mexican raw materials and cheap labor. A rapid rise in population accompanied the economic progress, as evidenced by the demographic increase that took place in the north between 1895 and 1910, which surpassed the growth achieved by other regions within Mexico. Important cities such as Chihuahua, Saltillo, Monterrey, and San Luis Potosí grew substantially faster than comparable urban centers in the interior. Along the border, Nuevo Laredo, Piedras Negras, Paso del Norte (Ciudad Juárez), and Nogales also experienced significant growth once the railroads connected them to zones of major economic significance.[34]

But progress in northern Mexico was not uniform. While the states of Tamaulipas, Nuevo León, Coahuila, Chihuahua, and Sonora grew economically and demographically, Baja California remained isolated, sparsely populated, and underdeveloped. Distance and geographic barriers kept the peninsula effectively separated from the rest of the republic, and its inhospitable terrain acted as a deterrent to human settlement. Such conditions accounted for Mexico City's designation of the region as a territory rather than a state. Few Mexican investors found the remote northwest border attractive, but Southern Californians, who had easy land and sea access to the peninsula, maintained a deep interest in exploiting its resources. People and products could easily cross back and forth at the Calexico–Mexicali and San Diego–

Tijuana borders, and it was only natural that residents of Baja California had more contact with the United States than with their own country. Attracted by the favorable policies of the Díaz government toward
foreign capital, Americans strengthened their economic foothold in
the peninsula, acquiring more land and obtaining mining and other
concessions. Foremost among American investors in Baja California
were Harrison Gray Otis and his son-in-law Harry Chandler, who controlled 832,000 acres of land through the California-Mexico Land and
Cattle Company.[35] Hence the American presence and Mexico's distant
and perennially feeble rule of its northwest territory encouraged some
expansionist-minded Southern Californians to keep alive the old idea
of annexation of Baja California to the United States.

The opportunity to once again promote the independence of the
peninsula arrived during the 1910s when revolution engulfed Mexico.
In early 1911, while Francisco Madero's forces attempted to capture
northern Chihuahua as a prelude to deposing the dictator Díaz, Mexican Liberal Party leaders Ricardo and Enrique Flores Magón sought
to launch a socialist-anarchist revolution in Baja California. The Flores
Magón brothers had been trying to overthrow Díaz for a decade. When
government repression forced them into exile in 1906, they continued
plotting insurrection in St. Louis, El Paso, and finally Los Angeles, relying on sympathetic groups such as the Industrial Workers of the World
to recruit adventurers and soldiers of fortune of various nationalities.
The Flores Magón effort to attract foreigners to the cause worked well,
and as preparations unfolded in January 1911 to launch an attack in
the Mexicali area, about 90 percent of the recruited revolutionists were
non-Mexicans. As embarrassing as that situation was in an era of pronounced Mexican nationalism, the Liberal Party commenced its offensive, and within a few months the insurgent forces, which kept growing
with each success, controlled the Mexican border between the Colorado River and the Pacific Ocean.[36]

Meanwhile, the Maderistas had captured Ciudad Juárez, where they
forced the federals to sign a treaty providing for Díaz's resignation and
new presidential elections. Díaz stepped down shortly thereafter and
Madero surged forward as the principal leader of the Revolution, but
the Flores Magón brothers refused to follow the moderate soldier-
politician, opting to continue their own radical struggle.

During the occupation of Tijuana, the latent filibustering spirit
among some of the foreigners in the Magonista army surfaced. Their
adventurism was partly encouraged by the interest expressed by many
Southern California newspapers in acquiring Mexican lands. "If Lower
California should wake up some morning to find the stars and stripes
floating over it," observed the *San Diego Sun* on May 12, "San Diego

would suddenly become more than ever a City of Destiny."[37] In early
June, amidst confusion and dissension then plaguing the Magonista
forces, "Captain" Louis James proclaimed the "Republic of Lower
California," complete with a provisional president (wealthy Southern
Californian Richard Ferris), a flag, and a constitution. Ferris's "republic" died as quickly as it started, however, because Ricardo Flores
Magón convinced Jack Mosby, one of his field commanders, to take
charge of the operations and stick to the original plan. Nevertheless,
the damage had been done, and things deteriorated rapidly for the
Magonistas. On June 17, a group of Mexican railroad workers loyal to
Madero forced them to evacuate Mexicali, and on June 22, Madero's
soldiers routed Mosby's men in Tijuana, sending the foreign adventurers scampering to the United States and effectively ending the socialist
revolution. The sensational publicity given these events at the time
created the perception that a filibustering venture disguised as a revolution had been foiled by the Mexican federal army. "The Liberal
army," commented the *San Diego Sun*, "has gone down in history with
the band of William Walker that terrorized the peninsula 50 years
ago."[38]

Subsequently, American authorities tried the Flores Magón brothers
and accomplices Richard Ferris, Jack Mosby, and Rhys Pryce for violation of the neutrality laws, but Ricardo Flores Magón was the only one
convicted. He served time in prison for the neutrality offense and was
then released, but within a few years he was put behind bars once again
for violating the U.S. Espionage Act. He died at Leavenworth in 1922
under mysterious circumstances.[39]

The Flores Magón episode created considerable controversy both in
Mexico and the United States. Mexican detractors of the Liberal Party,
especially in Baja California, accused Ricardo Flores Magón of betrayal
for participating in a conspiracy to wrest territory from Mexico. Support for his ideals in the Mexican labor sector and among intellectuals,
however, assured that in time his countrymen would view with greater
understanding how certain opportunists manipulated the Liberal
Party's movement for their own ends. Supporters of the Flores Magón
brothers would emphasize instead the important contributions of the
Magonistas to the Revolution of 1910. Indicative of the positive view
of Ricardo Flores Magón that evolved in later years is the internment
of his remains in 1945 in the nation's Rotunda of Illustrious Men.[40]
Closer examination of the evidence has likewise led historians critical
of the Flores Magón movement to modify their views.[41] It is now recognized that the stillborn "Republic of Lower California" was the work of
a small group of foreigners, some of whom were charlatans, and that
the Liberal Party leadership did not approve of filibustering. The presence of recruits from various nationalities among the Magonistas is

explained by Ricardo Flores Magón's adherence to an internationalist ideology that called for a Mexican workers' revolution linked with external radical movements. Although Flores Magón obtained some financial help north of the border, neither American capitalists nor the U.S. government influenced his struggle. Flores Magón's problems stemmed from letting too many soldiers of fortune join his army and later losing control over the actions of some of them.

Shortly after the Flores Magón episode, a less-dramatic but still-intriguing event with a filibustering twist underscored again the vulnerability of Lower California. In 1915 the U.S. government indicted Harry Chandler, an owner of the *Los Angeles Times*, along with six other persons, for conspiring to overthrow the established government of Baja California in violation of American neutrality laws. The attorney for the southern district of California charged that Chandler intended to create an independent state, an interpretation shared by others as well.[42] The affair began when Baltazar Áviles, a supporter of Pancho Villa, recruited volunteers along the U.S. side of the border to help Áviles regain the Baja California governship, an office the latter had lost to Carranza-follower Esteban Cantú, the military commander at Mexicali, during a bloodless coup in 1914. Chandler allegedly participated in the plot because Áviles had promised to forgive unpaid taxes and to protect the family's vast holdings in the Mexicali valley against land reforms recently announced by the Carranza government. At the trial, American prosecutors failed to present credible evidence establishing Chandler's complicity with Áviles, and the wealthy Southern Californian was acquitted. Defense attorneys destroyed the ill-prepared government's case by discrediting witnesses and implanting serious doubts about the conspiracy charges against Chandler. The justice department's bungling strengthened suspicions that the filibustering side of the story had remained unexposed.[43]

The involvement of Americans in the Flores Magón and Áviles incidents reinforced the view long held by Mexican government leaders that only Mexican colonization and economic control of Baja California would counteract the dangerous foreign influences. As early as 1911, provisional President Francisco León de la Barra promised to study methods of Mexicanizing the distant province and of building a railroad across the Colorado River to facilitate its contact with the mainland. The Revolution delayed those plans, but in the latter 1910s, Governor Cantú introduced large numbers of mainland colonists into the Mexicali Valley and resettled Mexican workers returning from the United States on land near Tijuana. In 1921, the Alvaro Obregón government began a colonization project that included the development of local resources and the building of a railroad from Magdalena, Sonora, to Ensenada, Baja California. By 1930, twenty-five miles of track

were completed, but the world depression forced a halt in the construction until 1938. With the slow progress on the railroad and the failure
to speed up national land reform during the 1920s, the colonization
plan languished. Ironically, the stimulus for population growth during
the period came not from Mexico but from the United States, where
Prohibition triggered a boom in tourism in the Mexican border towns.
Even so, many of the new residents who settled in Tijuana were Americans, and foreign businessmen clearly dominated the entertainment
establishments.[44]

In the early thirties, two developments in the United States alarmed
Mexican leaders. For a time, rumors circulated in the Congress that
the International Water Commission, an entity of the State Department, had recommended American purchase of Baja California. Then
U.S. Senator Henry F. Ashurst of Arizona introduced his fifth resolution since 1919 calling for the purchase of the peninsula along with
Sonora. The State Department denied the rumor, and Ashurst's idea
failed to garner significant support; just the same, throughout the decade resolutions and propaganda about Baja California persisted in
the United States, causing continued concern among Mexicans. Urging his government to immediately build roads in Baja California as a
means of tying the area to the mainland, Secretary of Communications
Juan Andreu Almazán warned in 1931 that "to oppose such works
would show an utter disregard of the very real and immediate danger
of a new mutilation of the Fatherland."[45]

Mexico's long-standing desire to remove foreign control of Baja
California and thereby eliminate the threat of U.S. annexation finally
materialized during the administration of President Lázaro Cárdenas
in the 1930s. This nationalist leader expropriated lands belonging to
the California-Mexico Land and Cattle Company, thus encouraging individual Mexican farmers to purchase plots and allowing villages to establish *ejidos* (communal holdings). By 1938, Americans had given up
ownership of 268,000 acres of land in Baja California. The Otis-Chan-
dler monopoly had been broken and Mexican colonists poured into
the area. In addition to his bold land policies, Cárdenas stimulated the
Baja California economy by allowing free foreign trade and by continuing the building of the railroad to Sonora.[46] With the completion of the
line in 1948, more Mexicans migrated to the region, causing the peninsula's population to rise to 286,000 by 1950. By virtue of the overwhelming concentration of the peninsula's population close to the border, the northern district became a state in 1952, while the southern
part remained a territory. A new age had arrived. At last Mexican control of a remote province long threatened by expansionist neighbors
was secure.[47]

SUMMARY AND CONCLUSION

Filibustering constitutes a central part of American expansionist aggression directed at Mexico. The periods of greatest intensity of unlawful invasions organized in the United States coincide with weakness and instability in Mexico, a condition that made that country's northern frontier exceedingly vulnerable to conquest. In the 1810s, Spain was consumed with wars of independence throughout Latin America, thus leaving remote areas like Texas short on military protection. Between 1821 and 1867, Mexico endured perennial political unrest, civil conflicts, depleted treasuries, separatist movements, war with the United States, and colonization by a European power. During the 1850s, when the most spectacular filibustering took place, Mexico's usual political problems were compounded by the recent trauma of the War of 1846–48 and its devastating consequences. It was an opportune moment for adventurers to seek further despoilation of Mexico's relatively unprotected border areas. The latter nineteenth century witnessed infrequent attempts at filibustering that did not get very far. A major factor in that lack of successs is the order and progress that prevailed in Mexico during the period, but equally important is the fact that the Porfirio Díaz government granted many generous concessions to foreigners, thus lessening the impulse to take Mexican land and resources by force. During the Mexican Revolution of the 1910s, cries for interventionism rose in the United States, and that, along with the confused state of affairs south of the Rio Grande and the continued isolation of perennially vulnerable Baja California, prompted some American adventurers to use the native insurrection to foment separatism.

It is remarkable that Mexico managed to hold onto its northern frontier, such as it became after 1848, in light of the persistence of the filibustering syndrome in American society even into the twentieth century. In retrospect, filibustering failed for a variety of reasons, including inadequate planning by the aggressors, insufficient human resources, poor judgment, lack of official support, and Mexican resistance. More than any other factor, firm opposition to the foreign invaders on the part of the Mexican people explains the collapse of countless invasions. Although separatist tendencies existed for generations along Mexico's northern frontier, the intervention of foreigners in such movements was hardly seen in a positive light, especially after the experience in Texas in the 1830s and the massive loss of territory in 1848.

Filibustering and pseudofilibustering added considerably to the legacy of distrust between Mexicans and Americans first engendered by diplomatic and military conflicts that led to changes in the boundary. Suspicions surfaced with regularity in Mexico City that Washington encouraged private attempts in wresting more Mexican lands. As long as the dark cloud of possible foreign conquest of Mexico hovered in the background, it was difficult to sustain amiable and productive international relations. Not until the late 1930s and early 1940s, when the entire northern frontier became more effectively integrated into the Mexican republic, did that fear begin to disappear south of the border. Along with other major changes in a traditionally conflict-ridden relationship, that development helped usher in a new climate of greater mutual respect and cooperation between the two neighbors.

CHAPTER 3

Border Indians

When the Spaniards pushed northward from central Mexico in the 1600s, they encountered Indians whose way of life contrasted sharply with that of highly urbanized groups like the Aztecs. Numerous nations and tribes with diverse linguistic and cultural characteristics lived in what today is northern Mexico and the southwestern United States. Anthropologist Edward H. Spicer has identified four types of native groups in the region, which he calls "*ranchería*," "village," "band," and "nonagricultural bands."[1] "*Ranchería*" people practiced farming and had fixed but scattered settlements. In numbers they constituted the largest category and included such groups as the Tarahumaras, Yaquis, Mayos, and Pimas. "Villagers" refers to those people who adhered to the Pueblo style of living in compact villages sustained by either irrigation or dry farm agriculture. "Band" Indians, such as the Apaches and Navajos, mixed agriculture with hunting and gathering, and lacked permanence in their settlement patterns. Numbering only a few thousand, "nonagricultural" people like the Seris formed roving bands that gathered wild foods, hunted, and fished for a living.

Extended contact with Spaniards, Mexicans, and Anglos not only altered the lifestyles of these heterogenous groups but set the stage for considerable conflict, given that the native Americans inhabited a region that came to be viewed by whites as a "borderland." For the indigenous inhabitants the only borders that ever mattered were the limits

of tribal living spaces. Although conflict often erupted when other natives trespassed on territory claimed by a tribe, the trouble tended to
be localized. That tendency changed radically when the white man organized the region according to his political and economic concepts.

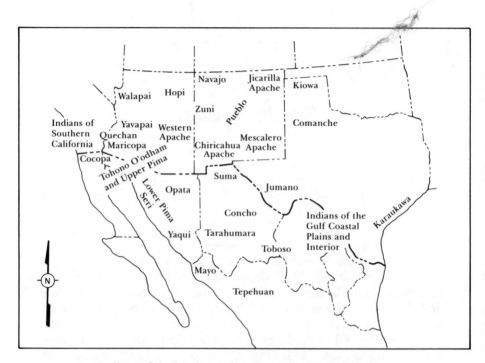

Indians of the border region. Drawn by Linda Marston.

Spain was the first to claim the borderlands, followed by Mexico, and
finally Mexico and the United States divided the area between them by
creating what seemed to the Indians a vague line called a "border." Native Americans were caught in that middle ground, sandwiched in by
aggressors who kept dribbling in from the south and the east. If the
initial encounter with whites marked one major turning point in the
history of the borderlands Indians, the creation of the U.S.-Mexico border marked another. The region's indigenous groups had to grapple
with external controls imposed by the white man, including the restriction of physical movement beyond approved international limits.
Those tribes that lived at or near the new border would find it especially difficult to adjust to the new way of life.

INDIANS AS A BORDER PROBLEM

The natives of New Spain's northern frontier strongly resisted the Spanish effort to change their culture and religion and to incorporate them into a new economic system. Among the early revolts that broke out were the Tepehuan uprising in Durango in 1616, the Tarahumara insurrection in Chihuahua in the 1640s, and the Pueblo rebellion in New Mexico in 1680. The Spaniards responded with force and intensified their efforts to congregate the Indians into missions and *pueblos*. In some areas this approach worked well, but in the plains and in the desert it failed to subdue fiercely independent and aggressive peoples such as the Apaches, Navajos, Utes, and Comanches. Not only did these groups refuse to submit to external control, they took the offensive against the whites, raiding their settlements and taking captives. By the latter eighteenth century, perennial Indian attacks heightened the concern of the Spaniards for the security of the borderlands, an area that was already threatened by the imperialistic designs of the French, English, and Russians.

Spain responded to the crisis by reorganizing its frontier defenses in the 1760s and 1770s.[2] Major changes included the creation of new *presidios* and the implementation of a cynical policy of "pacification by dependency" toward the indigenous peoples. Henceforth, Spaniards would endeavor to make treaties with individual bands, persuade them to settle near military stations where they would receive food rations, give them low-quality weapons for hunting, encourage trade, increase their appetite for Spanish goods, "hook" them on liquor, and use "divide and conquer" tactics where appropriate. The Spaniards hoped that these measures would result in the disorganization of Indian life and in the establishment of a dependency relationship, which is precisely what materialized, and for nearly twenty-five years peaceful relations came to exist between the two groups. In the early nineteenth century, however, that tendency was seriously disrupted as Spain's attention shifted to containing Mexico and other Latin American colonies then fighting for their independence. The political unrest led to a decline in Crown resources destined for the Mexican northern frontier and contributed to a general breakdown in the system established to deal with the Indians. The Sonora Apaches gradually drifted away from their settlements and resumed raiding, while Apaches from Arizona and New Mexico swept southward into Chihuahua, leaving behind destruction and desolation. With the rising Indian attacks going unchecked, many norteños, especially *sonorenses*, abandoned their homes in the ensuing years. Conditions continued to be much the same after Mexico achieved independence, for the young republic faced seemingly endless civil strife and seriously depleted economic resources. Repeated pleas from norteños for the authorities to contain the Indian assault went unheeded, bringing devastating results. According to Spicer, five thousand Mexicans along the northern frontier lost their lives and four thousand others left the area between 1820 and 1835.[3]

Along the Texas-Mexico frontier, population changes and political turmoil complicated the problem with the Indians. By 1830, Comanches and Kiowas were forced to raid throughout Texas and as deep into Mexico as Zacatecas due to loss of land and game brought about by the advance of the Americans into their homeland.[4] In the middle and late 1830s, as the Texans accelerated their drive toward independence from Mexico, many Mexicans felt the rebels used the Indians as an auxiliary to their movement, encouraging them to attack Mexican settlements. Those victimized complained that Texans supplied arms to the natives and that American traders readily accepted spoils taken by the Indians in their raids. The U.S. government also came under criticism for driving some tribes from the southern states and placing them in areas adjacent to the Arkansas and Red rivers, which they then used as bases to carry out raids in nearby Mexico. In an official investigation conducted by a commission of the Mexican government many years later, American political leaders of the 1830s and 1840s were accused of tolerating, permitting, and even stimulating such depredations into Mexico.[5] Of course, raiding was not a one-way proposition. Americans and Mexicans frequently invaded Indian territory, often killing people and taking captives. Usually the rationale for such attacks was "pacification" or retribution for Indian hostilities. One particularly deplorable practice found in New Mexico was the taking of native hostages who were then relegated to a life of servitude and peonage.[6]

Mexican concern over the Indian problem became so pronounced that President James Polk sought to use it as justification for absorbing Mexican territory. As negotiations to end the War of 1846–48 progressed in December 1847, Polk suggested that since Mexico was unable to protect its frontier, it might wish to transfer the region to the United States, allowing Americans to prevent the Indians "from committing . . . outrages and compel them to release . . . Mexican captives and to restore them to their families and friends."[7] Mexico rejected the offer, but once the Mexicans resigned themselves to the reality that the northern provinces would have to be ceded, they argued forcefully for a U.S. commitment to restrain the troublesome Indians situated to the north of the proposed boundary. The Chihuahua state legislature insisted that the peace treaty then under discussion include guarantees that Indians incorporated into the United States by the acquisition of Mexican territory would not be placed in a situation that would force them to raid in Mexico. Specifically, Chihuahua asked that Indians not be displaced from their territories, that they not be furnished arms for making war, and that no Americans be permitted to buy stolen goods or animals from the Indians.[8] American negotiator Nicholas Trist informed his government that in order to make the treaty acceptable to Mexico's northern states, it would be requisite for the United States to assume responsibility for the Indians. Despite opposition in the U.S. Senate, Article XI of the Treaty of Guadalupe Hidalgo incorporated most of the stipulations desired by Mexico. Henceforth, the 160,000 to 180,000 Indians who lived in the territory acquired by the United States would need to live by new rules, including restraining themselves from crossing a new political line that for them had little or no meaning.[9]

The United States faced the awesome task of establishing peaceful relations with the Indians, protecting its own citizens, and preventing plundering into Mexico. Vast expanses of barren terrain, weather extremes, remote mountain Indian enclaves, and the extent of the border complicated that challenge. Unable or unwilling to carry out the treaty commitments, the American government failed to stop Indian forays across the border. Between 1848 and 1853, Indian raids, originating mostly in the United States, led to the death of over one thousand Mexicans in the states of Nuevo León, Coahuila, and Sonora. Hundreds more were wounded or taken into captivity, and residents of these states sustained losses from theft of horses, cattle, mules, and other property. The people of Chihuahua also suffered considerable personal and property damage, although statistics are not available for that state. One consequence of the deplorable conditions was the further depopulation of many zones within northern Mexico.[10]

Major responsibility for the transborder incursions rested with people north of the border who profited by buying goods and captives from the Indians. According to James Calhoun, a well-known Indian agent in New Mexico, attractive female captives brought $150, and males about half that price. Mules sold for $20 to $30. Indians used some of the money obtained from such transactions to purchase arms that were generally better than the ones used by Mexican soldiers, thus complicating the defense problem for Mexico.[11]

Mexican officials filed numerous complaints against the United States, but Washington responded that everything possible was being done and that Mexicans should not expect greater protection than that offered U.S. citizens. Indeed, the people who lived in the American Southwest endured many of the same hardships as those who resided

south of the border. Comanches frequently attacked Texans, and
Apaches and Navajos regularly victimized New Mexicans and Arizonans. In 1850, a joint resolution of the Texas legislature asserted that
"vast numbers" of citizens had been killed and that "a vast amount" of
property had been stolen by Indians. In New Mexico, fifty-two long-
time residents declared in a petition that the Indian troubles had never
been worse.[12]

To deal with the problem, the U.S. government established many
forts from the Gulf of Mexico to the Colorado River, scattering four
thousand troops throughout the region by the early 1850s. Indian
agents busily negotiated treaties with various tribes, but these were
doomed to failure not only because of mutual distrust but also because
they brought few benefits to the Indians. Americans who lived in the
Southwest expressed dissatisfaction with their government's policies
and frequently complained about the lack of adequate protection. Texans, in particular, found it difficult to accept the government practice
of signing peace treaties, preferring instead a no-nonsense, ruthless
approach to subdue the Indians. For many Texans the only answer was
extermination.[13]

American agents who negotiated agreements with Indians routinely
insisted that the latter cease their raids into Mexico, but this objective
was difficult to accomplish. Indians resented any restriction on their
movement and thought it unfair to be required to give up profitable
enterprises that had been a way of life for generations. It also seemed
incomprehensible to the indigenous peoples for Americans to demand
that they stop attacking Mexicans, a common enemy. Such reasoning,
coupled with the inability of the U.S. government to back up its policies
with sufficient military power, guaranteed that the transborder raids
would continue. That is not to say that the United States made no significant effort to live up to its treaty obligations beyond the signing of
largely meaningless treaties with the Indians. American troops did engage the Indians in combat, and on occasion Indian agents and soldiers recovered Mexican captives and restored them to their families.
For example, James S. Calhoun handed over thirteen captives to Mexican officials in El Paso in June 1850, with five more being delivered at
the same place a year later.[14]

These gestures failed to impress Mexico, however. Mexicans insisted
that the American effort fell far short of actual needs and that a clear
lack of commitment existed in the United States to deal with the problem. Indeed, the U.S. Congress either failed to appreciate the gravity
of the situation or chose to ignore it, repeatedly turning down presidential requests to increase appropriations for military defense along
the border. Mexican historian Luis G. Zorrilla observes that the American policy of placing Indians on reservations failed because of the ab-

sence of resources and supportive mechanisms to ease the transition from a nomadic to a sedentary life. Americans also lacked the equivalent of the Spanish mission, notes Zorrilla, an institution that had proved successful in many areas for congregating Indians and keeping them stationary. Another American weakness was the shortage of military forces along the border. At the end of 1849, for example, Texas and New Mexico had only eighteen hundred soldiers. Later the number of troops increased, but they still fell short of the desired level, and the most effective force against the Indians—the cavalry—never numbered more than six hundred at any time between 1848 and 1853.[15]

As damages from Indian incursions into northern Mexico piled up, Mexico began to submit claims to the U.S. State Department. To the Mexican government, the enforcement of Article XI of the Treaty of Guadalupe Hidalgo constituted a small price for the United States to pay in the aftermath of the War of 1846–48, in contrast to Mexico's huge loss of territory. In fact, the Mexican minister in Washington informed the U.S. secretary of state in 1850 that Mexico's only advantage from that treaty had been the expected fulfillment of Article XI. For a time the Americans accepted the notion of being liable for damages caused by American Indians in Mexico, but as the Mexican claims escalated into the millions of dollars, Washington took a hard line against compensation. American officials pointed out that the United States had no policy to indemnify its own citizens for losses resulting from Indian raids, so Mexicans should not be entitled to receive special treatment. Washington also accused Mexico of placing too much responsibility on the United States and doing too little to protect itself.[16]

In truth, Mexico invested considerable resources to secure its border area. Beginning in 1848, it established a chain of military colonies occupied by over one thousand soldier-settlers, including hundreds of cavalry personnel. In 1852, Mexico's northern states formed a defense coalition, organizing companies of troops that fought various campaigns against the Indians for several years. Data gathered by the Mexican commission sent to investigate border conditions in 1873 showed frequent battles between Mexican fighters and Indians, including thirty-three encounters in Nuevo León and forty in Coahuila between 1848 and 1853, and from thirty to forty in Sonora between 1848 and 1851. In the state of Chihuahua, the legislature approved in 1849 the controversial practice of paying for Indian scalps and captives, encouraging many Mexicans and foreigners to engage in this savage activity for many years. Hunters received $150 for each dead Indian and $250 for a prisoner of war or a woman over fourteen years of age. Tragically, peaceful Indians and even Mexicans were often victimized in the process.[17]

To free itself from what it saw as an onerous burden, the U.S. government proposed to Mexico abrogation of Article XI of the Treaty of Guadalupe Hidalgo in exchange for payment of up to $4 million and the assumption of American claims against Mexico. But the Mexicans, who estimated actual losses at $39–$40 million, would settle for no less than $12 million and the assumption of debts due the United States. While the two countries haggled over the amounts, the depredations increased and so did the claims.[18] The issue eventually became part of the negotiating agenda taken to Mexico in 1853 by James Gadsden, whose main objective at the time was to resolve the dispute over the New Mexico–Chihuahua boundary. After prolonged negotiations, Mexico agreed to make the abrogation of Article XI part of the Gadsden Treaty, but in turn Gadsden accepted continued U.S. responsibility for the Indians, although not in as comprehensive a fashion as under the Treaty of Guadalupe Hidalgo. When the Pierce administration sent the Gadsden Treaty to the Senate for ratification, it advised modification of the statement agreed upon by Gadsden, urging new wording to reflect mutual obligation in the restraint of the Indians. The Senate, however, decided to absolve the United States altogether of the Indian responsibility by approving nothing beyond the abrogation of Article XI, and thus the Gadsden Treaty deprived Mexicans of a formal binding instrument for seeking relief from the Americans.[19]

In the years that followed, Mexico continued to press for compensation for its frontier citizens, arguing that the United States was still accountable for damages that had been inflicted since 1848. Washington countered with claims of its own citizens who had allegedly suffered even greater losses in Texas and in Mexico itself from a variety of causes. Not until the late 1860s did the two nations agree to set up a commission to settle the numerous claims that had accumulated over two decades, and in the 1870s awards were made to claimants from both countries.

Meanwhile, the Indians continued with their raids, darting across the line, striking at ranches or settlements, and then swiftly withdrawing to the other side, where pursuers were not supposed to follow. Mexico suffered most from this pattern, but Americans endured losses as well.[20] Tribes based in the mountains of Coahuila, Chihuahua, and Sonora frequently terrified residents of northwestern Texas, southeastern New Mexico, and Arizona. Of course Indians were not the only ones involved in the plundering. Bandits of both American and Mexican backgrounds took advantage of the lawless climate and general confusion to steal and kill on both sides of the border. Cattle theft along the Texas-Tamaulipas frontier became a particularly troublesome activity, eliciting desperate pleas from ranchers to their respective governments to provide added protection.

By the early 1870s the border situation had become so critical that it took center stage in U.S.-Mexican relations. Following a joint resolution of Congress, the United States appointed a three-member commission to investigate conditions at the Texas frontier. Shortly thereafter, Mexico appointed its own investigative commission. In its report, which focused on the Texas Lower Rio Grande Valley, the American commission alleged that raiding activity that originated in Mexico had caused losses in Texas amounting to $28 million and that cattle holdings along the border had declined by 75 percent. Mexican frontier officials not only did little to help, declared the American commission, but many of them participated in the illegal trade or simply chose to ignore it. The American commissioners recommended an increase of cavalry troops to bring relief to the area.[21] The Mexican commission studied the border problems at greater length than did the American panel, issuing a series of reports that sharply contradicted the above findings. Mexico's frontier had suffered far greater losses than the U.S. border area, asserted the Mexicans, and the United States was largely to blame because of its policies toward the Indians, particularly the practice of pushing Indians to the frontier, which encouraged them to prey on Mexico for a livelihood. Border Mexicans had repeatedly been victimized by horse and cattle thieves who used Texas as their base of operations. The Mexican commissioners strongly rejected the claims against Mexico presented by the Texans, arguing that the latter greatly exaggerated their losses. Most of the thieves who robbed the Texans were Americans of Anglo extraction, said the Mexican panel, and the few Mexicans who participated in this activity had been trained by Texans themselves. The Mexican commission further declared that Americans raised complaints against Mexico with the intent of finding excuses to annex more Mexican territory. In order to solve the problems, extradition procedures would need to be simplified, each government would need to do more to police its own borders, and above all, the United States would need to change its attitude from aggressive hostility to friendly cooperation.[22] To make sure that Mexico's viewpoint became known and understood in the United States, the Mexican government had the commission's reports translated into English and published as a volume in 1875.[23]

The reports of both countries succeeded in documenting a host of border problems, but they contributed little toward providing solutions. Marauders continued their destructive activities. To make matters worse, Mexican internal politics deteriorated during the period, contributing to the lawless border climate and making it more difficult to carry on normal diplomatic negotiations. In 1876, Mexico's established government was overthrown by Porfirio Díaz. That event reinforced the perception long held in the United States that Mexico's political system was hopelessly chaotic and that the interests of Americans could best be served by annexation of Mexican territory, or at least by establishing a U.S. protectorate along the border.[24] Díaz's inability to quiet the border delayed full U.S. recognition of his regime for a year and a half, heightening existing confusion and misunderstanding. By the late 1870s, the border friction ballooned into a full-scale crisis. Tensions rose particularly because the United States, unable to secure an agreement from Mexico for reciprocal crossings of the border to pursue marauders, unilaterally decided in 1877 to enter Mexican territory to punish offenders. Some ten to fifteen American transborder expeditions followed during the next two years, eliciting loud protests from Mexico. Later, when the center of border disturbances shifted from the Texas Rio Grande area to the New Mexico and Arizona borders, the two countries finally entered into an agreement permitting troops of either country to cross the boundary in pursuit of hostile Indians. A new era of cooperation had begun. The reciprocal crossing pact remained in force from 1882 to 1886, when most of the Apaches were subjugated, but subsequent sporadic incidents necessitated several renewals of the pact into the 1890s.[25]

Thereafter, conflict over Indian transboundary incursions faded as an issue in the relations between Mexico and the United States. The troublesome indigenous groups had largely been eliminated or banished to reservations, both governments had more effective administrative and military control of the region, and modernization had penetrated sufficiently to reduce the isolation of the borderlands. Long-awaited peace had arrived, but the remaining native Americans would face other problems for generations to come.

THE INDIAN DILEMMA

Fundamentally, the trouble faced by the United States and Mexico with the Indians of the border region stemmed from the impossible situation in which the Indians were placed by their white conquerors. The Indian territories became the frontier area for outsiders who aggressively moved in to claim land and resources. Spaniards, Mexicans, and Americans fought wars, signed treaties, created borders, and regulated life on the frontier with insufficient concern for the effect these momentous events would have on the indigenous inhabitants. That approach guaranteed conflict, but of course, the nature and degree of the friction varied depending on time, place, and actors. Spaniards, who had a sense of religious mission toward the Indians of the New World, typically encountered little resistance in their initial relations with native peoples, but as the newcomers commenced imposing regulations and restrictions, rebellions broke out, followed by suppression and subsequent Indian submission to European domination. Spaniards and Mexicans felt a duty to "civilize" the natives and to incorporate them into their societies, but invariably at the bottom of the social order. Anglos, on the other hand, generally pushed the Indians aside, forcibly isolated them, and when nothing else worked, exterminated them.[26]

The Indian response to domination ranged from peaceful integration to armed resistance. The California Indians, for example, accommodated themselves to the mission system, but the Tarahumaras of Chihuahua repeatedly rejected that way of life. To a significant extent, violence against the whites stemmed from the dislodging of the Indians from hunting grounds or fertile valleys that supported their way of life. In the first half of the nineteenth century, Anglos evicted several eastern tribes into western lands, and later they established ill-conceived reservations in the territories ceded by Mexico. Often, tribes were moved from one reservation to another for the convenience of the whites, causing bewilderment and resentment among the Indians. In many cases reservations lacked good agricultural land, water, or game, forcing the Indians to look elsewhere to meet basic needs. Not surprisingly, many chose stealing and plundering as the practical response to their difficult situation. Indians had been known to raid each other before they ever encountered whites, but the conditions imposed by the latter served to reinforce such practices.

An examination of those parts of the Treaty of Guadalupe Hidalgo that refer to the borderlands peoples incorporated by the United States illustrates the marginality of the Indians. Article XI, which focuses on the responsibility of the United States to restrain Indians from raiding in Mexico, took care of Mexico's main concern—protection from perennially unfriendly northern tribes and prevention of possible conflict with tribes that might be displaced within American territory in the future. But what of the rights of the Indians as newly incorporated subjects of the United States? Articles VIII and IX, which specifically mention citizenship, property, and religious rights for Mexicans, say nothing about Indians. It has been argued, however, that the term "Mexican" implied inclusion of the Indians, for Mexico itself had long counted Indians among its citizens, and a lengthy tradition existed dating to the Spanish period of protecting Indian communities from encroachment by outsiders.[27] Under this interpretation, Indians were entitled to all the rights guaranteed to the Mexicans of the Southwest, including protection from unlawful loss of land. But as students of the Southwest well know, the United States failed miserably to protect the rights of Mexicans, and the latter soon became second class citizens in U.S. society. If Americans neglected the Mexicans, who at least had the Mexican government to remind the United States of its obligations, how could they be expected to pay attention to the Indians, who lacked an advocate?

Hence, despite the protection implied for Indians of the Southwest in the Treaty of Guadalupe Hidalgo, these peoples fared no better than Indians from other parts of the United States. Lacking sorely needed assistance, the borderlands Indians suffered massive population decline, isolation, persecution, and economic dislocation. Early constitutions written by the southwestern states specifically disenfranchised the Indians, and the machinery set up to validate land claims bypassed most of them. For decades the federal government did little beyond embarking on pacification compaigns, signing meaningless treaties, and establishing ineffective reservations. Not until 1924 did Washington confer U.S. citizenship on the Indians. When confronted with the issue of Indian rights stemming from the Treaty of Guadalupe Hidalgo, the government maintained that no obligation had been incurred under that document. Of course the Indians themselves knew little about the treaty; it was American reformers of the late nineteenth century who first linked Indian rights to that treaty.[28]

When conditions became unbearable in the United States, several American tribes sought refuge south of the boundary; Mexico accepted these refugees on the condition that they stop raiding and that they help in pacifying other troublesome Indians. Driven by American troops, a small group of Karankawas left Texas after 1848 and crossed into Mexico. In 1850, a group of Seminoles, Kickapoos, and Muscogees asked for and received colonies in Coahuila after declaring that Americans had appropriated their lands in the United States. Because of unsettled conditions along the border, some of these Indians later moved deeper into Mexico. For example, the Seminoles and Kickapoos sent a delegation into Mexico City in 1852 to arrange for a reservation in the interior of Coahuila, which the Mexican government agreed to grant to them. The colony, located about 125 miles southwest of Piedras Negras, became known as "Nacimiento" and endures to this day. In 1854, U.S. troops reported that a tribe of Lipans and three bands of Mescaleros had settled in Tamaulipas and Chihuahua. Within a few years of their arrival in Mexico, most of the refugees abandoned their settlements, choosing to relocate elsewhere in Mexico or to return to the United States. Destitution and conflict with non-Indians forced them to pull stakes initially, and much the same conditions prompted subsequent moves.[29]

During their stay in Mexico, these Indians received blame for count-less atrocities committed in Texas, and on occasion, they were accused of perpetrating crimes in Mexico as well. The charges were often exaggerated, but there is an element of truth to them. Americans be-came particularly incensed at the aid given runaway black slaves by the Indians who had settled in northeastern Mexico. Seminole leader Caacoochie, better known as "Wild Cat," was one of the most successful liberators of the slaves. For years he cagily directed their flight through Texas and into Mexican territory, where many of them became part of the Seminole and Kickapoo tribes.[30]

Among the indigenous population of the U.S. Southwest, the In-dians of Texas were subjected to particularly harsh treatment, suffer-ing extermination or banishment after they came into contact with the white man. Sedentary tribes who submitted to the Spanish-Mexican systems lost much of their cultural identity, and thousands of Indians fell victim to diseases for which they had no immunity. By virtue of their nomadic and aggressive disposition, the plains Indians made poor subjects for mission life; thus they successfully maintained their independence and lifestyle, at least until Americans from the eastern United States encroached on their homeland. From the very beginning of their contact with Texas Indians, American-Indian antagonisms abounded. For example, as some of Stephen Austin's colonists made it to shore in 1821 after being shipwrecked, they were killed by Kar-ankawas. Hostilities with this tribe continued, until Americans and Mexicans forced the Karankawas to sign a treaty in 1827 after literally driving them to the sea. Facing further pressures, the tribe split into subgroups that scattered along the coast, went inland, or left for Mexico. Later soldiers and ranchers almost annihilated some of these roving bands.[31]

As Americans spread throughout Texas following secession from Mexico in 1836, frontier lands were taken or sold to settlers, with the result that Indians were constantly retreating to less-desirable areas. Cherokees and allied tribes who had settled on fertile lands in eastern Texas faced brutal attacks in 1839 following white agitation against them. Survivors fled to other parts of the United States and Mexico. Along the way some of the displaced bands encountered white troops and hunters who shot at them. With eastern Texas free of Indians, and with middle Texas occupied by more peaceful Wacos, Tawakonis, and Wichitas, the battle lines shifted to the northwestern plains, the land of the Comanches.[32]

In the 1830s, Comanches and Kiowas experienced great hardships when the American presence led to loss of land and diminishing game, forcing these Indians to increase raiding activity in Texas and in Mexico. That engendered harsh attacks from revenge-seeking Texans. Demoralized Comanche groups sought peaceful relations with the whites, and signing of peace treaties followed, but these were routinely disregarded by both sides and conflict continued. Annexation of Texas to the United States in 1845 put the Indians at a greater disadvantage, as Texas, unlike other western states, kept its land under state rather than federal domain, thus avoiding the responsibility of providing land for the Indians.[33] Texans expected the federal government to solve the Indian problem, but Washington could do little to bring about pacification without having land to give to the Indians. One thing federal agents did do was to advise the Indians that they must not raid in Mexico because that would violate an international treaty entered into by the United States. Of course the Indians felt compelled to disregard that admonition, but in so doing they had to contend with U.S. troops that guarded the frontier. From the Indian perspective, the situation had become impossible.

After prolonged indecision on assigning land to the Indians, the Texas legislature resolved in 1854 to create reservations, but as these lands were situated in the path of white settlement, the continuation of conflict was assured. Five years later the Texans decided on a drastic measure: forceful removal of the Indians from the state to a reserve north of the Red River. Major Robert S. Neighbors, the agent in charge of escorting the Indians out of the state, compared the exodus to that of the Israelites many centuries earlier. Henceforth Indians could not reside legally in Texas. Defying Texas law, some continued to rampage through the state and along the Mexican border, bringing desolation to countless communities. For example, the state of Nuevo León blamed over one hundred deaths to Comanche raids carried on between 1857 and 1870.[34]

By the mid 1870s, attention shifted from Texas to the Indian troubles farther west along the boundary. Approximately fifty thousand Indians lived in Arizona and New Mexico at the time the United States took over the Southwest in 1848. Most had a semi-nomadic lifestyle and strongly resisted the American effort to subdue them, with the notable exception of the peaceful and fully settled Pueblos of the upper Rio Grande area. The Navajos, a branch of the Apaches, constituted the largest group. Jicarilla Apaches inhabited northeastern New Mexico, along with bands of Utes who roamed into the area from their home in Colorado. Along the border lived the Mescalero and Lipan Apaches of southeastern New Mexico, the Chiricahua Apaches of western New Mexico–eastern Arizona, and the Tohono

O'odham (formerly Papago) and Yuma tribes of southeastern Arizona. These Indians created major problems for the United States by resisting white attempts to subdue them, by opposing efforts to relocate them, and by continuing the long-established practice of raiding. It took many years and hundreds of offensives conducted by American troops before the Arizona–New Mexico Indians were finally subjugated. In 1863–64 alone, 143 battles in New Mexico resulted in six hundred dead Indians and almost nine thousand Indian prisoners.[35]

The case of the Navajos illustrates the desperate measures taken by Americans to suppress Indian resistance. Following a chaotic decade that witnessed countless hostile actions and atrocities on both sides, the U.S. government practically starved the Navajos into surrender in the early 1860s. Thousands were then forcibly driven on foot in 1864 through three hundred miles of rugged terrain to a barren area in eastern New Mexico known as Bosque Redondo. Pathetic conditions at their new reservation led to two thousand deaths and forced the government to reverse its action, allowing the Navajos to return to their homeland in 1868. The experience became deeply etched in the memory of the tribe, whose members still bitterly refer to it as "The Long Walk."[36]

But problems with Navajos were exceeded by conflict with Apaches. In parts of Arizona, white-Apache relations deteriorated to the point where American settlers faced the prospect of being driven from their homes. Reduction of U.S. troops in the region during the Civil War partially explains the troubles, but a concerted campaign to imprison Apache chiefs significantly increased the anger of the Indians. The Apaches not only attacked Americans, they also raided Pimas and Tohono O'odham, as well as Mexicans from Sonora. In 1865 the military commander of Arizona reported that Tubac had been deserted and that only two hundred souls remained in Tucson. To the north, most white settlements faced annihilation or abandonment. Several years of living in that dangerous environment drove angry Arizonans to demand greater protection from the U.S. government, but the response from Washington, which called for a peace policy toward the Apaches, greatly disappointed many whites who saw extermination of the Indians as the only solution. Inevitably the highly charged atmosphere produced calamities. One tragic incident occurred in 1871 when a large mob from Tucson killed more than one hundred Apaches, including men, women, and children, during a dawn attack at Camp Grant, where the Indians had temporarily camped. Indignation and outrage expressed by people from the eastern United States forced a trial, but a Tucson jury acquitted the 104 participants, who included Anglo-

Americans, Mexican Americans, Mexicans, and Tohono O'odham among their number. Some of the mob members were prominent settlers.[37]

As a way of keeping the Indians and whites apart while seeking a permanent and peaceful solution to the conflict, the federal government created temporary reservations and refuge stations between 1866 and 1872. That practice was then replaced with a policy of concentrating the Indians in a few permanent reservations, some of them of considerable size, where the Indians were to receive material aid and instruction in farming.[38] By 1887 all the Indians of New Mexico and Arizona were officially settled in specified locations. New Mexico Apaches received two reservations—the 1,165-square-mile Jicarilla tract in the northwest, and the 741-square-mile Mescalero reserve near the Mexican border. In Arizona, the government brought together more than thirty-five hundred Indians from several tribes and placed them at the White Mountain Reservation. Problems soon developed at White Mountain because of the traditional hostility that existed among many of the bands and because white settlers coveted the resources found in the region. Consequently the government detached parts of the reservation over the next few years, and in 1896 what remained of White Mountain was split in two parts, the northern tract becoming the Apache Reservation and the southern part, the San Carlos Reservation. Major reservations established in northern Arizona during the period included the Hopi Reservation (1882) and the Hualapai Reservation (1883).[39]

The case of the Chiricahua Apaches, whose homeland straddled Arizona and New Mexico at the Mexican border, is of special interest because of the magnitude of violence that touched their lives and because they figured so prominently in U.S.-Mexican relations for a number of years. Historically the Chiricahuas had terrorized Spaniards and Mexicans on the Sonora-Arizona frontier, and when American miners, ranchers, and farmers settled in the area, they too felt the wrath of these Indians. The American colonists obtained some relief when the federal government established a reservation for the Chiricahuas in 1872, but raiding into Mexico went on as before. Problems on the Chiricahua reservation developed in 1876 when internal dissension among the Indians led to a fracas in which several whites died. As the situation deteriorated, the Arizona governor called for the removal of the Indians, and the federal government, which already questioned the wisdom of having a reservation of troublesome Indians so close to Mexico, followed suit by abolishing the reservation and relocating over three hundred Chiricahuas to San Carlos. Chiricahua Chief Gerónimo and his followers refused to go along and fled to Mexico. About the same time, Victorio, another major Chiricahua leader who had been living in Warm Springs, New Mexico, also rejected the San Carlos option, choosing instead to lead a nomadic and predatory existence along the border.

In the ensuing decade, Gerónimo, Victorio, and other Apache chiefs led their warriors in protracted and devastating attacks against Americans and Mexicans in Arizona, New Mexico, Sonora, and Chihuahua. During the reign of terror, hundreds died and considerable property was lost. In 1880, Mexican troops killed Victorio along with seventy-eight of his followers in the mountains of Chihuahua south of El Paso. Some of the survivors settled in Mexico and others returned to reservation life in Arizona. Four years later, Gerónimo and other renegade leaders returned to the Fort Apache region but stayed only a short time. In 1885, after U.S. troops harrassed Indians at Fort Apache over the manufacture of homemade liquor, the famous chief left for Mexico once more, taking with him a large number of warriors. By then an agreement existed with the Mexican government that allowed U.S. troops to cross the border to chase Indians, and Americans undertook a long pursuit of Gerónimo in the Sonora mountains, finally forcing him to surrender in 1886. Gerónimo's days as a guerrilla fighter along the border had come to an end. He and other Chiricahuas were sent by train to confinement centers in Florida. After a few years of prison life, the proud Gerónimo was reduced to a tourist attraction in major fairs and expositions around the United States; that too came to an end in 1909, when he died. Most of his people were sent to the Mescalero Reservation in New Mexico in 1913.[40]

Apache troubles did not end with the elimination or capture of the famous Chiricahua chiefs. As late as the 1920s, Apache warriors still used the rugged border mountains as a base from which to carry on marauding operations. One incident that received considerable press coverage occurred in 1926 in Sonora. A group of Apaches attacked a ranch, killed a woman, and kidnapped her child, prompting the husband and father, Francisco Fimbres, to begin a passionate and protracted campaign to punish the assailants. Fimbres sought his government's help in tracking down the Indians, but the authorities hesitated out of fear of arousing the recently pacified Yaquis. In 1929 Fimbres did receive some official assistance. However, his effort to rescue his son was unsuccessful. A proposed second, larger campaign involving the Mexican army received widespread attention in the United States, where newspapers dubbed the operation the "West's last Indian round-up." Hundreds of Americans and Canadians volunteered to join the chase, but the Mexican government, conscious of previous troubles with foreign adventurers on its northern frontier, approved the participation of only a few. The big "roundup" never materialized, due to political unrest in Mexico at the time and to the continuing concern over the presence of foreigners on Mexican soil. That forced Fimbres and other Sonora ranchers to continue on their own. In 1930 they killed five Apaches, and in 1935 they hunted down the rest of the suspected band, but Fimbres never found his son.[41]

In California, Indian-white relations involved considerably less violence owing to the presence of generally peaceful and sedentary indigenous groups. Many of these West Coast Indians were readily incorporated into the Spanish mission system but were later displaced by the process of secularization that occurred in early nineteenth century California. Further disruption ensued when Americans encroached on their lands following the Mexican cession of 1848. Treaties signed by half the Indians in California with the U.S. government called for the creation of reservations, but in 1852 the U.S. Senate refused ratification, effectively stripping the Indians of their land altogether. They also had little success with the Land Claims Commission, which confirmed only a handful of land grant claims to the Indians. Deprived of their traditional means of livelihood, thousands fled to white settlements to enter a life of servitude and destitution, and eventually large numbers perished from malnutrition and disease. In 1848, the Indians of California numbered between 150,000 and 200,000; by 1885 they had declined to only 17,000.[42]

The deplorable conditions among the California Indians moved American reformers to call for new government policies. Reports written during the 1880s and 1890s stressed Indian rights derived by historical presence as well as from the Treaty of Guadalupe Hidalgo. Best known among the works of the reformers is Helen Hunt Jackson's statement of outrage entitled *A Century of Dishonor: A Sketch of the United States' Dealings with Some of the Indian Tribes* (1881). In the San Diego area, sympathizers were prompted by the revocation in 1871 of an executive order that had established four townships for the Indians. Opponents of the Indian townships bitterly complained that white settlers had occupied the land in question and made some improvements. Their pressure worked and the president of the United States abolished the townships, although later the government did create many reservations in San Diego County. Even so, most were only between one and three square miles in size, and the greater part of the land was unsuited for cultivation.[43]

As awareness of the plight of the California Indians increased, additional lands were made available for their use. In 1928 Congress authorized the state's attorney general to bring suit against the federal government for its rejection of numerous treaties that had been signed in 1852. Sixteen years later the Indians involved in the case received $5 million in compensation from the Court of Claims.[44]

USE OF THE BOUNDARY FOR SURVIVAL: KICKAPOOS AND YAQUIS

Two Indian groups in the border region, the Kickapoos and the Yaquis, stand out for their use of the boundary to escape persecution and to maintain their ways of life. In the nineteenth century, the Kickapoos, a U.S. tribe from the Great Lakes region of the United States, witnessed the migration of a portion of its population into Mexico, while the Yaquis, a Mexican tribe from northwestern Mexico, sent some of its people to the United States. Both groups experienced considerable conflict with authorities from their own countries and lost much in the process. Nevertheless, long after their exodus from their homelands, the border Kickapoos and Yaquis retained their identities as indigenous peoples and kept their ties with the mother tribes. For both groups, the boundary has been of fundamental importance.[45]

Friction with other Indians and with succeeding waves of European and Americans caused the Kickapoos in the Great Lakes area to migrate westward, and by the 1820s splinter bands had moved into Texas. When Texas became an independent republic in the 1830s, the Kickapoos, who had experienced violent clashes with the Texans, fled to Oklahoma and to Mexico. About 80 settled at Morelos, Coahuila, a town some forty miles south of Eagle Pass, Texas. In 1850 they were joined by about 500 Kickapoos from Missouri, who brought along a group of Seminoles and American Blacks as well. Two years later, however, most of the Kickapoos left for Oklahoma, leaving only 20 in Mexico. In 1862 an estimated 1,300 Kickapoos left Oklahoma and Kansas to settle in Mexico, but part of the group disliked what they found and returned to the United States. Another major migration occurred in the early 1870s when American troops, seeking to eliminate Indian raiding along the Texas border, forced the removal of several hundred Kickapoos from Mexico. By 1875, only about 350 Kickapoos remained south of the border. Finally, in the late 1890s two groups returned to Mexico when the U.S. government instituted new land policies at the Oklahoma reservation that worked against the interests of many Kickapoos.[46]

Among the root causes of the recurring Kickapoo migration between the United States and Mexico in the nineteenth century was constant confrontation with whites. Often the Kickapoos found themselves caught in the middle of factional fighting in American society. For example, during the Civil War, one Kickapoo band chose to go to Mexico rather than join the forces of the South or the North. On their way, while in Texas, some local Confederates attacked them, forcing them to hasten their trip across the border. That incident, which occurred in 1862, left the Kickapoos with strong anti-Texan feelings. Those bitter sentiments were reinforced in 1863 when another band of Kickapoos, who were also on their way to Mexico, had to fight an attack by Texas Rangers and Confederates at Dove Creek, Texas.[47]

These encounters led the Kickapoos to think of the Texans as among their worst enemies, and a prolonged era of raiding of Texas settlements followed. Trouble between the Texans and the Kickapoos from Mexico reached such serious proportions that the U.S. Congress launched an investigation in 1872. The investigative committee concluded that the Kickapoos were operating under the protection of Mexican officials, and the only solution was to induce them to leave Mexico and migrate to Indian Territory in Oklahoma. Efforts followed to peacefully persuade the Kickapoos to abandon their settlement in Coahuila but to no avail. American agents sent to negotiate the proposed departure not only encountered opposition among the Kickapoos themselves but among Mexicans who saw these Indians as protectors against marauding tribes, such as the Comanches and Mescaleros. Indeed, the Kickapoos fought numerous campaigns alongside Mexicans against these traditional enemies of the non-Indian population of northern Mexico. Many Kickapoos served in the Mexican military, and in return for the service rendered to Mexico, they received land concessions and sanctuary from their enemies in the United States.[48]

Upon seeing the futility of attempting the peaceful removal of the Kickapoos from Mexico, a force of four hundred Americans led by Colonel Ronald S. Mackenzie crossed the border without permission from the Mexican government and invaded the Kickapoo village near Remolino, while the men were away on a hunting expedition. The Americans took some forty frightened women and children to San Antonio, Texas, and later to Oklahoma. When the U.S. government refused to return the captives, several hundred Kickapoos bowed to the pressure and removed themselves from Mexico in order to join their kidnapped kin in Oklahoma. Other Kickapoos left Mexico in later years, but those who remained continued their raiding in Texas, perpetuating the instability that had long existed along the border.[49]

During the Mexican Revolution, the Kickapoos once again found themselves in the middle of a conflict that did not concern them but that they could not escape. For some time they fought with the forces of Pancho Villa but later joined those of Victoriano Huerta. At one point a contingent of Carrancistas (followers of Venustiano Carranza) burned their village and forced them to flee into the mountains. For years the Kickapoos left their settlement at night fearing attacks from revolutionaries or federal troops. Peace finally arrived around 1920, and the Kickapoos once again resumed their traditional life of farming, ranching, and hunting.[50]

For a quarter century following the Mexican Revolution, the Kickapoos enjoyed relative stability in their Nacimiento settlement, but by the mid-1940s troubles began to appear that once again disrupted their lives and forced them to resume their old migratory ways. Water shortages, mechanization, conflicts with neighboring ranchers, and plant diseases reduced their agricultural productivity, prompting many to seek employment elsewhere. By the 1960s, almost all the Kickapoos had joined the stream of workers from Mexico who annually crossed the border to work in the United States.[51] Their way of life assumed the character of international migrant farm workers, complete with a way station at the Rio Grande. For years they have left Nacimiento for part of the year to travel to the United States, stopping temporarily at the "Kickapoo Village" underneath the international bridge that connects Piedras Negras, Coahuila, with Eagle Pass, Texas. The Kickapoos retained rights to cross into American territory based on possession of a letter signed by an American military officer in Illinois in 1832 that guaranteed the tribe recognition and protection by the U.S. government. Reportedly some still possess a xerox copy of that letter and use it to cross the border. Most simply identify themselves as "Kickapoo" to U.S. immigration inspectors familiar with their status and migration patterns. From Eagle Pass the Kickapoos follow the crops in Texas, Florida, the Midwest, and the Northwest. Only a few families remain in Nacimiento during the picking season.[52]

Recently, important government decisions have come about that offer hope for changing the migratory lifestyle in which the Kickapoos have been locked for the last several decades. In 1977, Texas, once enemy territory, recognized them as a tribe, paving the way for state assistance. Then in 1983 the U.S. government passed the "Texas Band of Kickapoo Act," which extended them official recognition at the federal level, thus making them eligible to obtain reservation land in Texas and to receive government services provided to U.S. Indians.[53]

Looking back, the border Kickapoos can take pride in their perseverance and triumph over potent forces that repeatedly threatened their survival as a group. Their legacy of disruptive migration actually began before they made contact with whites, for their original homeland could support human life only up to a certain level. Interaction with Americans resulted in the breakup of the Kickapoos into various roaming bands. Those who settled in Mexico lived a precarious existence, for the American enemy was uncomfortably close, and the possibility of eviction from their adopted homeland always concerned them.

The government of Mexico from the very beginning explicitly agreed to let the Kickapoos maintain their traditional language and culture, although it did require them to abide by the laws of Mexico and actively participate in frontier defense against "barbarous" tribes. In sum, the strong will of the Kickapoos, their adaptation to changing circumstances, and their use of the boundary to gain advantage helped to overcome many crises. Those collective experiences will ease the adjustment to yet another new situation as they settle permanently in Texas as an officially recognized U.S. "band."

Like the Kickapoos, the Yaquis of Mexico have survived as a distinct people despite forced fragmentation and dispersal. Moreover, a portion of the Yaqui population used the border as bands of Kickapoos had done before them, crossing it to escape persecution. Whereas the Kickapoos took refuge in Mexico, many Yaquis found asylum in the United States.

The emigration of the Yaquis from their homeland in Sonora to other parts of Mexico and to the United States began in the 1880s during a rebellion against the Mexican government led by Chief Cajeme. Following a long tradition of resistance against attempts by outsiders to dominate them, the Yaquis during this period sought to assert their autonomy as an independent nation. Cajeme kept them in a perpetual state of war, causing many to flee the fighting. Others took advantage of the new railroad that connected Sonora with the United States to move northward in search of employment. Eventually, in 1897, Cajeme was captured and executed, beginning a process of fragmentation for the Yaqui nation.[54]

Another major Yaqui revolt occurred in 1895, prompting Porfirio Díaz to initiate a policy of extermination for some and forced labor in the *henequen* plantations of far-off Yucatán for others. More Yaquis fled to safer areas of Sonora, and hundreds migrated to Arizona, settling among the Tohono O'odham and among whites in Nogales and Phoenix. During the administration of Sonora Governor Rafael Izábal, who carried out the most determined campaign to deport Yaquis to Yucatán, approximately one thousand Yaquis entered Arizona. Some denied being Yaquis to elude the Mexican Rural Police and make it to the border.[55] Another exodus occurred in 1916–17, when the government renewed the campaign against the Yaquis.[56] Trouble erupted again in the 1920s with a last-ditch government attempt to flush the Yaquis from the mountains, prompting more Indians to flee to the United States. Slowly peace returned to the Yaqui homeland, inducing some to leave Arizona and resettle in Mexico. In subsequent decades small numbers of Yaquis continued to trickle across the border, but the bulk of the migration had taken place by 1920.[57]

The Yaquis who settled in Arizona arrived both individually and in groups that had unified for mutual support and protection during the years of pronounced persecution. Some of the immigrants took jobs as farm laborers around Tucson, Phoenix, and Yuma, and others worked with the railroads, moving throughout the U.S. Southwest. They found it difficult to transplant traditional family and community institutions because of their fragmented situation and their precarious economic status in the United States. Yet they managed to retain a strong identification with the Yaqui nation, although their way of life came to differ somewhat from that of the main group in Sonora.[58]

In the 1930s, President Lázaro Cárdenas initiated a new era for the Yaquis by establishing an Indigenous Community in their traditional tribal lands, which included the right to run their own local government. Later, federal aid became available for agricultural development, and the Yaquis experienced some economic advances. However, lack of water for irrigation and other needed resources kept most at subsistence level, despite the availability of good land. By contrast, large commercial farmers south of the Yaqui River who had external capital, imported technology, and access to water provided by government-built dams prospered greatly. Indeed, the Yaqui Valley became one of the most productive zones in Mexico, but the benefits of this development bypassed the indigenous population.[59] In Arizona, assistance from Washington in the 1960s led to the establishment of Yaqui farming enterprises, including the creation of cooperatives. Though lack of land ownership and poverty remained perpetual problems, and despite internal dissension and conflicts with American government bureaucrats, the Arizona Yaquis managed to maintain their customs and traditions and to make improvements in their living conditions.[60]

Like the Mexican Kickapoos, therefore, the Arizona Yaquis overcame the hardships of life in exile to remain an Indian community with significant ties to the parent group on the other side of the border. Despite three and a half centuries of calculated efforts by whites to destroy their cultural heritage, Yaquis in Arizona and in Sonora have refused to be absorbed into the mainstream of society on either side of the border. That they have endured is a tribute to their strong will and sense of self-determination.

As historian Evelyn Hu-DeHart has observed, they "stand out for

having waged the most . . . enduring and successful war against in-
voluntary absorption."[61] Of course in recent years their lives have been
deeply influenced by the controls exercised by government officials
and by increased interaction with groups outside their communities.
Thus the objective of maintaining cultural distinctness has become
much more difficult, but "they have not yet surrendered the ethos of
resistance."[62] At present there are about thirty thousand Yaquis; most
live in the Yaqui River area, but there are several thousand scattered
throughout Mexico and about six thousand residing in the United
States.[63]

BORDER INDIANS TODAY

After four and a half centuries of contact with the white man, some
twenty-five indigenous peoples in the borderlands remain as distinct
groups within U.S. and Mexican societies. Their numbers have been
substantially reduced from the time of initial contact, but most have
achieved a degree of stability that has allowed for group continuity. An
estimated one-third of the approximately 1 million Indians in the
United States reside in Texas, New Mexico, Arizona, and California.
New Mexico and Arizona together account for 20 percent of the total
U.S. Indian population.[64] About forty-four thousand Indians live in the
U.S. counties adjacent to the boundary, as Table 3.1 indicates. Included
in that figure are Kickapoos, Tiguas, Mescaleros, Yaquis, Pimas,
Maricopas, Yumas, and various California tribes. On the Mexican side,
some eighty thousand indigenous peoples, including several Baja
California groups, Kickapoos, Tohono O'odham, Ópatas, Seris, Yaquis,
and Tarahumaras, live in the states of Baja California Norte, Sonora,
Chihuahua, and Coahuila. The Tarahumaras of Chihuahua, number-
ing some fifty thousand, constitute the largest Indian group in the
Mexican border area.[65]

Conditions among the borderlands Indians reveal widespread isolation, economic deprivation, and political powerlessness. A report by
the U.S. Commission on Civil Rights published in 1973 characterized
the living standards of New Mexico and Arizona Indians as "grim," noting "few hopeful signs or positive action" for future improvement.[66]
The commission found deplorable economic problems, with unemployment rates at just under 40 percent in New Mexico and between
50 and 60 percent in Arizona. Educational data revealed achievement
levels of Indian children at two to three years below, and dropout rates
far above, those of the general population. Lacking adequate health
care, Indians had a high infant mortality rate and a short life expec-
tancy. The application of justice toward the Indians was found to be

Table 3.1
Indian Population in U.S. Border Region, 1980

	Number	Percentage of U.S. Indian Population	Percentage of State Indian Population
United States	1,364,033	100.00	
Border states			
Texas	50,296		100.0
New Mexico	106,585		100.0
Arizona	154,175		100.0
California	227,757		100.0
Total	538,813	39.5	100.0
Border counties			
Texas	3,663		7.3
New Mexico	3,980		3.7
Arizona	18,940		12.3
California	17,499		7.7
Total	44,082	3.2	8.2

SOURCE: U.S. Bureau of the Census, *Census of Population.*

unfair. For example, Indians had a much higher arrest rate on drunk charges than non-Indians. In Phoenix, Indians accounted for about one-fourth of all the male and half of all the female arrests on alcohol-related offenses, although the Indians comprised less than 1 percent of the city's population! In their testimony before the Civil Rights Commission, Indians charged that law enforcement was harsher in rural areas and in "border towns" than in the cities.[67]

As severe as the situation is among American Indians, conditions are worse south of the border. Despite increased governmental attention to their problems in recent decades, serious difficulties continue to plague Mexican Indian groups from one end of the border to the other. Unemployment, poor housing, substandard education, bad health, and exploitation at the hands of outsiders are some well-known problems. Anyone who has visited urban centers like Ciudad Juárez or Chihuahua City in the last few years has seen the effects of economic displacement for Indians such as the Tarahumaras. Increasing numbers from this tribe have migrated from their mountain homelands to the cities, seeking to eke out an existence by selling candy, cigarettes, and the like on the streets. Barefoot women wearing their traditional tribal dress routinely stake out sidewalk spaces, where they tend their children while attempting to sell their goods to passersby. Some try to carry on such activities or to beg near the international bridge between Ciudad Juárez and El Paso, but the police frequently drive them off to remove them from the sight of American tourists.

Recent reports from Chihuahua indicate that the Tarahumaras face one of the most difficult periods in their history. Commercial exploitation of their mountain homeland, bad harvests, and government neglect caused a crisis situation to develop in 1983. Logging activity in the Sierra Madre has particularly hurt them, driving away game traditionally used for food. A document distributed by the Catholic Church indicated that infant mortality had risen 60 percent and nearly four-fifths of the Tarahumaras were afflicted by tuberculosis. Church leaders called for donations totaling 4.5 million *pesos* to buy nearly three hundred tons of corn for emergency distribution to several mountain communities.[68]

SUMMARY AND CONCLUSION

The historical experience of the Indians of the U.S.-Mexico border region has varied significantly since the arrival of the whites. Because of their cultural heterogeneity, some groups accommodated peacefully to the lifestyles introduced by Spaniards, Mexicans, and Americans, but others violently resisted external dominance. What distinguishes the indigenous peoples of the borderlands from other, nonborder Indians is their misfortune of having been conquered in cycles and their having to abide by restrictions imposed by the creation of an international boundary meant to separate two nation-states. Groups whose homelands straddled that border or whose traffic lanes cut across it had to contend thereafter with a major disrupter of their ways of life. Dispossessed of lands they had occupied for centuries and forced into reservations that frequently had inadequate resources to support them, many tribes had no choice but to prey on whites; if the border could be used to their advantage, so much the better.

The difficult situation of the Indians led to prolonged violence, and predictably, tragedy befell both Indians and non-Indians. Transborder Indian raiding generated so much friction between the United States and Mexico that war seemed a real possibility in the 1870s. Reciprocal agreements to cross the boundary in pursuit of raiders finally eliminated the problem for both countries, but that policy took a heavy toll on the Indians. They emerged from those troubled years decimated in numbers, segregated from the mainstream society, and destined to live marginal lives in a modern industrial world. Yet many groups managed to survive as culturally identifiable groups, and to this day they fiercely resist absorption into U.S. or Mexican society. That determination to endure despite continuous assaults on their way of life constitutes one of the major stories in the heritage of the borderlands.

Viewed in historical perspective, the situation of the Indians of the U.S. Southwest resembles in some important ways that of Chicanos. As a result of a war of conquest, Indians and Chicanos were involuntarily incorporated into the United States. It mattered little that the rights of Chicanos were explicitly and those of Indians implicitly protected by the Treaty of Guadalupe Hidalgo; both groups became second-class citizens in American society, with Indians occupying an even lower position than Chicanos. Countless separate treaties signed by the U.S. government with individual tribes proved largely meaningless because they were seldom observed. Only after several generations did the United States recognize the injustices suffered by the Indians. Programs established in recent years meant to redress those wrongs have helped, but as a group the Indians of the Southwest still find themselves at the bottom of the social order. The same is true of Indians in the Mexican border zone.

It has been some time now that the border itself ceased to be an issue of concern for the Indians, although reminders of nineteenth-century history remain. One case in point is the Kickapoos, who continue to cross the boundary with regularity while living in the settlement they established in the Mexican state of Coahuila in the 1850s during their early days in exile. The Yaquis of Sonora-Arizona maintain contact across the border much the same way that Mexicans and Chicanos carry on kinship and economic relations in the region. A modern-day trend is illustrated by the Tarahumaras, who have gravitated from their homes in the Chihuahua mountains to border cities in search of economic opportunity. With the overcrowding and serious unemployment that already exists at the border, these Indians face severe problems. Thus the dilemma of the past continues. A century ago, the overriding concern was how to establish peaceful relations with the Indians; today the question is how to prevent further disruption of their way of life, how to lessen exploitation, and how to improve their standard of living in an era of continuing economic crises.

CHAPTER 4

Border Chicanos

Since the Texas Revolution in 1836 and the U.S.-Mexico War of 1846–48, the experiences of borderlands Mexican Americans, or Chicanos, have been profoundly affected by the political boundary that separates the two countries. With the detachment of Mexico's northern frontier, approximately one hundred thousand Mexicans residing in Texas, New Mexico (including Arizona), and California became subjects of the United States, forcing permanent severance of political ties with the motherland. The choice of the Rio Grande as the dividing line had the immediate effect of partitioning various population clusters that had formed along that stream since Spanish settlement in the eighteenth century. Later, shifts in the course of the river produced further disruptions in community life and physical displacements of local populations, affecting the interests of Mexican Americans in numerous ways.

Throughout the latter nineteenth century, immigrants from Mexico expanded the Mexican-origin population in the southwestern United States, and with the outbreak of the Mexican Revolution in 1910, that initial migration flow evolved into a major movement that continues to the present day. Consequently Mexican Americans have become a major component in the population of the U.S. borderlands.

An unfortunate element in the history of Mexican Americans in the U.S. border region has been their strained relations with the dominant society. The record reveals an enduring pattern of racial, ethnic, and cultural confrontation, much of which is directly traceable to border tensions. Armed clashes, raids, thefts, rapes, lynchings, murders, and other outrages became commonplace in border areas from Texas to California. In time the violence subsided, but Mexican Americans in the borderlands remained a second-class population in the United States, even until recent years.

This chapter examines the unique circumstances of border Mexican Americans by discussing key aspects of their lives since they came in contact with Anglos. Attention is directed in particular to the effect on the group of living in a boundary zone, physically close to Mexico but decidedly distant in many ways from their roots. To give a sense of what border Chicanos have thought and felt about their peculiar condition, I have drawn from selected historical events, characters, and situations that seem to me to personify the border experience. My aim, then, is to interpret the condition of border Chicanos rather than to narrate the historical record.

BORDER CONFRONTATION AND VIOLENCE

Relations between *norteamericanos* and *mexicanos* in the borderlands have evolved significantly since initial contact in the early nineteenth century. When Anglos began dribbling into New Spain's northern frontier, the native settlers welcomed them. Immigration, regardless of its source, meant greater protection against hostile Indians, and expanded population implied increased economic activity in an area ripe for development. Anglo traders, merchants, and trappers brought much-needed goods that the mother country would not or could not supply. Small in number and dependent on the frontier Mexicans for their livelihood, the first wave of Anglo immigrants integrated themselves into the local society. Peaceful ethnic relations prevailed, although the Anglos often had problems with government authorities who sought to enforce, albeit unsuccessfully, the strict trade and immigration policies of the Spanish Crown.

The character of Anglo-Mexican relations on the frontier began to change in the 1820s, when *norteamericanos* arrived in greater numbers following Mexico's independence from Spain. The newcomers became more assertive in promoting their personal interests and in seeking greater autonomy from Mexico City; underlying those efforts was a desire, which became more pronounced as time passed, to annex Mexico's northern provinces to the United States. In Texas, where Anglos outnumbered *tejanos* by six to one by the end of the decade, assertiveness gave way to aggressiveness as the Anglos constantly expressed resentment toward Mexican rule and contempt for the Mexican way of life. As frontiersmen who had long advocated greater autonomy for their province, many tejanos joined the Anglo-Texans in opposing the centralist policies of the Mexican government, but given prevailing Anglo attitudes toward Mexicans, that union was far from an ideal coalition. A historic Anglo-led movement for Texas independence followed in the 1830s, ushering in a decade of conflict with Mexico and pronounced ethnic hostility on the Texas-Mexico border that lasted several generations. Confrontations generated by ethnic friction and economic competition also broke out in New Mexico, Arizona, and California after the acquisition of these provinces by the United States as a result of the War of 1846–48. The Anglos who moved into the region soon imposed a political, social, and economic system that promoted their interests and relegated those of conquered Mexicans and Indians to secondary consideration.

The period from 1848 to 1920 was particularly difficult for the frontier Mexicans who had become part of the United States through annexation and for their compatriots who later immigrated from Mexico. These people became politically powerless, economically impotent, socially marginalized, racially stigmatized, and culturally maligned. Ethnic tension and class friction frequently gave way to violent encounters, as shown in Table 4.1. Clashes were particularly pronounced along

Table 4.1
Anglo-Mexican American Conflict
in the Border Region, 1830–1916

Year(s)	Place	Incident(s)
Protracted "Microviolence"		
Entire Period	U.S. Southwest, including the border area	This ninety-year period witnessed hundreds, perhaps thousands, of small-scale encounters between Anglos and Mexicans, with the latter, because of their subordinated status, predominantly the victims. Incidents include discrimination, harassment, miscarriages of justice, land invasions, swindles, thefts, rapes, murders, and lynchings.
Violence on a Larger Scale		
1830s–1840s	Texas	Instability stemming from Texas rebellion from Mexico leads to widespread persecution of tejanos.
1848	Border towns	"Forty-niners" harass Mexican settlements and steal from local residents; American slave chasers cross into Mexican territory.

Table 4.1
Anglo-Mexican American Conflict
in the Border Region, 1830–1916 *(continued)*

Year(s)	Place	Incident(s)
Early 1850s	New Mexico	About two thousand native New Mexicans leave their homes and cross the border into Mexico when Anglos encroach upon their lands.
1856–57	Los Angeles, California, area	"Juan Flores Revolution." San Quentin escapee Juan Flores leads a gang that kills a sheriff, triggering harassment of Mexican suspects, arrests, and at least nine hangings. The gang is captured and Flores is executed.
1857	South Texas	"The Cart War." Anglo cartmen attack Mexican competitors, killing seventy-five.
1859–60	Brownsville, Texas	"Cheno Cortina Raids." Juan Nepo-muceno Cortina and sixty followers engage Anglo lawmen in a series of skirmishes motivated by racial tensions. Fifteen Americans and eight Mexicans die in the raids.
1870	Arizona-Sonora border	"Mission Camp Affair." A theft allegedly committed by a Mexican leads to reprisals and shootouts, resulting in the death of four Anglos and two Mexicans.
1870s	All along the border	The old problem of transborder Indians raids and bandit depredations flares up into a crisis in U.S.-Mexico relations. Countless clashes in the 1850s, 1860s, and 1870s result in hundreds of deaths, widespread destruction of property, and repeated violations of national sovereignty.
1871	Mesilla, New Mexico	"Mesilla Riots." Nine men, most of them Spanish-speaking supporters of politician Colonel J. Francisco Chávez, are killed in a political dispute. Additionally, forty to fifty are wounded.
1873	Lincoln County, New Mexico	"Lincoln County War." Range war between rival Anglo cattlemen traps Mexican *vaqueros* in the middle. Thirteen Mexicans die along with many Anglos.
1875	Corpus Christi, Texas	Bandit activity precipitates attacks on Mexican settlers. Many die.
1877	El Paso, Texas	"The Salt War." Mexicans from San Elizario rebel against Anglo entrepreneurs who take over community's salt deposits. Texas

Table 4.1
Anglo-Mexican American Conflict
in the Border Region, 1830–1916 *(continued)*

Year(s)	Place	Incident(s)
		Rangers are brought in to reestablish peace but are repelled. Several Anglos and several Mexicans die in a series of violent clashes and summary executions.
1880s	Panhandle, Texas–New Mexico border	Retaliating for the murder of an Anglo sheepman, Texas cowboys rampage in Tascosa, killing several innocent Mexicans and lynching others suspected of complicity in the murder. Gunman and folk hero Sostenes l'Archeveque, of French-Mexican descent, is identified as the killer and is executed in a trap.
1889–90	Northern New Mexico	"Las Gorras Blancas Raids." In an attempt to preserve the old Hispano way of life, "Las Gorras Blancas" raid Anglo settlements, destroying considerable property and precipitating injuries from shootings.
1915–16	Texas-Tamaulipas border	"Plan of San Diego raids." Raids associated with the Plan of San Diego keep the Texas Lower Rio Grande Valley in continuous turmoil. Raiders include Mexican revolutionaries, Mexican American guerrillas, and bandits of various backgrounds. U.S. troops, Texas Rangers, local lawmen, and vigilantes retaliate against the attackers, sometimes crossing into Mexico to avenge losses. Hundreds die in the raids.
1916	Texas-Chihuahua border	"Santa Ysabel Massacre." Villistas kill sixteen Americans at Santa Ysabel, Chihuahua. Racial riot erupts in El Paso.

the border, where uneasy international relations added fuel to the explosive ethnic climate. The frequent military engagements triggered by the secession of Texas from Mexico had left bitter memories, and more than any other event, the U.S.-Mexican War left a legacy of enmity among the people of the borderlands. Mexicans in the annexed territories were free from the neglectful and often oppressive control of Mexico City, but in the new American social order they had become at best inconsequential bystanders and at worst colonial subjects in their own land. Anglos assumed the role of conquerors, demanding subservience from the Mexican population in the annexed territory while contemplating extension of the border deeper into Mexico.

Of the many violent encounters that took place along the border during the nineteenth century, the El Paso "Salt War" of 1877 perhaps best illustrates how the imposition of the boundary gave rise to conditions that the local Mexican population found hard to accept, thus setting the stage for transborder conflicts that carried ethnic overtones. The "Salt War" was essentially a rebellion at San Elizario, Texas, a town located about twenty miles east of El Paso–Paso del Norte, which involved the participation of up to four hundred Mexicans from both sides of the Rio Grande. Three Anglos and three Mexicans died in the disturbances, and many others suffered personal injury or loss of property. For a time San Elizario and the adjoining communities of Socorro and Ysleta were practically evacuated, with Mexicans finding refuge south of the Rio Grande and Anglos retreating to El Paso, Texas.[1]

The uprising stemmed from the efforts of an Anglo entrepreneur to stake a claim near San Elizario on salt deposits that the people of the region had long considered community property on the basis of old grants made by the Spanish government.[2] In the 1850s a similar dispute had arisen at the Salina de Andres, a salt deposit in New Mexico some seventy miles from El Paso, when Texas resident James Magoffin confiscated salt, carts, and oxen belonging to residents of Dona Ana County on their return home from the site. In both the San Andres and the San Elizario cases, Mexicans from the El Paso–Paso del Norte area and points in Chihuahua had helped to build roads to the deposits, mined the sites, and ignored what they considered outrageous attempts on the part of outsiders to appropriate the deposits and charge for the salt. The intrusion of the Anglo entrepreneurs seriously affected the welfare of the border community and intensified racial animosities that had existed since the U.S. invasion of the area in 1846.[3]

Just as the local people from both sides of the border had worked jointly to mine the salt deposits, so they stuck together during San Elizario's uprising of 1877. "The inhabitants of the adjacent towns on both sides of the river . . . are intimately connected by the bonds of a common faith, like sympathies and tastes, and are related in numerous instances by marriage," reported the board appointed by the president of the United States to investigate the rebellion. "Hence each would naturally support and defend the other, if occasions . . . demanded their aid, to any sacrifice."[4] The strength of the bonds across the border is evidenced by the participation of some 150 to 200 Mexicans from south of the river in the disturbance. The importance of the latter's role is illustrated by the fact that the members of the squad who executed three Anglos identified by the rebels as the principal culprits in the controversy were all from Mexico. Further, the people from the

Mexican side not only gave sanctuary to scores of tejanos branded as "rioters" but ignored repeated pleas from U.S. authorities to extradite seventeen self-exiled Mexican Americans accused of various "crimes" during the uprising.[5]

Various witnesses testified before the investigating board that the uprising was motivated not only by the salt issue but also by resentment of Anglo authority in the area. One letter signed by six Anglos and three Mexicans from San Elizario stated that local Sheriff Charles Kerber had "been treated with cool contempt" when he had tried to collect state and county taxes, and that "the mob" had cried that "they had been fooled long enough, that . . . they had no use for . . . the American government."[6] Another letter signed by the same six Anglos reported that "armed men promenaded the town, shooting and crying 'Death to the Gringos.'"[7] One Anglo deputy sheriff wrote that among the threatening cries uttered by the insurgents was the following: "Death to all white men [who] . . . try to uphold the laws of the State of Texas or of the United States."[8] Other witnesses repeatedly emphasized that if U.S. troops were not sent to the area, the lives of all Anglos would be in danger.[9] "It seems that we have no claims on our government and we have to give up all our property for the sake of a lot of greasers [*sic*]," wrote Sheriff Kerber in a moment of despair over what he considered to be too slow a response by the U.S. government to the local crisis.[10]

An important lesson taught by the San Elizario incident was that the border had little meaning for Mexicans of the Rio Grande region. "The people on the left bank of the river were supposed to be American citizens and their cousins a hundred feet away on the other side of a sometimes nonexistent stream were supposed to be Mexicans," writes C. L. Sonnichsen. "Most of them paid no attention. They and their ancestors had passed and repassed the river at their pleasure for ten generations, and the idea of a 'boundary' set up by a handful of gringos who had moved in only twenty-five years before was a little comic."[11] Fundamentally it was that prevailing sentiment among the border Mexicans that kept authorities from ever punishing the "rioters," or the Anglos who lost property from recovering their losses. Without the cooperation of the people from the Mexican side, who not only sympathized with the insurgents but harbored them, U.S. officials could do nothing except establish Fort Bliss as a permanent military installation at El Paso, Texas, to guard against recurrence of similar incidents in the future.

Mexican-Anglo ethnic confrontations, which declined somewhat at the turn of the century, resurfaced with great force during the 1910s, when the Mexican Revolution created extremely unsettled conditions along the two-thousand-mile border separating the two nations.

Mexico's civil unrest not only brought injury and property loss to Americans who lived south of the boundary, but the ferment also spilled over into Texas, New Mexico, Arizona, and California, spawning a strong reaction among the Anglo border population. The unstable climate set the stage for repeated incursions of Mexican revolutionaries and bandits into U.S. territory and punitive or "defensive" movements by American troops into Mexico. Such events produced repeated violent incidents along the entire border and added to the existing anti-Mexican hysteria in the United States. The most tragic clashes occurred in 1915–16 in the Lower Rio Grande Valley, when adherents to the "Plan de San Diego," a document that called for Mexican insurgency in the Southwest, repeatedly raided Texas settlements.[12]

With the end of the Mexican Revolution in 1920, the nature of Anglo-Mexican ethnic relations changed. Deep-seated differences continued to exist and racial confrontations surfaced from time to time, but large-scale violent encounters, the pattern during preceding generations, became less common. Perhaps the single most important factor that accounts for this transformation was that threats to national sovereignty ceased to be a major issue between Mexico and the United States, causing the border area to shed its traditional role as a staging ground for imperialistic invasions, unlawful incursions, Indian depredations, bandit raids, and other confrontational activity. The disappearance of armed movements in the binational frontier zone diminished significantly the intense nationalistic feelings aroused in previous eras that frequently carried over into the sphere of ethnic relations. Population growth and the onset of modernization in the border region also helped to ease tensions by reducing the ill effects of geographic isolation. Overt frontier lawlessness gave way to more subtle and "acceptable" forms of conflict, bringing forth a significant decrease of incidents that could flare up into serious disorderliness.

PSYCHOLOGICAL DIMENSIONS OF THE CHICANO BORDER EXPERIENCE: THE NINETEENTH CENTURY

The Mexicans who became part of the United States through annexation had considerable problems adjusting to an Anglo-imposed social and cultural system fundamentally different from their own way of life. The new political order offered the freedom, personal security, and economic prosperity they had not known under Spanish or Mexican rule, but those lofty promises failed to materialize. Instead, the status of Mexicans in U.S. society became one of conquered subjects and foreigners in their own homeland. They found themselves pressed on one side by the Anglo conqueror and restricted on the other by a border that legally and symbolically disjoined them from their Mexican roots.

The dilemma of these people is poignantly illustrated by the experience of tejanos, those Mexicans who found themselves within the jurisdiction of what became the Republic of Texas. When the Texas independence movement broke out, tejanos had to choose between the rebellion and loyalty to the motherland. Another alternative for them was neutrality, and it is apparent that the overwhelming majority of tejanos chose this course, hoping that nonalignment would spare them from the ravages of war. Yet neither neutrality nor alliance with one side or the other shielded them from the unfortunate fate that befalls frontier ethnic or racial minorities trapped in conflict-ridden zones created by altered borders.

Anglos deeply distrusted the loyalty of the tejanos, despite the presence of men like Lorenzo de Zavala and Juan Seguín in prominent positions in the rebel army and government. Some Anglo leaders, fearing that tejanos, Indians, and Black slaves would form an alliance against them, called for the occupation of tejano settlements suspected of Mexican sympathies, and others urged the segregation of tejanos from "white men" in the military ranks. Neutral Mexicans were often seen as enemies, as exemplified by an order given by the Anglo mayor of Nacogdoches to all able-bodied tejanos to join the rebel army or leave Texas.[13]

Anglo ambivalence toward tejanos was reflected in official documents of the Texas Republic. On the one hand the Texas Constitution of 1836 guaranteed tejanos equal rights along with the rest of the population, but the Declaration of Independence had concluded that Mexicans in general were "unfit to be free, and incapable of self-government." The contradiction in the two documents could only be resolved by viewing tejanos completely apart from Mexicans who lived south of the Rio Grande (where political instability prevailed), but few Anglo-Texans could or would consciously draw that distinction. To them, Mexicans were Mexicans, adversaries of the Anglo population, and likely enemies of the Texas Republic.[14]

Such attitudes bred intense persecution, particularly during periods of heightened conflict between the Texans and Mexico. For example, following the battle of San Jacinto, tejanos in large numbers were driven from the towns of Victoria and Goliad. In the early 1840s, many tejano families left San Antonio to avoid continued harassment by Anglo mobs and also to escape expected battles between Mexican troops and Texan forces. During a period of relative calm, they returned to their homes but had to face an unfriendly Anglo reception. Many refugees from such towns as Victoria, San Patricio, Nacogdoches, and Goliad found their lands occupied by Anglo squatters, who felt these migrants had forfeited their right to the land by failing to fight for the Revolution.[15] Under these circumstances, the tejanos had little hope of recovering their lands.

Tejanos had little room to maneuver within the dilemma that afflicted them during those difficult years. The Anglos demanded that they support the movement for independence, yet even those tejanos who did precisely that could not be free from problems with the arrogant and suspicious Texans. On the other hand, Mexico also expected the tejanos' loyalty, but the frequently insolent and abusive conduct of the Mexican soldiers seriously undermined sympathies for the motherland. Several incidents illustrate the tejanos' difficult position of being subjected to this dual jeopardy. In 1835, Mexican troops disarmed and mistreated residents of Goliad; the following year, Anglos plundered the town, forcing many to flee. The people of Nacogdoches endured repeated thefts from both sides. On one occasion, Juan Seguín's ranch in San Antonio was robbed by Mexican troops, only to be burned the next year by Anglos. Victoria resident Fernando de León, a supporter of the republic, suffered arrests from both sides in 1835 and 1836, each time for allegedly "conspiring" with the enemy.[16] At least one Texas newspaper understood the predicament faced by the tejanos, observing that although these people lived on the frontier, ever exposed to attacks by Mexican troops, they received "no protection from our government," thereby being "compelled to temporize with both parties, or be subjected to the insults and depradations of each."[17]

It is unfortunate that few tejano documents are available that elucidate the feelings of this group regarding their dilemma. Juan Seguín, one of the few whose writings survive, leaves us a brief but revealing memoir. As someone made to feel "a foreigner in my native land," his story vividly illustrates the painful ambivalence felt by those who fought alongside the Anglos against Mexico, only to discover later that the new masters of Texas had nothing but contempt for the tejano way of life. Reflecting on the intolerable conditions that had forced him to seek exile in Mexico after his distinguished service in the Texas Revolution, Seguín wrote in 1858:

> I embraced the cause of Texas . . . filled an honorable situation in the ranks of the conquerors of San Jacinto, and was a member of the legislative body of the Republic. I now find myself, in the very land, which in other times bestowed on me such bright and repeated evidences of trust and esteem, exposed to the attack of . . . enemies . . . who . . . engender strife [and] falsify historical facts.[18]

Seguín lamented the treatment received by his fellow tejanos at the hands of Anglo ruffians, and the enmity thrust upon him for coming to their defense.

> At every hour of the day and night, my countrymen ran to me for protection . . . Sometimes . . . force had to be resorted to. How could I have done otherwise? Were not the victims my own countrymen, friends and associates? Could I leave them defenseless, exposed to the assaults of foreigners, who, on the pretext that they were Mexicans, treated them worse than brutes?

> Could I be expected to stoically endure their outrages and insults? Crushed by sorrow, convinced that my death alone would satisfy my enemies, I sought shelter amongst those against whom I had fought [Mexicans]: I separated from my country, parents, family, relatives and friends, and what was more, from the institutions, on behalf of which I had drawn my sword, with an earnest wish to see Texans free and happy.

> I had to leave Texas, abandon all, for which I had fought and spent my fortune . . . Unable any longer to suffer the persecutions of some ungrateful Americans, who strove to murder me, I had determined to free my family and friends from their continual misery on my account, and go live peaceably in Mexico. For these reasons I resigned my office [as mayor of San Antonio], with all my priviledges and honors as a Texan.[19]

Seguín's treatment by Anglo-Texans is in sharp contrast with that accorded José Antonio Navarro, another prominent tejano, who, unlike Seguín, never deviated from his staunch support for Texas and militant opposition to Mexico. Coincidently both men left Texas in the early 1840s, but for very different reasons. Seguín sought asylum in Mexico when he could no longer function in an Anglo-dominated environment. Once in Mexican territory he was arrested and given the choice of staying behind bars or fighting on the side of Mexico. Caught between a sword and a rock wall, Seguín decided to join the Mexican forces, a choice that heightened the wrath against him among Anglo-Texans. Navarro also became a prisoner of the Mexicans, but his arrest resulted from participation in the attempted Texan invasion of New Mexico in 1841, commonly known as the Santa Fe Expedition. Unlike the other prisoners of that expeditionary force, Navarro was given an extended prison term and singled out for cruel treatment. That was the price paid by those tejanos who chose to collaborate actively with the Anglo insurgents against the mother country. Navarro's sufferings and staunch support for Texas independence brought sympathy and

admiration from Anglo-Texans, and when he returned to his homeland in 1845 following an escape while on parole in Vera Cruz, he received a hero's welcome. Meanwhile, Seguín led other tejano exiles like
himself against the Texan rebels. Later he served as a scout and guerrilla fighter on Mexico's side during the War of 1846–48, after which
he left military service and decided to take his chances by returning to
his native Texas. Although scorned by those who considered him a
"traitor," Seguín was nonetheless permitted to live out his life quietly
in the land of his birth.[20]

The racial strife engendered by the Texas Revolution was greatly
exacerbated by the War of 1846–48. Victory by the United States
opened the way for Anglo immigration into southern Texas, but
tejanos managed to maintain numerical superiority in the Lower Rio
Grande Valley, an area that remained isolated for several decades.
Greater numbers in the valley, however, did not prevent the subordina-
tion of tejanos to the newcomers, although numerical majority did
allow greater opportunities to maintain Mexican culture and traditional community institutions than in the interior of the state. The
close proximity to Mexico also permitted the valley tejanos to retain
intimate economic and social ties with fellow Mexicans south of the
river, many of whom had relatives on the American side. Since initial
colonization of the area by the Spaniards in the eighteenth century, the
settlements on both sides of the Rio Grande had developed as closely
interdependent units within a relatively self-sufficient and independent-minded regional society. The establishment of the new boundary
brought some disruption to that traditional integration, but the fundamental links uniting the two peoples remained fairly intact.

That is not to say that valley tejanos identified with Mexico politically.
It seems apparent that they had little desire to be part of Mexico, and
it is fairly certain that they had great ambivalence about being a part
of the Texas Republic. As frontiersmen long isolated by distance, geography, and governmental neglect, the people of the valley on both sides
identified primarily with their immediate surroundings. Residents on
the Texas side of the river had no choice, however, but to recognize the
political reality that resulted from the events of the 1830s and 1840s.
The river that had been their lifeline for nearly a century had been imposed as the line of demarcation between the two nations, and that fact
necessitated a new political orientation for those settlers who lived on
the north bank. Yet culturally and socially, the new border made little
difference for most valley tejanos, for they held on to their traditional
lifestyle. If, politically, valley tejanos had to think of themselves as part
of the United States, in many other ways they continued to identify
with Mexico. Nationality, customs, kinship, and traditions bound them
to the motherland, and it was only natural that they saw themselves as

an extension of the population that lived in the Tamaulipas border frontier.[21]

One of the strongest bonds linking the Mexicans of the transborder Lower Rio Grande Valley was the need to defend themselves against the oppression of the Anglos. That harsh reality created a feeling of solidarity that transcended the boundary, bringing a measure of security and assertiveness to valley tejanos not found among their outnumbered and isolated compatriots to the north. The presence of the border itself placed valley tejanos in a better position to resist with greater intensity and determination the abuses of the Anglos, for moral and material support was readily available nearby, *al otro lado*. In the worst of cases, sanctuary from Anglo persecution could always be found in Mexico.

The spirit of valley resistance to external domination is well illustrated by the struggle led by Juan Nepomucena Cortina in 1859–60 in the Brownsville-Matamoros area. Assisted by hundreds of tejanos and volunteers from Tamaulipas, Cortina fought a "war" against Texas Rangers and U.S. troops that produced some 250 deaths and damages in the thousands of dollars. The mistreatment of a former family servant and the hanging of a friend served as Cortina's immediate motive for striking against the Anglos, but that personal grievance made up only a part of a set of outrages he had seen committed against tejanos. As a young man he had been a member of a local irregular force that helped the Mexican military attempt to repel the U.S. invasion of the valley in 1846. Important battles were fought near his home, and atrocities were committed in nearby settlements. The memory of the war and the continuous despoilation of tejanos thus contributed to his animosity toward Anglos. One especially troublesome point of contention in the valley, as elsewhere, was the aggressiveness and duplicity of the Anglos in seeking to obtain land that had belonged to the local people for generations, some even dating to Spanish colonial days. Cortina's own family encountered problems establishing title to their land in the Brownsville area.[22]

Cortina did not seek to drive the Anglos from the region or to overthrow their governmental authority. Thus he was not a revolutionary or a separatist, although as a young man he had been exposed to the sentiment for regional separatism that developed in his native Tamaulipas against Mexico's central government. Possessed of an often adventurous spirit, Cortina took part in Jose María Carvajal's movement to establish the "Republic of Sierra Madre" in the early 1850s.[23]

At the height of his quarrel with Anglo authorities, Cortina issued a series of proclamations that revealed his disillusionment with Texas, a land that had betrayed those who, like his family, had chosen to remain on the U.S. side with the hope of enjoying peace, freedom, and equality. Cortina's mother became a U.S. citizen in 1849, but whether her famous son followed suit is not entirely clear. Yet several pieces of evidence support the view that he did indeed take on U.S. citizenship. Because Cortina lived in Texas for several years before and after the signing of the Treaty of Guadalupe Hidalgo, a document that had bestowed U.S. citizenship within a year to Mexicans who chose to remain north of the boundary, it seems logical that he was one of those people so affected. Most of Brownsville's residents seem to have considered him a U.S. citizen, judging from references to him in the legal case that followed the raid of 1859. The Mexican Claims Commission that investigated conditions along the border in the 1870s denied Mexico's responsibility for Cortina's actions, based on the premise that he was a U.S. citizen. Finally, Cortina's own comments regarding democratic ideals and equality of opportunity that supposedly flowed from the U.S. Constitution imply that he viewed himself as a U.S. citizen at the time of the raid, although in later life he opted for Mexican citizenship.[24]

Despite his problems with Anglo-Texans, Cortina had faith in the American government and expressed a desire to make it work for all its people, particularly tejanos. He blamed a few evil and abusive men for the plight of his countrymen and, at one point, expressed hope that newly elected Governor Sam Houston would restore justice in Texas.[25] Cortina's sense of betrayal in the land that had promised freedom for Mexicans and his anguish toward Mexico is revealed in one of his proclamations to fellow tejanos.

> The ills that weigh upon the unfortunate Republic of Mexico have obliged us for many heart-touching causes to abandon it [Mexico] and our possessions. . . . Ever diligent and industrious, and desirous of enjoying the longed-for boon of liberty . . . we induced to naturalize ourselves in [the United States] . . . flattered by the bright and peaceful prospect of living therein and inculcating in the bosoms of our children a feeling of gratitude towards a country beneath whose aegis we would have wrought their felicity and contributed with our conduct to give evidence to the whole world that all the aspirations of the Mexicans are confined to one only, *that of being freemen.*

> Having secured this ourselves, those of the old country, notwithstanding their misfortunes, might have nothing to regret save the loss of a section of territory [the lands ceded to the United States in 1848], but with the sweet satisfaction that their old fellow citizens lived therein, enjoying tranquility. . . . All has

been but the baseless fabric of a dream, and our hopes having been defrauded in the most cruel manner in which disappointment can strike, there can be found no other solution to our problem than to make one effort, and at one blow destroy the obstacles to our prosperity.[26]

Certain behavioral patterns in the life of Cortina exemplify the ambivalence and contradictions that many tejanos and other Mexican Americans had to confront in the United States. Cortina and other members of the upper classes, who normally distanced themselves from those socially beneath them, sometimes found themselves defending the interests of the poor in the face of Anglo oppression. In Mexican society it was rare for a person of means to side with the downtrodden. Along the border, however, strong nationalistic sentiments at times prompted the affluent to champion the cause of their humble countrymen who suffered mistreatment and exploitation at the hands of the hated *gringos*. Injury inflicted by a foreigner to any Mexican, regardless of his or her class standing, stirred strong feelings of ethnic solidarity. Group honor demanded counteraction, at the very least expressing indignation or filing formal protests against the perpetrators of the offenses. Cortina was one of those affluent *fronterizos* so outraged by the actions of the Anglos that he chose violence as the way to strike back. Little evidence exists that Cortina had an ideological affinity with the class interests of the dispossessed; rather, he seems to have been motivated by ethnic unity, regional loyalty, a sense of social justice, youthful restlessness, and frontier adventurism.

Cortina's ability to function in various spheres of border society constitutes one of the most fascinating aspects of his life. His family background allowed him to move freely in upper-class circles, whereas his struggle against the *gringos*, coupled with his "Robin Hood" reputation, endeared him to the working class. Throughout much of his adult life, he operated outside the law on both sides of the border; yet in the eyes of Mexican authorities, the tension-filled frontier environment in which he lived mitigated the errant behavior, thus permitting Cortina to hold impressive positions in Mexico, such as lawman, government official, and military leader.

Cortina was a man of remarkable leadership abilities, whose natural constituency was the Mexican border population but whose interests he could not represent in the assertive style that he preferred without placing himself in a state of limbo vis-à-vis the Texas power structure, as well as the Mexican government. Thus his future as a leader lay not in Texas, where he was needed but where he could not function, but in Mexico, where his talents and passions for leadership could find full expression. Tejanos who had occupied privileged positions during earlier eras, when Spain and Mexico had governed Texas, found it especially difficult to accept their subordinated status in the Anglo system. Some, including Cortina, recognized the futility of attempting to rise to positions of leadership in Texas. Mexico was a troubled land, but it placed no racial or cultural barriers for strong-willed, capable men from the elite sector who wanted to rise to positions of power.

Cortina's decision to leave Texas gave him an opportunity to function outside of the troubled border area and helped him make the notable transition into the world of politicians and high-ranking soldiers in the state of Tamaulipas. Yet long after he had assumed a "respectable" life, suspicions remained that he continued in his old ways, engaging in unlawful activities such as cattle rustling. Eventually those accusations bore fruit for his enemies. In 1875 Mexican officials jailed him for suspected theft, and later they exiled him to Mexico City, effectively removing him from the border region. In 1890 he returned to the border for a visit and was given a hero's welcome by the people who remembered him as a defender of Mexican rights.[27]

IDENTITY AND LANGUAGE

Cortina and Seguín are examples of border Mexican Americans who took extreme measures to deal with the disruption in their lives brought on by the imposition of the international boundary. Variations of the same ambivalence that troubled these two leaders have disturbed most U.S. Mexicans since the mid-nineteenth century. Chicanos long have struggled for acceptance in the United States, often at the price of denying their heritage. This behavior is well illustrated by the rejection of the term "Mexican" by many within the group. Such repudiation stems from the decidedly negative connotation "Mexican" has had in the United States. The early nineteenth-century Anglo-Americans, and especially Texans in the border region, labeled Mexicans as "halfbreeds," "intellectually inferior," "indolent," "dishonest," "immoral," "treacherous," and "backward." Such unflattering descriptors were routinely used in early newspapers, magazines, and books. Later, movies and television continued the tradition of using popular stereotypes and racist caricatures to portray Mexicans and Mexican Americans. These characterizations became firmly etched in the American mind, continuing even to the present day.[28]

Under such circumstances, many Mexican Americans along the border and elsewhere sought to establish some distance between themselves and their Mexican roots, particularly when interacting with

Anglos. By blurring, minimizing, or obliterating their Mexican genetic and cultural inheritance, Mexican Americans discovered that they received better treatment from members of the dominant society. Thus began the practice of passing off as "Spanish" rather than "Mexican." By calling themselves "Spanish," defensive Mexican Americans "purified" their blood, "whitened" their appearance, and "Europeanized" their heritage. Later, other terms such as "Latin," and more recently "Hispanic," were also used as substitutes for "Mexican."[29] (By contrast, young activists in the 1960s demonstrated their pride in being Mexican by adopting "Chicano" [a derivative of "Mexicano"] as their preferred self-referent term.).

The tendency to avoid association with the term "Mexican" is evident in the names chosen for community organizations. For example, the largest Mexican American organization in the country chose to call itself the League of United Latin American Citizens (LULAC). LULAC emerged in 1929 from a unity meeting involving several Mexican American groups that did not use the term "Mexican" to identify their organizations: the League of Latin American Citizens, the Knights of America, and the Order of the Sons of America. It is also significant that LULAC was born in Corpus Christi, not far from the border, in an area known for its extreme anti-Mexican sentiment. Other visible organizations established during the World War II period such as the Community Service Organization, the American G.I. Forum, and the Political Association of Spanish-Speaking Organizations carried on the tradition of avoiding the label "Mexican."

It was only in the late 1950s and 1960s that "Mexican American" began to appear in names given to community and political organizations. By then, racial discrimination in the United States had softened and Mexican Americans had become a less oppressed group. Awareness that the true heritage of the group came from Mexico rather than from Spain had increased, easing the acceptance of a self-identifier like "Mexican American." Better-educated and more-experienced leaders did not hesitate to assert themselves before the Anglo establishment. Thus a political group in California formed the Mexican American Political Association in 1959, students established the United Mexican American Students in the late 1960s, and tejano activists created the Mexican American Democrats in the 1970s. Nonetheless, the rejection of "Mexican" was still widespread among Mexican Americans. Regardless of the milder racial climate, negative images, distorted perceptions, and destructive stereotypes toward Mexicans and Mexican Americans remained very strong in the mainstream culture, causing large numbers of people of Mexican background to jump at the opportunity to adopt "less offensive" labels. By the 1980s, the term "Hispanic" had become widely accepted throughout the United States, and it quickly caught on in the Mexican-American community as well.

The ambivalence mirrored in the use of varied self-referent terminology is also reflected in uncertainty over language. Historically, Chicanos have struggled to have the dominant culture recognize Spanish as a functional language in the Southwest, and especially along the border where the interaction with Mexico is intense. The view of the dominant society—that to be Mexican is to be inferior—has extended to language as well: speakers of Spanish have been perceived as inferior to speakers of English.

Until the 1960s, it was common for children to be punished in schools for speaking Spanish. School officials pointed to the need to learn English as the reason for inflicting sanctions, but to Spanish-speaking students the message was a devastating one: using Spanish and practicing or exhibiting Mexican cultural traits were negative forms of behavior that should be eliminated. Outside of the schools that message was reinforced with negative characterizations of Mexicans in American popular culture. Consequently, generations of Mexican-American children grew up confused about and ashamed of their heritage, causing serious damage to their self-esteem and personal pride.

The advent of bilingual education in the 1970s introduced a more enlightened approach to the education of Spanish-speaking children, but the program has since been plagued with many problems, including lack of resources, teacher shortages, inadequate training of teachers, improper use of teaching techniques, and hostility to the program on the part of the Anglo majority. Bilingual education has become one of the most controversial issues along the border, deeply dividing the Mexican-American and Anglo communities.

Opposition to bilingual education goes hand in hand with recent efforts to make English the "official" language of the United States. Groups such as U.S. English and English First have campaigned hard to convince a large portion of the American public that the use of languages other than English fosters fragmentation in the country and threatens future political stability. Led by California, by the mid-1980s about twelve states had declared English as their official language, sending a message to Hispanics and other language minority groups that they should rid themselves of their native tongues as quickly as possible. Thus far, similar measures in the legislatures of Texas, New Mexico, and Arizona have failed to pass, but the debate on the issue in these states is bound to increase in the future.

For border Chicanos, the "English-only" controversy is particularly unsettling because Spanish (excluding Indian languages) is the native language in the region. It has been spoken for centuries, and because of the continuing symbiosis with the Mexican side of the border, it will remain a very functional and even necessary language for many years to come. Many opposed to the "English-only" initiative feel it is a deliberate campaign to undermine the development and advancement of Hispanics in the United States. There is, however, divided opinion among Mexican Americans on this issue. Reports suggest that most persons of Mexican descent in the border states actually favor the declaration of English as the official language of the country, although it is far from certain whether the Mexican-American community at large fully understands the possible negative educational and legal implications of such an action.

OTHER BORDER-RELATED DILEMMAS

During their long struggle to become full participants in American society, Chicanos have often questioned whether there is a place for them in the United States other than at the bottom of the social order. There have been times when Anglo hostility and rejection have actually driven large numbers of Mexicans back to Mexico, as evidenced by the migrations southward across the border of approximately three thousand New Mexicans and tejanos between 1848 and 1850; about ten thousand Sonorans during the California Gold Rush period; and in the best-known movement of all, close to a half-million Mexicans from throughout the United States during the Great Depression. In addition, countless individuals seeking refuge for a variety of reasons have made the trek southward before and since those larger movements.

Yet it is highly significant that for most of those displaced people, the stay south of the border has been a short one. Few have made Mexico their permanent home, opting for an eventual return to the United States. What is more, they have been joined in their northward journey by millions of other Mexican nationals with aspirations to greater opportunity than they have enjoyed in their own country. The inescapable conclusion is that whatever the degree of antagonism, rejection, and marginalization found north of the border, life has been better in the United States than in Mexico.

The forces that have driven masses of Mexicans across the border have also conditioned and shaped their attitudes toward their homeland, their adoptive society, and the border itself. Above all, Mexicans have come to see the boundary as an escape valve for poverty and lack of economic opportunity in Mexico. Therein lies one of the most acute dilemmas that has confronted the Chicano community.

Chicanos have long been deeply troubled over the issues of migration from Mexico to the United States. As products of the process themselves, today's Chicanos naturally feel deep sympathy toward poor Mexicans who cross the border in search of economic opportunity. Chicanos directly extend the immigrants a helping hand, following a universal tradition of compassion toward foreigners who find themselves in a strange land. On the other hand, many Chicanos, just like other sectors of American society, have questioned whether the United States has reached the saturation point with regard to immigration. At the border, that concern has existed for many years, along with the related objection to the U.S. policy that permits "green card" commuters (Mexicans who have U.S. residency status) to live in Mexico and work in U.S. border cities. Labor unions, made up and led predominantly by Mexican Americans, have been particularly vocal in their demands to have the "green card" system eliminated and to close the border to the undocumented traffic.

Border labor leaders have long argued that both legal and illegal commuters depress U.S. wage scales, increase unemployment, serve as strikebreakers, and make union organizing and maintenance difficult. The struggle of the unions to force "green carders" to move to the United States led to hearings by the U.S. Select Commission on Western Hemisphere Immigration in 1968, to unsuccessful restrictive legislation introduced by Senator Edward Kennedy, and finally to a U.S. Supreme Court decision in 1974 that legalized the alien commuter program.[30] After the Supreme Court ruling, the unions then focused their attention on restricting the flow of undocumented workers. In 1974, Mexican American labor leaders in El Paso applauded a periodic U.S. Immigration Service "crackdown" on Mexican nationals who worked illegally in the United States. "It is about time something was done to keep illegal aliens from taking our jobs," stated Vice President Martin Reyes of the El Paso Building Trades Association. "For too long we have been at a disadvantage. Only eight percent of the jobs in El Paso are done with union labor."[31] A decade later, border union leaders sought passage of legislation that would impose penalties on employers who hired undocumented workers. In part because of union lobbying efforts, the long-debated Simpson-Rodino bill finally became law in 1986, ushering a new era of immigration control in the United States. The landmark legislation combines employer sanctions with other strong measures designed to curb the migrant flow, and at the same time grants amnesty to illegals who have lived in the United States continuously since January 1, 1982.

The debate on the Simpson-Rodino bill and its many predecessor proposals clearly revealed the divisions in the Chicano community over the migration issue. Across the nation, Hispanic politicians and middle-class organizations like the League of United Latin American Citizens, the National Council of La Raza, and the Mexican American Legal Educational Defense Fund strongly raised their voices in opposition to such bills. At the grass roots level, however, polls indicated considerable Hispanic support for tough immigration legislation, to include sanctions against employers who hire undocumented workers (see Table 4.2). The discrepancy between the views of Hispanic leaders and the Hispanic population at large is to some extent explained by economics: the political leadership and the activist organizations are made up largely of businesspersons and professionals who face no direct threat from the presence of undocumented persons. On the other hand, working-class persons, who predominate in the Hispanic population, must compete to a certain degree with the immigrants and consequently many feel more inclined toward restrictive legislation.

Table 4.2
Hispanic Views on Immigration Reform

	Polls		
	FAIR[a] (National sample)	Los Angeles Times[b] (California Hispanics)	SWVRP[c] (Texas Hispanics)
Tougher laws			
Favor	47%		
Oppose	15%		
Unsure	22%		
Employer sanctions			
Favor	60%	34%	60%
Oppose	33%	57%	40%
Unsure	8%	8%	0%

[a]Federation for American Immigration Reform poll, conducted in 1983 by telephone. Size of Hispanic sample: 1,600.
[b]Conducted in 1983. Size of Hispanic sample: 568.
[c]Southwest Voter Registration Project. Poll results as reported in the *El Paso Times*, May 1, 1984.

The divided views of Chicanos toward Mexican immigrants is very much related to their ambivalence toward Mexico itself. Even in the frontier days of the early nineteenth century, the people of Mexico's Far North held mixed perceptions about the motherland. Culturally they very much identified with their Mexican heritage, but their political allegiance was weak and their critcism of policies formulated in Mexico City was strong. The waves of immigrants who have come from Mexico into the United States since the mid-nineteenth century have adopted similar outlooks. For them the border has come to represent a line that separates progress from backwardness, order from chaos, lawfulness from lawlessness, honesty from corruption, and democracy from domination by a privileged few.

Recurring economic and political crises in Mexico during the last century have caused Mexicans on both sides of the border to lose faith in the ability of Mexican leaders to solve that nation's problems. Cynicism toward the governmental apparatus has grown to alarming proportions in recent years because of Mexico's deep financial crisis and blatant fraud in the electoral process.

Mexican currency, reflecting the condition of the country's economy, has become the symbol of failure, especially along the border. Immigrants have close familiarity with changes in the value of the peso in relation to the dollar, for countless devaluations have occurred since the peso equaled the dollar in worth back in the 1880s. It is those devaluations that prompted many of them to leave Mexico in search of the life that accompanies the earning of American dollars. Along the border, Chicanos laugh right along with Anglos when jokes are made about "no pesos accepted here."[32] Denigration of Mexican currency is often accompanied by expressions that imply contempt and pity for Mexico, a country said to be so riddled with inefficiency, incompetence, and corruption that it failed in the early 1980s to take advantage of a unique opportunity to profit greatly from its oil bonanza. Instead, it created for itself one of the most disastrous economic crises the world has ever witnessed.[33]

Consistent with prevailing views on both sides of the border, Chicanos relate Mexico's economic failures to atrocious government, particularly at the federal level. The political system imposed by the Partido Revolucionario Institucional (PRI), Mexico's ruling party for the last six decades, is seen as undemocratic and corrupt. The heavy-handed manner in which the PRI has maintained itself in power has disgusted many Chicanos, and some have publicly criticized government actions south of the border.[34] This departure from traditional practice of not saying negative things about Mexico openly in the United States derives from the massive fraud observed in a number of recent elections throughout northern Mexico, in particular the Chihuahua elections of 1986. The important point for this discussion is that the unfavorable image of the Mexican political system in the United States has worsened, and that image is one more burden Chicanos must carry as they struggle to find acceptance in a society that has always denigrated their heritage.

Another burden endured by Chicanos is the often cool and even hostile treatment encountered when they visit Mexico. Many Mexicans seem to feel that Chicanos are in some ways "traitors" to Mexico, having abandoned the motherland in preference to life in the land of the *gringos*. Mexicans from the middle and upper classes especially see

Chicanos as people from *campesino* (peasant) and working class backgrounds who, through their assumption of a *pocho* (culturally cor-
rupted) style of life, embarrass all Mexicans. Chicanos who speak no
Spanish are criticized for failing to learn the language of their parents,
and those who speak "Spanglish" (a mixture of Spanish and English)
draw contemptuous comments for their "mongrelized" mode of expression and "lack of culture." Those who "show off" American
clothes, personal articles, or flashy cars while in Mexico are deeply resented for their imitative American materialism and alleged feelings
of superiority toward Mexican nationals.

Despite the rejection from Mexicans and their own ambivalence vis-
à-vis Mexico, Chicanos have always looked south of the border in their
search for identity and cultural pride. During the height of the
Chicano Movement in the 1960s and 1970s, it became very popular to
study Mexican history, culture, and art. Many young Chicanos proudly
proclaimed themselves descendants of the Aztecs, followers of Emili-
ano Zapata and Pancho Villa, and admirers of the great painters Diego
Rivera, José Clemente Orozco, and David Alfaro Siqueiros. Pilgrim-
ages to the pyramids and to Mexico City were organized by college
groups, and summer study at Mexican universities became fashiona-
ble. In a very real sense the outward embracing of Mexico represented
a repudiation of American society. After decades of experiencing rejection in the United States, Chicanos felt a strong need to identify with
their Indian-Mexican roots and to show how their heritage was as good
if not superior to that of White Anglo-Saxon Protestants (WASPs).

Although the discovery of Mexican history and culture did much to
enhance pride and self-esteem among Chicanos, there were certain
realities in contemporary Mexican society that deeply disturbed them.
They quickly learned that Mexicans generally looked down on
Chicanos, that the poor in Mexico were even more oppressed than the
poor in the United States, and that the Mexican political system left
much to be desired. Chicanos found it difficult to reconcile the contradictions they observed in Mexico with their negative feelings toward
American society. Confusion, disillusionment, and resignation to their
condition in the United States were natural consequences of the "back
to our roots" experience for many who had romanticized the land of
their forebears.[35]

One sector of the Chicano population with a better understanding
of the realities of Mexico consists of leaders of several community organizations, national associations, labor unions, and academia, as well
as a few elected officials. These spokespeople sought to establish informal relations with Mexico in recent years. Whatever apprehensions
they had about the Mexican government, they recognized an opportu-

nity to derive some benefits from direct contact with Mexican officials. Frustrated by their lack of political power in the United States, this loosely tied group established links with Mexico City both to legitimize their leadership status in the United States and to gain Mexico's support for Chicano issues. The contact began in 1971, when the Luis Echeverría administration, sensing the growing political force of Chicanos in the United States, initiated a series of meetings to discuss issues of common concern. The Chicano leaders responded enthusiastically to that initiative, feeling that the U.S. government would have to take notice of their "recognition" by a foreign state and consequently take them more seriously in U.S. domestic politics. Access to the international media in Mexico City provided a means to make Chicano problems widely known and to embarrass Washington for its unresponsiveness to the group's needs. Of course Mexico stood to gain from the Chicano connection as well. By befriending Chicanos, Mexican officials hoped that a sizable pro-Mexican lobby would emerge in the United States, making it much easier for Mexico to negotiate with Washington on issues ranging from immigration and trade to sales of petroleum.[36]

The Chicano-Mexico relationship, however, involved complications for both parties. Close identification with Mexico risked a severe anti-Chicano backlash in the United States, where historically many Anglos have viewed Chicanos as less than "true" Americans. Political, social, and economic gains made by Chicanos in recent years could be put in jeopardy in possible retaliatory actions against the group by the U.S. government. Mexico risked alienating Washington by appearing to be manipulating a U.S. minority group to promote its interests, some of which appeared to clash sharply with U.S. policies. These considerations slowed the Chicano-Mexico relationship somewhat, but it was the Mexican economic crisis of 1982 that brought it practically to a halt. A drastic shift in priorities in Mexico City relegated the Chicano "connection" to low priority status during the early part of the Miguel de la Madrid administration. Scholarship programs for Chicanos to attend Mexican universities, established during the Echeverría and López Portillo administrations, suffered cutbacks as a direct result of the crisis.

Despite relative inactivity in the dialogue during the De la Madrid years, it seems clear that both parties wish to see the contact continue. It appears, however, that in the future Mexico will emphasize education and cultural ties with Chicanos and steer away from any activities that will place it on a collision course with Washington. De la Madrid has stated explicitly that Mexico will continue its long tradition of avoiding actions that might be interpreted as interfering with U.S.

domestic politics. As Chicanos gain more strength in the U.S. political system, they too will see less of a need to engage in a politically motivated relationship with the Mexican government.

The underlying reasons behind the efforts of Chicano leaders to maintain links with Mexican officials and the often-passionate concern of Chicano youth of the 1960s and 1970s for cultural identification with Mexico provide further evidence of the enduring ambivalence of the Chicano population as an ethnic minority in the United States. In short, because of unique historical, social, cultural, and social circumstances, Chicanos have found it very difficult to fit into American society, and because of their physical separation from Mexico, they ceased long ago to be a part of Mexican society. Thus Chicanos have been a group that fit on neither side of the border, destined to live a defensive lifestyle vis-à-vis both their adoptive society as well as their country of origin.

SUMMARY AND CONCLUSION

The creation of the U.S.-Mexico border in the mid-nineteenth century separated those Mexicans who lived north of the Rio Grande from the motherland, converting them into an ethnic minority in the United States. Henceforth they would live an "in-between" life, removed from their natural Mexican *ambiente* and unable to function as full participants in U.S. society. Those who lived close to the boundary maintained many social and cultural ties with Mexico, and that provided a measure of security in a hostile environment. Yet by keeping old customs, traditions, and language, border Chicanos enlarged the distance that separated them from the Anglo-American mainstream.

Another effect of the border for Chicanos has been its role in precipitating friction and violence. Conflicts between the United States and Mexico over myriad issues in the region placed the Chicano border population in an uncomfortable middle ground. Territorial disputes, banditry, irredentism, and revolutionary activity engendered intense nationalism and anti-Mexicanism among the Anglo public, continuously placing the group on the defensive. As border violence subsided, the character of Chicano–Anglo relations changed, and the conflict between them became less intense. Nevertheless, generally speaking the two groups have continued to live in separate worlds.

Changing conditions in the borderlands in recent decades have resulted in improvements in the status of Chicanos. The region is fast becoming more similar to the U.S. heartland as a result of large-scale migration of capital and people to "sun belt" areas. That has increased economic opportunities for southwestern Hispanics and has sped up the process of integration into the dominant culture. An indication of that trend is the impressive growth of Hispanic political power in the Southwest. Yet the basic pattern of Chicano ambivalence vis-à-vis the U.S. mainstream remains. Controversial border-related issues like migration, bilingual education, and "English-only" movements assure that Chicanos will face unsettling dilemmas in their lives for years to come. For border Chicanos, the psychological consequences of continued separation from the U.S. mainstream and of mixed emotion toward Mexico will remain deep and acute.

CHAPTER 5

Norteños and Fronterizos

The recession of Mexico's frontier to the Rio Grande in the nineteenth century had far-reaching consequences for the provinces immediately to the south of the new boundary. After the transfer of Texas, New Mexico, and California to the United States, the states of Tamaulipas, Nuevo León, Coahuila, Chihuahua, Sonora, and Baja California assumed the role of guardians of Mexico's territorial limits, with the settlements on the Rio Grande constituting the first line of defense against the American menace. Mexicans in the border area faced new challenges emanating from the imposed proximity to the powerful and aggressive nation next door. Economic pressures and unwelcome cultural influences compounded long-standing frontier problems such as isolation and danger from Indian attacks. Enduring remoteness and the ensuing economic orientation toward the United States would place the border region in a unique position vis-à-vis the rest of the republic.

This chapter focuses on the special characteristics of *norteños* (northerners) and *fronterizos* (borderlanders) that serve to distinguish them from their compatriots in other parts of Mexico. Since pronounced regionalism is a basic hallmark of the North, attention is given to tensions between *norteños* and the central government. The trend toward increased external relationships is also examined. Finally, American influence on *norteño* lifestyles are assessed in relation to national desires to reduce the process of "demexicanization" perceived to prevail in the border region.

EL NORTE

To understand the heritage of the Mexican borderlands, it is important to consider some of the unique features of northern Mexico.[1] Physically, the area is characterized by vast open spaces, rugged mountain terrain, desert lands, and few rivers and lakes. The harsh natural conditions acted as a deterrant to effective colonization from the south for many years, and the border states remained sparsely populated well into the twentieth century. Until the advent of modern transportation, the North was practically cut off from the Mexican interior, and population centers in the region itself were isolated from each other.

Different ethnic patterns are also noticeable among norteños. Because of the limited Indian population and its strong resistance to assimilation into the Mexican way of life, little *mestizaje* (Spanish-Indian miscegenation) took place in the region. Consequently, norteños as a group are more white than their compatriots to the south. The large number of *mestizos* now found throughout the North are largely a product of recent migrations from the interior. Norteño elites are descended to a significant degree from pioneer Spanish and Mexican families who arrived centuries ago.

In contrast to economic tendencies in the interior, ranching and mining dominated the economy of El Norte for many generations, leading to the development of certain occupational patterns that promoted individual and group self-sufficiency, mobility, and independence. Peonage thrived to a lesser degree in the North because of the absence of *encomiendas* (Spanish system of exacting tribute from Indians) and the less-exploitative character of local *haciendas* (large estates). Agricultural workers also had the option of becoming sharecroppers, thus increasing their independence from *hacendados*. *Vaqueros* (cowboys) enjoyed the freedom to move about, seeking the best *rancho* to practice their trade. As in the rural areas, urban norteño workers also enjoyed better conditions and higher wages than in the South. In short, traditional patterns of paternalism and rigid control of workers were ameliorated in the North by different environmental and economic circumstances.

Mexicans recognize a norteño culture distinct from that of other parts of Mexico. Norteños are said to be different in their manner of thinking, speaking, acting, and dressing. A strong spirit of struggle, determination, adaptability, and hard work is attributed to norteños because of the harsh conditions traditionally encountered in the region. Additionally, the people of the North have been affected by the modernizing influences of the United States; thus more progressive ideas and institutions are said to have developed in El Norte. Remoteness from the central government in Mexico City has bred regionalism and independence, and norteños have demonstrated in a strong way their dissatisfaction with national policies at various points in Mexican history.

In the mid-nineteenth century, separatist movements erupted in various northern provinces. The attempts to establish a "Republic of the Rio Grande" in 1839–40 and a "Republic of Sierra Madre" in the early 1850s serve as indicators of the level of dissatisfaction among norteños with central authorities. To a degree, the separation of Texas and subsequent loss of New Mexico and California to the United States is explained by chronic local insurgency that weakened Mexico City's control in those provinces. Norteños had plenty of reasons to rebel against the federal government, and that made the conquest of the territory in the mid-nineteenth century easier for the United States.

Northern rebelliousness exploded again in the 1910s, when Mexico endured one of the world's great revolutions. Significant events that preceded the unrest occurred in the northern provinces, and major battles were subsequently fought in countless northern cities. It is fitting that the first important encounter between *federales* and *revolucionarios* took place in the border town of Ciudad Juárez in May 1911. That battle resulted in the deposing of the dictator Porfirio Díaz and the ascension of the "Apostle of Democracy," Francisco Madero. Most importantly, norteños produced a majority of the major leaders who fought the Revolution, and subsequently several of them became presidents. Apart from Madero, who hailed from Coahuila, other northerners who assumed the highest office in the postrevolutionary years were Venustiano Carranza (Coahuila), Eulalio Gutiérrez (Coahuila), Roque González Garza (Coahuila), Adolfo de la Huerta (Sonora), Alvaro Obregón (Sonora), Plutarco Elías Calles (Sonora), Emilio Portes Gil (Tamaulipas), and Abelardo L. Rodríguez (Sonora). The most famous personality of the period, Francisco "Pancho" Villa, was also a norteño (Durango and Chihuahua).

More recently the North has once again sent shock waves throughout Mexico by rebelling against the Partido Revolucionario Institucional (PRI), the party in power since 1929, in countless local and state elections. The most significant losses for the ruling party took place in 1983 in Durango City, Chihuahua City, and Ciudad Juárez, where the conservative Partido Acción Nacional (PAN) won the mayorships and city councils of all three cities. Then in 1985 voters in Ciudad Juárez elected three PAN members to the federal Congress. By the end of that year, the PAN had achieved unprecedented power in Chihuahua, the largest Mexican state: it controlled the seven most important cities and had six state representatives (out of fourteen) and ten seats in the federal Congress. The PAN had also given the PRI a tough fight in the governor races in Nuevo León and Sonora, but massive electoral fraud in those states derailed the opposition candidates.[2]

The losses of 1983 and 1985 in the North severely shook the ruling party, and a decision was made not only to prevent the PAN from winning further elections but to recover the offices the PRI had lost. This was to be accomplished using whatever means necessary. The opportunity to implement the hard-line policy came in July 1986 in Chihuahua, where the PRI used ballot stuffing and other blatantly fraudulent tactics to smother the opposition.[3] According to the official results announced by the PRI-controlled Chihuahua Electoral College, the PRI overwhelmingly won the governorship, all fourteen seats in the state legislature, and sixty-five of the sixty-seven mayorships. The only PAN victory officially recognized was the mayorship of Nuevo Casas Grandes; the other mayorship (of Gómez Farías) was awarded to the leftist Partido Popular Socialista.[4] The people of Chihuahua were expected to believe that the ruling party had suddenly recaptured the support of the voters after the lopsided repudiation throughout the state during the previous two years.

The PAN and its supporters reacted angrily to the official results, holding a series of demonstrations, marches, blockades of streets and highways, hunger strikes, and even picketing of President Miguel de la Madrid when he met with President Ronald Reagan in August 1986 at the White House. The depth of the discontent was evident in the size of the demonstrations and the bold takeover of international bridges in Juárez–El Paso. One gathering in front of the Juárez City Hall drew an estimated thirty thousand people, while thousands of protesters occupied the bridges for days at a time on several occasions. For six weeks following the elections the political climate in Juárez and Chihuahua City remained extremely tense.[5] In Parral, violence erupted in mid-August, including shootings and damage to property, prompting state authorities to issue arrest warrants for the PAN mayor and five other party activists. Feeling that their lives were in danger, they fled to El Paso and asked for political asylum in the United States.[6] Elections-related violence in the last two years has also been reported in other places, including Piedras Negras, Agua Prieta, Mexicali, and Durango City.

As of this writing, a PAN-led coalition of five political parties, embracing rightist as well as leftist orientations, and ten civic organizations has been formed to press for political changes in Mexico. Called the National Democratic Movement, the coalition includes the PAN, the Partido Socialista Unido de México, the Partido Socialista Democrático, the Partido Revolucionario de los Trabajadores, and the Partido Mexicano de los Trabajadores.[7] It is difficult to say how successful this confederation will be, or even to speculate how long it will maintain internal unity given the vast ideological differences that exist among the component parties. However, the fact that these groups joined together to fight a common enemy is of major historical significance in Mexican politics. Whatever happens within or outside of this movement in the years to come, norteños will be in the forefront of change, just as they have been during previous national crises.

The most compelling explanation for the latest norteño rebellion against central authority is the harm caused to the economy of northern Mexico by the national economic collapse that began in 1982. Though norteños and other Mexicans realize that the drop in oil prices and other unfavorable developments in the international economy have much to do with Mexico's misfortune, they nonetheless feel that government mismanagement and corruption played a significant role in precipitating and prolonging the crisis. The antigovernment reaction has been strongest in the North because the area, with its close economic ties to the United Stats, has been hardest hit by the devastating devaluation of Mexican currency. In February 1982, the dollar-peso ratio stood at 1:27; subsequently it plummeted to 1:69 (August 1982), 1:149 (February 1983), 1:204 (December 1984), 1:350 (September 1985), 1:690 (August 1986), and 1:1,270 (May 1987).

The drop in the value of the peso resulted in a drastic reduction of the purchasing power of norteños. Their pesos could no longer buy American products, on which they had long been dependent. To add insult to injury, the central government in 1983 instituted a currency exchange controls program that made it very difficult for norteños to transact business with the American side. With the nationalization of the banks, businessmen found it increasingly difficult to carry on normal financial dealings, and worst of all, capital for investments became very scarce. Consequently, the economy of the North almost came to a standstill, and many people, particularly along the border, found themselves in a near state of panic.

Norteños thus expressed their discontent with the central government by voting for the PAN in many towns and cities. It is not clear to what extent norteños embrace the conservative ideology of this party, but it seems apparent that the PAN's emphasis on the need for more honest and efficient government has struck a powerful chord with voters. Whether the PAN continues to win elections in the North and along the border will largely depend on the condition of the economy. Since the recovery is proceeding slowly and the peso continues to slide, it is likely that the PRI will encounter tough challenges in the North in the future. Locked as they are to the American economy, norteños could face further deterioration of their standard of living, and the political arena will be their forum for expressing frustration and dissatisfaction.

THE EVOLUTION OF FOREIGN DEPENDENCY

The Mexican border states became economic dependencies of the United States in the latter nineteenth century, in particular during the years when Porfirio Díaz held the presidency of Mexico. Díaz encouraged foreign capitalists to look to Mexico for big profits by offering them numerous concessions. Americans readily answered the call, investing heavily in transportation and mining, two industries that changed the economic character of the North. It was primarily U.S. capital that financed the construction of major railroad lines from the interior to the northern border, making it possible to substantially increase the export of Mexican raw materials and labor to the United States, and to expand the import of American manufactured goods into Mexico.

The revitalization of the mining industry during the period is evident in the rise of gold and silver production. In 1877 the value of gold production stood at 1.5 million pesos and that of silver at 24.8 million pesos; by 1908 the figure for gold was 40 million pesos and for silver 85 million pesos. American companies operated large mines in Coahuila, Chihuahua, and Baja California. Most prominent among the foreign concerns were the Guggenheims, who owned mines and smelters throughout the northern states. In Cananea, Sonora, entrepreneur William Greene ran one of the world's premier copper operations, employing thousands of Mexican workers.[8]

Apart from railroads and mining, Americans also invested in agriculture, ranching, commerce, and urban industries. Numerous American company towns and colonies sprang up in Baja California, Sonora, and Chihuahua, stimulating economic activity and providing employment for local people. Thus large numbers of Mexicans in the North became directly dependent on foreign capital for their livelihood, and as the years went by many of them determined that their dreams could best be fulfilled working for American companies rather than for Mexican employers.

The reality of pronounced economic dependence on the United States among the people of northern Mexico is best illustrated by the skewed relationship that developed between the Mexican border towns and their counterpart communities across the Rio Grande. Before the conversion of that stream into a boundary, towns such as Matamoros, Reynosa, Mier, Guerrero, and Paso del Norte (now Ciudad Juárez) supported themselves on the basis of agriculture, ranching, and limited regional trade. Isolation had, by necessity, given rise to economic self-sufficiency. After the war of 1846–48, Anglo-American entrepeneurs penetrated the border markets with vigor, engendering a dependence on foreign products that would grow steadily as the population of the area increased. Before 1848, local residents could conduct trade northward with only minor impediments, but after the establishment of the new border, Mexico applied its tariff laws to goods brought in from across the Rio Grande, an unwanted development that substantially increased the cost of living on the Mexican side. Consequently, many families migrated to nearby U.S. communities. Those who remained on the south bank asked Mexican authorities to allow the duty-free importation of foreign products to prevent further outmigration and to stimulate local commerce. Mexico City responded in the affirmative, but the concessions granted to the border were insufficient to meet local needs, prompting the states of Tamaulipas and Chihuahua in 1858 to establish a Zona Libre, or Free Trade Zone, along their border frontiers. At the time the central government exercised reduced control over its provinces, allowing these states to make those decisions on their own.[9]

Free trade helped fronterizos cope with the Anglo-American economic competition, but the Zona Libre was a hotly contested political issue in the interior of Mexico, because it was regarded as a regional privilege that created unfair competition for national products. Many Mexican officials also objected to the loss of tariff revenues. In addition, the Zona Libre aroused the ire of American merchants and the U.S. government when commercial activity favored the Mexican side and when smuggling into the United States proved difficult to control. Along the Chihuahua frontier the Zona Libre was an on-again off-again proposition for several decades because of frequent changes in government in the state capital. Yet with or without the Free Zone, foreign goods penetrated the Mexican side, for even at times when duties had to be paid, these could easily be avoided through the payment of *mordidas* (bribes) to customs inspectors. Internal and external pressures induced Mexico to finally abolish the Free Zone in 1905, but the continuing need for tariff exemptions would prompt fronterizos to petition repeatedly for its return. Free trade reemerged in Baja California and portions of Sonora in the 1930s, and another variation of the concept was introduced in other border areas in the 1970s, allowing for duty-free importation of certain approved products for resale on the Mexican side.

Viewed historically, it is clear that free trade has benefited fronterizos, albeit to the detriment of the national economy and at the cost of economically tying the border region closer to the United States. Regardless of the existence or nonexistence of the Free Zone, however, Americans have maintained hegemony over Mexican border consumers. That reality has caused Mexicans in the interior to view fronterizos as a different breed within the nation's society, a group whose lifestyle has been conditioned by their "addiction" to foreign tastes and products. The problem has long been recognized by the federal government, which has sought unsuccessfully to integrate the northern frontier economically to the rest of the republic.

In the late 1950s, Mexico City conducted studies of spending patterns of border Mexicans and confirmed the acute integration with the American side. A decision was made to promote the consumption of greater quantities of national goods by the border citizenry, and in 1961 the government began a comprehensive program to develop the border. Manufacturers from the interior received tax and transportation incentives to send more of their products to the north. Additionally, modern shopping centers were constructed in the border cities. The results of these programs have been mixed. Business activity in the border area increased markedly in the 1960s and 1970s, with a corresponding slowdown of the Mexican "parade" to American stores. Much of the consumption on the Mexican side, however, still involved products imported (legally or illegally) from the United States.[10] Only recent peso devaluations that drastically cut the purchasing power of the national currency could stop fronterizos from patronizing American stores or purchasing foreign goods in Mexican stores.[11]

The economic dependence of Mexico's fronterizos on the United States is also evident in the reliance of the border communities on tourist industries. Tourism per se is a beneficial addition to any economy, but certain activities that emerged locally have seriously marred the image of the border zone. Historically, cities like Juárez and Tijuana have been seen by many on both sides of the boundary as wide-open recreation centers for foreign visitors, appealing particularly to American military personnel eager for thrills from sex, liquor, drugs, and other vices. This aspect of border life has been popularized in books and the media, much to the detriment of local residents, who have been subjected to unkind criticism from both sides of the border. Given the powerful image formed by many of the Mexican border communities as "sin cities," it is important to place the development of border nightlife in proper perspective and to underscore the ties that have existed to American investors and clientele. In the broadest sense, this facet of the border economy started because of frontier economic necessity and has thrived because of a continuing consumer demand and a favorable operating climate. Moreover, it needs to be understood that vice is usually found in large doses in border areas and ports throughout the world, especially in regions visited by affluent tourists.

The "culture of sin" took root in the Mexican frontier during the last few years of the nineteenth century, when a depression, triggered by external forces, devastated the local border economies. Foremost among the causes of the disruption of that period were restrictions imposed on border trade by the Mexican government, a series of peso devaluations, and in the case of the Chihuahua frontier, severe shortages of Rio Grande water for agricultural use precipitated by excessive appropriation by farmers in New Mexico and Colorado. Fronterizos desperately needed new sources of income. Coincidentally, many Anglo-American "merchants of sin" at about the same time needed safe pastures to relocate their operations when they were driven out of countless communities throughout the United States during a period of moral reform in that country. It is in that context that operators of brothels, gambling joints, and bars in El Paso moved to Juárez at the turn of the century. The construction of such prominent tourist facilities as the bull ring in 1903 and the race track in 1905 reflect the transformation of the Juárez economy as the twentieth century began. Steadily, foreign capital played a crucial role in the building and maintaining of the border tourist industry.[12]

During the Prohibition era (1918–33), American investors poured substantial amounts of money into the Mexican frontier, capitalizing on the demand for liquor and entertainment not legally or readily available north of the border. Results of a Juárez Chamber of Commerce study in 1926 indicated that persons with English surnames controlled about 40 percent of the value of forty-one structures in the city. Two prominent companies, the D & H and D & W distilleries, moved their plants from Kentucky to Juárez, while according to a local newspaper, "nearly all of the bars formerly in El Paso and many other parts of the United States relocated in Juárez."[13] Although the spending of dollars stimulated economic activity on the Mexican side, a great portion of these funds found their way back to the United States because of the heavy dependence of fronterizos on American stores for their daily necessities.

The boom in tourism created in the 1920s began to dissipate once the effect of the Great Depression began to be felt along the border in 1930 and 1931. Greater declines in the tourist trade followed when Prohibition came to an end in the United States in 1933 and when the

Mexican federal government closed gambling casinos and related establishments during a wave of moral reform.

World War II brought another major upswing in tourism in the Mexican border towns. Millions of American servicemen and civilians patronized Mexican shopping centers, bars, and brothels, thus providing new revenues for the struggling border communities. The new earnings allowed fronterizos to make civic improvements and stimulated nontourist activities that aided in the diversification of the economy. Yet the heavy reliance on the entertainment sector, especially its seedy component, strongly reinforced the image of the border cities as "Centers of Vice," "Sodoms," "Gomorrah Cities," and other such epithets.

Today liquor, drugs, and prostitution no longer provide the magnetism they once did for visitors from north of the Rio Grande. The emergence in the United States of topless and bottomless bars, X-rated movies, sexual permissiveness, and availability of drugs has diminished the thunder of the Mexican border nightlife. Even so, foreigners continue to frequent diversion centers on the Mexican side, and in the process, many needy Mexicans dependent on tourism, particularly women who work as prostitutes, must endure humiliations and indignities in their struggle to make a living.

Although foreign-based tourism has been a prominent industry at the Mexican border for several decades, an even more important and longer-standing source of income has been jobs available north of the boundary. During the late nineteenth century, when northern Mexico and the American Southwest experienced rapid economic growth, Mexicans in significant numbers began working for *norteamericano* companies on both sides of the border. The towns adjacent to the boundary became strategic recruiting points of Mexican labor, and soon a system developed by which large numbers of fronterizos, both documented and undocumented, used the area as a jumping point, or springboard, to cross into the United States to work. Over time that labor system became institutionalized and continues to function to the present day. Transborder workers include commuters who cross the boundary on a daily basis and migrants who penetrate deeper into American territory, working on a seasonal basis and making periodic return trips to their border home bases.[14]

It is difficult to know the actual size of the Mexican worker commuting traffic because of problems with the collection of data. The U.S. Immigration and Naturalization Service (INS) gathers statistics on legal commuters and on apprehended undocumented migrants. Each set of data has limitations, but together they give a general idea of the volume of the "springboarder" traffic—and the degree of direct dependence of the Mexican side on jobs in the United States.

Mexican worker commuters consist of persons who hold U.S. residency cards (popularly known as "green cards"), persons who illegally use local crossing permits (issued to shoppers, students, businesspeople, tourists, and others) to work, and persons who cross the border without any documentation. In 1981 the INS counted forty thousand "green carders" from one end of the border to the other (Table 5.1). This figure represents a very conservative estimate of the overall "green carder" traffic, for many such crossers refuse to identify themselves as commuter workers simply because they are suspicious of INS intentions in gathering that information.

Table 5.1
Number of Mexican Green Card Commuters, 1981

Major ports	
Nuevo Laredo–Laredo	1,759
Piedras Negras–Eagle Pass	1,689
Juárez–El Paso	7,554
San Luis–Yuma	7,919
Mexicali–Calexico	6,954
Tijuana–San Ysidro	10,592
All other ports	3,720
Total	40,187

SOURCE: U.S. Immigration and Naturalization Service, *Commuter Report, 1981*, Washington, D.C. Cited in El Paso Chamber of Commerce, *El Paso Area Fact Book*, sec. 12, pp. 8–9.

The number of people who use local crossing permits to work and those who totally lack documentation is impossible to determine. The best available clue is the INS data on apprehension of Mexican illegal aliens along the border. Out of 820,357 apprehensions of illegal aliens recorded in 1981, 89 percent took place in the U.S. border districts (Table 5.2). It is difficult to know what portion of the 89 percent consists of border commuters (as opposed to migrants headed for the interior of the United States), but a reasonable estimate would be from one-third to one-half; thus for 1981, between 271,718 and 410,179 apprehensions of improperly documented, job-seeking border commuters took place. Of course, many of those apprehensions involved multiple counts of individuals apprehended more than once during the year. Further, not all persons apprehended crossed the border for job-related reasons. Taking those facts into consideration, I will speculate that 150,000 persons commute daily to jobs in the United States without the necessary documentation.

One more category of workers needs to be considered in estimating

Table 5.2
Undocumented Immigrants Required to Depart, 1981

		Percentage of Total
U.S. total	820,357	100.0
Border districts	727,536	88.7
Harlingen	30,650	3.7
San Antonio	92,540	11.3
El Paso	133,588	16.3
Phoenix	73,377	8.9
San Diego	397,381	48.4

SOURCE: U.S. Immigration and Naturalization Service.

the total worker commuter traffic: U.S. citizens who live on the Mexican side and, just as the others, cross the border daily to work in American border cities. Using as a point of departure the fact that seven thousand such workers commute from Juárez to El Paso, I will venture to guess that twenty-five thousand U.S. citizen commuters live along the entire Mexican border.

Thus, adding the three categories (40,000 "green carders," 150,000 crossers lacking proper documents, and 25,000 U.S. citizen commuters), an estimated 215,000 workers who live on the Mexican side are directly dependent on employment in the United States. Assuming that each of these workers supports an additional 4 persons, the number of people dependent on U.S. jobs increases to 1,075,000.

Another very important sector of the Mexican labor force that relies on the U.S. economy for their livelihood are the people who work in predominantly American-owned assembly plants known as *maquiladoras*. These factories, which began operations in the Mexican border cities in 1965 at a time of heavy unemployment in the region, numbered 680 and employed 184,400 border workers by 1984. Most plants are concentrated in Juárez, Tijuana, Mexicali, and Matamoros (Table 5.3).

The maquiladoras demonstrate in a dramatic way the external dependence of the Mexican border. In Ciudad Juárez, now the assembly "capital" of the world, an estimated three-fourths of the economically active population is tied in directly or indirectly to the maquiladoras.[15] The overwhelming foreign orientation of the Juárez economy becomes evident if maquiladora workers are combined with border commuters and employees of tourist-related activities. One source reports that

Table 5.3
Assembly Plants in Mexico, 1970–1984

	Number of Plants			Number of Employees		
	1970	1974	1984	1970	1974	1984
Entire republic	—	474	680	—	75,614	211,200
All border municipalities	120	449	585	20,327	70,738	184,400
Matamoros	23	45	38	2,565	8,964	20,300
Nuevo Laredo	17	17	13	3,472	5,516	3,700
Piedras Negras	5	15	18	1,240	3,094	3,900
Ciudad Juárez	22	89	159	3,165	17,484	75,200
Nogales	5	48	46	1,202	8,517	17,300
Mexicali	22	71	71	5,002	8,714	10,900
Tijuana	16	101	143	2,190	10,024	24,400
Other border municipalities	10	63	97	1,491	8,425	28,700

SOURCES: Martínez, *Border Boom Towns*, 133; American Industrial Parks, Inc., El Paso.

those three sectors account for at least two-thirds of the total earnings of the local labor force.[16] Assembly plants have not only increased the economic dependence of the border region, they have affected all of Mexico. These industries have become the nation's second largest earner of foreign exchange, surpassing tourism but still significantly behind petroleum exports. If for some reason the maquiladora program should disappear or significantly reduce its operations (for example, as a result of changes in U.S. tariff laws brought about by pressures placed by U.S. labor unions), Mexico and the border zone in particular would experience a crisis of immense proportions.

Apart from the issue of external dependence, critics of maquiladoras have pointed out that the original purpose of the program, to alleviate the pronounced male unemployment at the border, has not been accomplished, since the employees are overwhelmingly women who have only recently joined the work force. Detractors of the program add that with rapid industrial expansion have come attendant social ills, such as inadequate housing, an alarming shortage of social services, increased crime, and family disintegration. Many also feel that maquiladoras tend to encourage more migrants from Mexico's interior to head toward the border, thus contributing to an existing overpopulation problem. For example, with a current population of nearly 1 million each, Juárez and Tijuana are among the most overcrowded cities in Mexico.

From the standpoint of the United States, the availability of large numbers of Mexican workers close by has been an important factor in the growth and development experienced by the American border-lands. This reserve army of labor has been built up over the decades by a combination of push-pull tendencies that have characterized the economies of Mexico and the United States. One significant factor has been the efforts of those who benefit from cheap labor to induce large-scale migration to the border. For years, American corporations sent labor recruiters deep into Mexico and to the border cities seeking work-ers for North American railroads, mines, and agriculture. The U.S. government, often with the cooperation of Mexico City, aided Amer-ican employers in securing labor by overlooking violation of labor laws, ignoring or bending immigration legislation, and instituting contract labor operations such as the Bracero Program during World War II. These various currents have fed on each other to bring about a steady migration stream involving millions of human beings caught in an ir-reversible social process.[17] This situation has been especially favorable to employers who derive large profits from the rock-bottom wages they pay workers who have no documents. Middle- and upper-class people in the U.S. borderlands also benefit from low-cost maids, gardeners, and other service workers, not to mention the availability of compara-tively low prices for certain consumer goods, such as food products, that involve the participation of undocumented labor at some stage. These benefits to American society are usually forgotten during hard times north of the boundary, and pressures build up to seal the border to north-bound migrants. Such a pattern has been in evidence during the recurring recessions experienced by the United States in the 1970s and 1980s.

AMERICAN CULTURAL INFLUENCES
ON THE MEXICAN BORDER

From the Mexican view, the overwhelming reliance of the border econ-omy on the American side has not only subjected the region to disrup-tive economic cycles that originate abroad, it has also tended to pull border residents within the cultural orbit of the United States. That condition has kept fronterizos on the defensive vis-à-vis the rest of Mexico. It has long been traditional for Mexicans from the interior to criticize fronterizos for their alleged complacency concerning illegal practices that permeate the border dollar economy; their alacrity to learn the English language; and their tendency to adopt *norteamericano* consumption habits, customs, and dress styles. As early as 1828, one Mexican observer commented on the negative effects of the proximity to the United States for residents of the frontier town of Nacogdoches,

Texas: "Accustomed to the continued trade with the North Americans, they have adopted their customs and habits, and speak Spanish with marked incorrectness."[18] Similar comments regarding the border would be repeated by interior Mexicans time and again in subsequent eras. The Prohibition, World War II, and Korean War years produced particularly strong verbal attacks from Mexicans, who expressed outrage at what they considered to be excessive levels of immorality and "demexicanization" at the northern frontier, prompting angry rebuttals from leading border residents. For example, one writer from Juárez wrote the following in 1948:

> Some stupid reporters from faraway regions say Juárez is the headquarters for gangsters, gamblers, smugglers, thieves, or drug pushers, marijuana and morphine users, and alcoholics. But if we read their writings carefully, we find that none of their arguments are good, that they cite no concrete facts, that those cited are not verifiable, and if an event is true it is exaggerated; that they lie, are badly informed or badly mistaken in their impressions, and that in most cases these writers are imprudent or ignorant, and many of them do not even know the city.[19]

Other writers have reacted with less emotion but with equal resolve to reassure their compatriots in the interior that they remain culturally loyal to the motherland. "We hope that the whole Republic comprehends us and understands our *mexicanidad*, for through our service clubs and scientific organizations . . . we defend our language, art, customs, religion, songs, and everything else that distinguishes our people and makes us feel proud of living on the border to carry out our role of first defenders of our native soil," stated an editorial written by the Juárez Union of Professionals and Intellectuals in 1954.[20] "In Juárez we breathe and live in an environment of profound *mexicanidad*," wrote an essayist in 1957. "People known as *pochos* do exist, but it can be said with absolute certainty that they number but a few in the city and that they more than likely are offsprings of Mexicans born on the other side, who have tried to adopt the forms and styles of life in the neighboring nation."[21]

The continuing concern over "demexicanization" at the border is exemplified by attempts from Mexico City to increase awareness in the frontier cities of Mexico's history and culture. As part of the National Border Program (PRONAF) of the 1960s, the government constructed museums, arts and crafts centers, and auditoriums to exhibit native artifacts and art and to hold musical, dance, and educational events that reflect traditional and contemporary life throughout Mexico. To complement that effort, the Secretaría de Educación Pública has targeted the border region for greater dissemination of books on Mexico and for the development of programs through the schools to strengthen national identity.[22]

The government's preoccupation with "demexicanization" is most dramatically illustrated by the creation of the Comisión Nacional para la Defensa del Idioma Español (National Commission for the Defense of the Spanish Language), whose "main goal was the protection of Spanish from the onslaught of English, insofar as this language had presumably derrogated and deformed the national standard. By emphasizing language in the enhancement of patriotic values, the central authority of Mexico intended to reactionate a dormant national consciousness and infirm ethnic identity."[23] The Comisión has directed its efforts primarily to three areas designated as "disaster" zones: (1) the three largest Mexican cities, that is, Mexico City, Guadalajara, and Monterrey; (2) centers of tourism; and (3) northern border cities. In Ciudad Juárez, the Comisión during 1979–82 disseminated films and books, held theatrical presentations, and assisted in the building of a new public library.[24]

The government initiatives to reinforce Mexican culture are commendable, but because of the limited resources invested, in reality they have done little to change existing conditions at the border. As long as the U.S. economy dominates the Mexican frontier, foreign cultural and linguistic influences will be forcefully felt. It is to the advantage of fronterizos to link themselves with the dollar economy, to learn English, and to become familiar with American lifestyles. That tendency has never been as enticing, and perhaps as necessary, as it is at present, given that Mexico continues to suffer from one of the most serious economic crises in its history. Regardless of what interior Mexicans think concerning the perceived "demexicanization" at the border, fronterizos will continue to look northward in their quest for material improvement. Such has been their destiny since the border's creation, and the future promises no alteration in that long-established pattern.

However, if fronterizos link their economic interests and consumption patterns with the United States, it does not follow that they reject their "Mexicanness." A recent study conducted by Mexico's Colegio de la Frontera Norte (formerly CEFNOMEX) revealed that feelings of national identity are actually stronger among residents of Ciudad Juárez and Matamoros, where foreign linguistic influences are most pronounced, than in interior centers like Acapulco, Uruapan, Zacatecas, and Mexico City. It is significant that among the seven cities surveyed, national identity sentiments were the weakest in Mexico City.[25] Assuming the validity of these findings, Mexico should find comfort in the degree of allegiance to the motherland among fronterizos. The traditional attacks on fronterizos for alleged "disloyalty" and "lack of cultural integration" appear to be based on stereotypes and misconceptions.

SUMMARY AND CONCLUSION

The people of northern Mexico have long been seen as a special breed by other Mexicans because of their isolation from the rest of the republic, their different cultural strains, and their close association with the United States. Residents of border cities in particular have been subjected to considerable criticism for their adoption of American customs and heavy consumption of U.S. products. Though the charge that the process of "demexicanization" is rampant in the North is exaggerated, by necessity and circumstances norteños have had intense interaction with the United States. Large segments of the population of cities like Nuevo Laredo, Ciudad Juárez, and Tijuana function directly in the American economy by working in maquiladoras, in tourism, or in a variety of jobs in the U.S. border cities. Over generations tens of thousands of fronterizos have actually used the Mexican border cities as jumping-off points for eventual emigration to the United States. It is not far-fetched to characterize many fronterizos as "Chicanos in the making," for their experience at the border prepares them well for life in the United States should they decide to emigrate.

Long concerned over the close ties of norteños and fronterizos with the United States, Mexico City determined in the 1960s that the time had arrived to seriously seek to integrate the border economy to the rest of the country. Border cities assumed high priority within the grand scheme of decentralized national development, which led to the creation of economic and cultural programs intended to improve the standard of life and to reinforce Mexican culture and customs. The strategy has achieved some significant results. Border urban centers have expanded their economic base and have improved their appearance. The old "sin city" images of Ciudad Juárez and Tijuana have changed dramatically as prostitution and related illicit activities have diminished or shifted to the American side. Such developments as these have instilled a sense of pride among fronterizos that was absent in previous eras.

Yet despite the efforts from Mexico City to pull the border region into the national fold, norteños and fronterizos remain a society apart from the restt of Mexico. The economic crisis of the 1980s has actually deepened the foreign orientation because of the declining economic opportunities within Mexico. For the first time since the years of the

Mexican Revolutiuon, significant numbers of middle- and upper-middle-class Mexicans from the North and elsewhere have emigrated to the United States, causing a "brain drain" in their homeland whose impact is bound to be felt with great force in the future. Further, many wealthy Mexicans have taken substantial amounts of money out of the country, leaving the economy starved for capital. Between 1976 and 1985, an estimated $53 billion left Mexico, much of it deposited in banks in the U.S. borderlands.[26]

In the political arena the norteños have already made their weight felt in vigorously protesting the absence of honest elections in Mexico. The "National Democratic Movement" begun in Chihuahua in 1986 involving the participation of conservative and leftist parties is bound to have a significant effect on Mexican politics. There is a real potential that other parts of the nation will join the norteños in pressuring the government to democratize the system. Once again the North is living up to its reputation of forcefully expressing its independence and challenging central authority on issues of fundamental importance to all Mexicans.

CHAPTER 6

Contemporary Border Issues

As in the past, the U.S.-Mexico borderlands continue today to generate friction within each nation and in the sphere of binational relations. But whereas frontier conditions spawned lawlessness and disorder a few generations ago, current issues are vastly different. Recent population growth, urbanization, industrialization, and other modernizing forces have transformed the once-isolated and sparsely inhabited borderlands into one of the most rapidly developing regions of the United States and Mexico. Many borderland cities now function as prominent sites for the international transit of goods and services, for manufacture and processing, and for labor exchange. Without the economic symbiosis of the border, it is inconceivable that the region would have become so attractive to the recent waves of entrepreneurs and immigrants.

These profound changes have produced new challenges for both nations. Americans and Mexicans, keenly aware of problems of overutilization of scarce resources, overpopulation, poverty, undocumented migration, and delicate economic interdependence, continue to struggle to prevent serious deterioration of cross-border relations. Even if a friendly atmosphere cannot always prevail at the frontier, its residents recognize the compelling reasons to preserve a spirit of neighborly coexistence.

GROWTH IN THE BORDERLANDS

Dynamic economic development in the last several decades has spurred rapid population and urban growth in the borderlands. The region is no longer a remote desert zone dotted with tiny outposts. Near the border and directly adjacent to it are many major urban centers supported by a vibrant economy that is fueled by increasing amounts of capital and an ever-rising stream of national and international migration.

Table 6.1 details the accelerated population growth experienced by the U.S. and Mexican border states since mid-century. In 1950, the combined population of Texas, New Mexico, Arizona, and California was 19.7 million; three decades later that figure had risen to 41.9 million. On the Mexican side, the combined populations of Tamaulipas, Nuevo León, Coahuila, Chihuahua, Sonora, and Baja California grew from 3.8 million to 10.7 million during the same period. Taken together, the U.S. and Mexican states now have a population of over 52

Table 6.1
Population of Mexican and U.S. Border States, 1950–1980[a]

	1950	1960	1970	1980
Mexican border states				
Tamaulipas	718,167	1,024,182	1,456,858	1,924,484
Nuevo León	740,191	1,078,848	1,694,689	2,513,044
Coahuila	720,619	907,734	1,114,956	1,557,265
Chihuahua	846,414	1,226,793	1,612,525	2,005,477
Sonora	510,607	783,378	1,098,731	1,513,731
Baja California	226,965	520,165	870,421	1,177,886
Total	3,762,963	5,541,100	7,848,180	10,691,887
U.S. border states				
Texas	7,711,194	9,579,677	11,198,655	14,229,191
New Mexico	749,587	1,302,161	1,775,399	2,718,215
Arizona	681,187	951,023	1,017,055	1,302,894
California	10,586,223	15,717,204	19,971,069	23,667,902
Total	19,728,191	27,550,065	33,962,178	41,918,202

SOURCES: *Censos Generales de Población* (México, Dirección General de Estadística), 1950–1980; *Censuses of Population* (U.S. Bureau of the Census), 1950–1980.

[a]Mexican figures are at best conservative estimates of the actual population in the border states. The Mexican census is well known for serious undercounting of people, especially in rural areas. U.S. census data suffer from the same problem, but to a much lesser extent.

million, with more than half of that number living within a 2,000-mile-long, 400-mile-wide belt bisected by the boundary.

American cities in the interior borderlands with particularly high growth rates for the period include Houston, Albuquerque, Phoenix, and Tucson. (Table 6.2). At the border, El Paso and San Diego experienced the most impressive growth, recording populations of 425,259 and 875,538 respectively in 1980 (Table 6.3). While interior Mexican borderlands cities such as Monterrey, Saltillo, Chihuahua City, and Hermosillo have also seen their populations rise dramatically, border cities like Ciudad Juárez and Tijuana have witnessed phenomenal growth. According to official statistics, Ciudad Juárez grew from 122,566 to 567,365 and Tijuana from 59,950 to 461,257 between 1950 and 1980; unofficial figures, however, place the current population at approximately 1 million for each city.

A number of factors, such as public sector spending, global economic competition, labor costs, climate, and geography, have combined to produce the recent dramatic expansion of the borderlands' urban population. During the World War II era, a trend began in the United States to disperse defense installations to make their destruction more

Table 6.2
Population of Selected Cities in the Interior Borderlands, 1950–1980[a]

	1950	1960	1970	1980[b]
Mexico				
Monterrey	339,282	601,085	830,336	1,090,009
Saltillo	98,603	127,772	191,879	321,758
Torreón	147,233	203,045	257,045	363,886
Chihuahua	112,468	186,089	363,850	406,830
Hermosillo	54,503	118,051	206,663	340,779
United States				
San Antonio	408,442	587,718	654,153	785,410
Houston	596,163	938,219	1,233,535	1,594,086
Corpus Christi	108,287	167,690	204,525	231,999
Albuquerque	98,815	201,189	244,501	331,767
Phoenix	106,818	439,170	584,303	789,704
Tucson	45,454	212,892	262,933	330,537
Los Angeles	1,970,358	2,479,015	2,811,801	2,966,850

Sources: *Censos Generales de Población* (México, Dirección General de Estadística), 1950–1980; *Censuses of Population* (U.S. Bureau of the Census), 1950–1980.
[a]Mexican figures are at best conservative estimates of the actual population in the border states. The Mexican census is well known for serious undercounting of people, especially in rural areas. U.S. census data suffer from the same problem, but to a much lesser extent.
[b]1980 data for Mexican cities are for *municipios*.

Table 6.3
Population of Major Twin Cities along the Border, 1950–1980[a]

	1950	1960	1970	1980
Matamoros	45,737	143,043	186,146	238,840
Brownsville	36,066	48,040	52,522	84,997
Reynosa	34,076	134,869	150,786	211,412
McAllen	20,067	32,728	37,636	67,042
Nuevo Laredo	57,669	96,043	151,253	203,286
Laredo	51,510	60,678	69,024	91,449
Piedras Negras	27,578	48,408	46,698	80,290
Eagle Pass	7,267	12,094	15,364	21,407
Ciudad Juárez	122,566	276,995	424,135	567,365
El Paso	130,485	276,687	322,261	425,259
Nogales, Sonora	24,480	39,812	53,494	68,076
Nogales, Arizona	6,153	7,286	8,946	15,683
Mexicali	64,658	281,333	396,324	510,664
Calexico	6,433	7,992	10,625	14,412
Tijuana	59,950	165,690	340,583	461,257
San Diego[b]	334,387	573,224	697,471	875,538

SOURCES: *Censos Generales de Población* (México, Dirección General de Estadística), 1950–1980; *Censuses of Population* (U.S. Bureau of the Census), 1950–1980.
[a]Mexican figures are at best conservative estimates of the actual population in the border states. The Mexican census is well known for serious undercounting of people, especially in rural areas. U.S. census data suffer from the same problem, but to a much lesser extent.
[b]San Diego is not a true border "twin-city," but its city limits do extend to the border.

difficult in the event of attack by the Soviet Union or other unfriendly Communist nations. That policy, coupled with the need for open spaces for ground training and good weather for airplane and missile testing, led to the growth of existing bases and the creation of new ones throughout the Southwest. In addition, new defense-related industries proliferated, bringing prosperity to cities like San Antonio, Albuquerque, and Phoenix. The public spending spree evident in the defense industry also made itself felt in other areas. Washington assisted states and localities in building superhighways and other infrastructure, making possible the urban sprawl so characteristic of countless modern southwestern cities. Other regions of the nation also benefited from the expansion of government spending for these activities, but not to the extent seen in the Southwest.[1]

Growing international economic competition in key industries such as electronics and textile manufacturing has also played an important role in stimulating growth in the Southwest. As Japan and other nations captured larger shares of world markets, U.S. industries sought more favorable settings within the country to produce goods at cheaper rates so as to remain competitive. Thus a trend began to shift operations from the labor-expensive and "stifling" business environment of the Midwest and Northeast to the more inviting climate of the Southwest. At the same time, many multinationals moved labor-intensive operations abroad, including the Mexican side of the border, where abundant labor at rock-bottom rates could be found. State and local governments throughout the Southwest took full advantage of these developments, offering numerous incentives to businesses and industries seeking new homes or looking for expansion possibilities. Cheaper and "more disciplined" labor, tax concessions, less regulation, and a "friendly" business climate served as the principal enticements. Good weather in the Southwest has also been promoted as an important advantage to companies weary of lost time during the often-brutal winters in the U.S. "Frostbelt." Executives in particular have found the "outdoor" lifestyle of the mild Southwest especially appealing. In short, the Southwest, along with the other regions of the "Sunbelt," has devised a successful formula to generate substantial economic activity south of the thirty-seventh parallel.[2]

Several of the same factors that have brought prosperity to the U.S. border area have been operative on the Mexican side as well. World War II, the Korean conflict, and the Vietnam War triggered an extraordinary demand for Mexican raw materials and cheap labor found in the Mexican borderlands. Because of its proximity to the United States, northern Mexico was the principal beneficiary in the growing movement of goods and people across the boundary. Border cities in particular benefited from a substantial increase in tourism, stimulated chiefly by a great expansion of U.S. military personnel in bases very close to the international line.

Keenly aware of trends in migration of U.S. capital to centers of low-cost labor, Mexican entrepreneurs, in cooperation with the federal government in Mexico City, enticed multinationals to establish assembly plants, or maquiladoras, in most of the border cities. Thus, since the mid-1960s, corporations such as General Motors, Ford, Chrysler, R.C.A., Zenith, and many other giants have opened operations in these cities, yielding huge profits because of the pro-business environment and availability of cheap labor. In early 1985, maquiladora workers made about $1.03 an hour, a sum, according to industry reports, representing a savings of $14,520 a year per employee over hiring U.S. workers. Under such circumstances, border maquiladoras increased in number from 120 in 1970 to 680 in 1984, a 466 percent rate of increase. The number of employees in the maquiladoras grew from 20,327 to 184,400 during that fifteen-year period (see Table 5.3).

As on the U.S. side, government spending is also an important cause of recent growth in the Mexican borderlands. The impact of public expenditures is particularly evident in the projects developed under the Programa Nacional Fronterizo (National Border Program), a program carried out in the 1960s, whose purpose was to beautify the border cities, to stimulate tourism, and to promote the consumption of Mexican products among the border citizenry. Mexico City has also invested heavily in public works ranging from highways to public service buildings, thus expanding employment opportunities for the vast border labor force. In short, public capital outlays have contributed greatly to transforming Ciudad Juárez, Tijuana, and other cities adjacent to the boundary into important economic centers within the Mexican Republic.

GROWTH AND THE FRAGILE BORDERLANDS ECOLOGY

Apart from economic considerations, the emergence of large cities in the arid borderlands has been made possible by utilization of modern technology to overcome environmental disadvantages inherent in the region.[3] Scarcity of water in particular has been a long-standing problem, but new methods now claim large amounts of water from underground sources, as well as divert it from rivers and lakes situated both nearby and far away. Energy-producing resources and raw materials for construction have been extracted from the landscape in appreciable quantities. Without a doubt the ability of cities to grow and prosper despite considerable environmental handicaps has been one of the most remarkable developments in the history of the borderlands. The region, however, has paid a high ecological price, raising serious questions about environmental practices and policies.

In the first half of the nineteenth century, both Mexico and the United States developed massive projects in the borderlands to provide water for agriculture. The zones of intensive cultivation under irrigation that arose between World Wars I and II often became the most-favored locations for the development of large cities. It is striking that the growth of these cities has had little relationship to the earlier agricultural economy; instead, millions of people have moved to these places for reasons quite unrelated to irrigated agriculture. They have thereby created large desert cities surrounded by older farming lands but with almost no subsistence connections to the natural environment. Many tracts of land once devoted to field crops have been converted to suburban residential developments, permanently removing farm land from productivity.

Both horizontal and vertical extensions of urban zones into hinterlands and into life zones with different habitats and resources has accompanied the success of many borderland cities. Los Angeles has been one of the most effective cities for bringing outlying regions into its dominance. In order to exist, it has had to overcome its aridity by gaining control of water resources hundreds of miles away and has even established rights to water falling in Colorado on the western slope of the Continental Divide. The dramatic effects upon the ecology of the Owens Valley arising from the diversion of water to Southern California are well known.

Phoenix and its satellites provide another example of urban extensions; here developers have built numerous subdivisions around artificial lakes, canals, fountains, and other aqueous artifacts in seeming defiance of the desert's ecological realities. Like Los Angeles, Phoenix has had to establish its hegemony over water resources far from its city limits. Phoenix has withdrawn so much groundwater from the Santa Cruz and Gila river valleys that the topography of the region has actually subsided. The opening of the Central Arizona Project will drain even more water from the already overutilized Colorado River.[4]

Mexico's efforts to build and sustain urban economies in the arid North is reflected in the construction of numerous dams and reservoirs since the 1930s. Torreon and its satellite cities in Coahuila and Durango are examples of areas whose growth resulted from large water projects. This zone now boasts over 1 million people in one of the most barren locations of North America. Irrigation projects financed by the government have also affected large areas of Chihuahua, Sonora, and Sinaloa.

The ever-increasing need for water in arid urban zones has generated considerable interregional conflict. California and Arizona in particular have contested the waters of the Colorado River in often-bitter legal battles.[5] Currently El Paso and the state of New Mexico are feuding in the courts over whether El Paso has a right to water from underground wells just across the state boundary. The issue has stirred such strong feelings that people from southern New Mexico have promoted economic boycotts of El Paso.[6] Water controversies have also erupted in the international arena because of the designation of rivers as part of the boundary between the United States and Mexico and because of the spanning of the boundary by underground water deposits. Since the late nineteenth century, both countries have disputed the distribution and use of the waters of the Rio Grande and the Colorado and Tijuana rivers. The Treaties of 1906 and 1944 failed to anticipate certain difficulties brought on by rapid population growth and increased irrigation, as in the case of the Rio Grande at El Paso–Juárez, or sub-standard quality of water delivered from one country to the other, as exemplified by the Colorado River in the Mexicali Valley. Contention over resulting problems damaged transborder diplomatic relations well into the 1970s.[7]

The salinity crisis in the Mexicali Valley in the 1960s raised the issue of the use of groundwater in border zones, a matter omitted from treaties that covered apportionment of surface waters. Recent studies indicate that serious depletion of various border groundwater deposits is taking place, presenting the possibility that some border population centers will run out of water within a generation if the two countries fail to institute an effective binational management plan.[8] The most acute groundwater problem exists in El Paso–Juárez, where the combined population of the two cities has grown from 146,000 in 1940 to 1,500,000 today. Between 1903 and 1976, the groundwater level declined by seventy-three feet in El Paso and eighty-five feet in Juárez. As the area continues to experience rapid growth, the reserves continue to fall by an estimated 1 percent annually, leading some to predict that the area will face severe shortages of water as early as 1995.[9] One possible source of future local contention is the grossly unequal consumption of groundwater by the two cities. El Paso County, with its farms, golf courses, and large tract-home lawns, consumes about six times the amount of water used by the municipality of Juárez, which has twice the population. Frequent water shortages south of the border heighten the awareness of the disadvantageous situation in which *juarenses* (residents of Juárez) find themselves, although these shortages do not originate with a current lack of water but rather the inability to pump it from the ground and deliver it to those who need it. Water lines do not reach many of the outlying *colonias* inhabited by the poor. As a result, crises erupt every summer in Juárez when a large number of infants become seriously ill drinking contaminated water and some subsequently die from dehydration.[10]

In recent years, water pollution has become an alarming problem along the California-Mexico border. Imperial Valley residents have complained for some time about the waste materials dumped at Mexicali into the Rio Nuevo, which flows northward into the Salton Sea. According to scientific studies, the water is so polluted that it presents grave danger for the spread of diseases like hepatitis, typhoid, and encephalitis.[11] At San Diego–Tijuana, raw sewage has flowed for decades into the United States via the Tijuana River, polluting the beaches and causing severe harm to agricultural lands and water wells. Tijuana built a plant in 1962 to treat the sewage, but over the years there have been frequent breakdowns, forcing heavy dependence on facilities in San Diego. The people of San Diego remain pessimistic about a permanent solution to the problem, despite the fact that Tijuana inaugurated a new $20 million plant in early 1987.[12]

Apart from water contamination, some border communities suffer from high levels of air pollution. Although natural phenomena, such as temperature inversions that occur in the desert climate and topography that tends to trap polluted air in narrow spaces, partly explain the problem, human activities have a far more serious effect. Industrial waste, auto emissions, pesticide use, agricultural dust, open burning, and unpaved streets are some of the more significant contributors to the contamination of the air. Small communities such as Presidio-Ojinaga and Del Rio–Ciudad Acuña attribute their relatively mild problems mostly to burning and dust, but at El Paso–Ciudad Juárez, polluting practices of residents combine with natural causes to produce serious levels of pollution at various times during the year.[13] Friction is often generated when one side of the border accuses the other of causing most of the problem. For example, El Paso is constantly blaming its inability to meet U.S. Environmental Protection Agency standards on the pollution that blows in from Mexico, which irritates *juarenses*.

INTERNATIONAL MIGRATION AND BORDER RELATIONS

In many ways the greatest source of contention for Mexico and the United States in recent times has been the issue of cross-border undocumented migration. Throughout the twentieth century, Mexico's border cities have not only acted as important way stations for Mexican migrants on their way to interior points in the United States; they have also provided a base from which many workers commute on a daily basis to jobs north of the border. During periods of economic recession and depression in the United States, Americans have taken measures to curb the flow, seriously affecting economic conditions on the Mexican side. Strained local relations in the "twin city" complexes have been natural consequences of such actions.

Since 1900, hundreds of thousands of migrants have repeatedly found themselves stranded on the Mexican side when U.S. immigration officials have closed the border in response to decreased demand for labor in the United States. Such policies upset Mexican municipal authorities because of the problems created by a "floating" population not native to the border cities. Human suffering was especially acute during the Great Depression, when close to half a million Mexicans were "repatriated" back to Mexico. A large portion of them became stranded at the border waiting for transportation to the interior of Mexico. During those years of economic hardship, both Mexican nationals and Mexican Americans encountered many problems attempting to cross the international bridges at the Texas border. Harrassment, and at times mistreatment of people by U.S. immigration officials, was reported in the press and in personal testimonies.[14] Bridge inspectors, who routinely asked embarrassing and insulting questions, often prevented legally admitted Mexicans living north of the border from reentering the United States. At the time, American labor unions escalated their efforts to prevent Mexicans who had jobs in the United States from crossing the Rio Grande. Many commuter workers were fired from their jobs and replaced by U.S. citizens, mostly Anglo-Americans. In Juárez, this practice prompted boycotts of American commerce, which lasted until tensions eased and the situation returned to normal.

One of the most serious immigration incidents along the border occurred in El Paso–Juárez in October 1948, when thousands of people gathered on the Mexican side waiting to secure permits to cross into the United States under the Bracero Program (bilateral program that provided Mexican workers to American employers on a yearly basis). As prolonged binational negotiations were underway to settle a wage dispute between Texas growers and the Mexican government, workers grew restless. The growers, anxious to get pickers for their already overripe crops, put pressure on U.S. immigration authorities to open the border. Clearly in violation of binational agreements with Mexico, the United States unilaterally allowed some seven thousand undocumented migrants to wade the Rio Grande for several days, "arresting" them at the river and immediately "paroling" them to growers who were waiting with trucks to take them to the fields. Upset by this blatant manipulation of its people, Mexico called a temporary halt to the Bracero Program.[15]

In the 1970s, actions taken by the United States again gave rise to border incidents that took their toll on good transboundary relations. During the recession of 1974–75, the U.S. Immigration and Naturalization Service carried out one of its periodic crackdowns on Mexican commuters "suspected" of holding jobs illegally in El Paso. Rigid and at times harrassing inspections at the bridges led to charges that "Gestapo methods" were being employed. Border crossing declined significantly with an accompanying downturn in business in El Paso and in Juárez. Both cities saw a repetition of practically the same scenario in March 1979, except that this time the drama took a violent turn, catching U.S. officials by surprise. Mexican women who lost their crossing cards at the hands of inspectors they considered abusive led demonstrations that effectively shut down the border traffic for two days. In the confusion and chaos that ensued, during which an American flag was torn down from its pole and thrown in the Rio Grande, one young girl died.

Officials worried that the altercations at the El Paso–Juárez bridges might escalate into something far more serious, given the tensions that existed at the time over the construction of the "Tortilla Curtain," the much-publicized border fence intended to slow down the crossing of undocumented migrants. The "Tortilla Curtain" became a highly charged issue that triggered demonstrations along the border and angry commentary throughout Mexico. As originally proposed, the high wire fence would be topped with sharp blades to "cut the toes" of anyone attempting to scale it. Perhaps more than anything else, that feature in the design of the fence (which was later dropped) stirred the passion of Mexicans and Mexican Americans alike.[16]

The intensity of the reaction to the new fence took officials by surprise once again, but anyone familiar with the sentiments of border people toward highly visible border enforcement symbols and practices would have anticipated the resentment. Over the years many local residents had taken a dim view of horse-mounted Texas Rangers at the Rio Grande, border patrol observation towers, automated roving patrols, and wire fences. Juárez ex-mayor René Mascareñas, who lobbied U.S. officials in the 1950s to remove the border patrol observation towers on the banks of the Rio Grande, expressed the feelings of many fronterizos regarding structures that divide the two cities.

> I don't like the idea of fences. We don't live between East and West Germany. The communist wall that is there is a slap in the face to any nation that boasts of being democratic. We want greater fluidity and communication between us. We don't want barriers; we don't want barbed wire fence. We brag we are two neighborly countries, two friendly nations, and that this is the longest border in the world where one does not see a single soldier, a single rifle, a single bayonet, or a single affronting or discriminatory sign. Besides, if a fence is put up, it won't last, because Mexicans have much ability to tear it down.[17]

Despite opposition from both sides of the border, the much-discussed "Tortilla Curtain" was built in El Paso and in San Ysidro, California, in 1979. But as Mascareñas had predicted, the fence in El Paso became a victim of vandalism and chronic hole-cutting. For a time the INS diligently repaired the damage but then gave up in frustration. El Paso's "Tortilla Curtain," with its abundant person-sized holes, is now practically useless as a deterrent to illegal migration.

Underlying much of the negative reaction to Mexican immigration in the United States is the perception that undocumented workers have a pronounced deleterious impact on American society. Over the last several decades, opponents of Mexican immigration have charged repeatedly that Mexicans send money out of the United States; cause unemployment; depress wages; retard unionization; become welfare recipients; create social problems; and utilize costly educational, health, and other community services. Some have claimed that the expense to American taxpayers is in the billions of dollars. Other critics have stated that Mexicans, in contrast to European immigrants, will not assimilate into the U.S. mainstream, which could lead to separatist tendencies in the Southwest, where most of the immigrants live.[18]

The negative view of the economic impact of Mexican immigrants prevailed until the 1970s, when field studies produced different conclusions. Scholars pointed out that the number of illegal aliens believed to be in the United States was greatly exaggerated and that their presence actually resulted in many benefits to the host society. It was discovered that, in economic terms, Mexican immigrants contributed far more to the United States than they took through payments sent abroad or through welfare and other social services received in communities where they resided.[19]

The new research has underscored the complexity of the undocumented migration issue. Old notions and assumptions have been discarded in light of empirical evidence that points in new directions. Yet much remains to be done to understand the problem fully. One important question that requires serious inquiry is to what extent the impact of undocumented migration along the border differs from its impact in the interior of the United States. Available evidence indicates that although the presence of undocumented persons brings many benefits to U.S. border communities, a number of negative consequences also result. There is, for example, a strong correlation between border overpopulation and surplus of labor and (1) the incidence of poverty, (2) low wages, (3) substandard working conditions, and (4) low levels of unionization in such cities as Brownsville, Laredo, and El Paso. "Poverty exists (along the border) in patterns similar to poverty throughout the rest of the country in that it is primarily concentrated among the racial and ethnic minorities of the region," writes Ellwyn R. Stoddard. "But unlike poverty elsewhere in America, its situation is complicated by an international boundary running through it with a perpetual migrant stream feeding it from economically developing Third World nations to the South."[20]

Regional comparisons of wealth distribution in the United States indicate that as one gets closer to the border, per capita income sharply drops; further, health and social problems increase. Official figures released in 1978 showed McAllen-Pharr-Edinburgh, Texas, with a per capita income of $4,323; Laredo, $4,529; Brownsville–Harlingen–San Benito, $5,024; El Paso, $5,639; and Las Cruces, New Mexico, $5,675.[21] Unemployment in the Texas border towns is consistently and substantially greater than in the state's interior, at times reaching over 12 percent in El Paso and over 20 percent in Laredo. With respect to health, reports indicate that in some border areas the incidence of infant mortality, influenza, pneumonia, tuberculosis, and other infectious diseases ranged from 125 percent to 250 percent higher than national rates.[22]

The concentration of poor Mexican workers at the border is, of course, only partially responsible for poverty and social problems in the area. Geography, isolation, lack of resources, and the barriers presented by the demarcation line have, until recently, precluded significant economic growth and development in American border cities. And although the region is now experiencing rapid growth, it remains far behind most other areas in the United States in industrial development. Existing industries are, for example, concentrated chiefly in extractive, agricultural, light manufacturing, and service sectors. Such industries typically pay low wages, regardless of border proximity. A history of antiunion sentiment, characteristic of the southern and southwestern regions of the United States generally, has likewise kept wages and other benefits low. Additionally, the fact that many border Mexican Americans have their origins in poor, rural areas of Mexico accounts partly for the bleak socioeconomic indicators of the region. Pervasive discrimination against Chicanos has interacted with all these factors to produce a less-than-favorable economy (for workers) that does not rest solely on the concentrated presence of Mexican employees. Yet the easy availability of cheap labor on the U.S. side, and even cheaper labor on the Mexican side, where workers are more abundant, has hindered social and economic advances among the people of Mexican descent in the U.S. border zone.[23] In the future, perhaps the Simpson-Rodino law will curtail the flow of undocumented workers sufficiently to ease some of the pressure on the Chicano border population.

THE BORDER FLOW

The pronounced interdependence that exists along the border has made it essential that interruptions in the normal flow of people and trade across the boundary be avoided or at least kept to a minimum.

Fronterizos in particular have sought to maintain an orderly and harmonious climate to prevent damage to the area's delicate economy and to existing neighborly relations. Yet historically many controversial issues and incidents have arisen at the border, and many unwise policies have been implemented by government officials that have seriously disrupted movement across the boundary.

Economic rivalry between the two sides has been a major source of contention for generations. For example, the presence of the Free Zone on the Mexican side at various times during the latter nineteenth century created antagonism among U.S. merchants and led to strained relations. Americans claimed that free trade gave Mexicans an unfair advantage and that attendant smuggling of merchandise into the United States harmed American interests. The issue became a political football on both sides of the border and was not resolved until 1905, when the Porfirio Díaz government abolished the Free Zone in response to external and internal pressures.[24] With the economy of the Mexican side badly damaged by the absence of free trade, the U.S. side became the dominant partner in the area's binational commercial relations, triggering great resentment among Mexican merchants.[25]

As the two sides have competed for the border trade, the protectionism practiced by each, especially during hard times, produced strife. During the Depression of the 1930s, for example, many people from El Paso vigorously urged the closing of the international bridges at an early hour to reduce the spending of dollars in Juárez. This effort was only one of many previous borderwide attempts (some of which achieved temporary success) to close the gates to U.S. citizens who had frequented liquor and gambling establishments in the Mexican border towns since the start of Prohibition in 1920.[26]

An illustration of local controversy integrally linked to border economics is the now "classic" transportation "war" between El Paso and Juárez. For several years the two cities feuded over the reinstatement of the almost-a-century-old international streetcar service that ended with a labor dispute in 1973. Many prominent Juárez merchants objected to the streetcars because they transported large numbers of Mexican shoppers to El Paso but carried few Americans to Juárez. Supporters of the streetcars, including El Paso officials and some Mexican leaders, generated considerable conflict when they bypassed the sentiments of influential *juarenses* by seeking to arrange for resumption of the service directly with Mexican state and federal officials. At one point the prostreetcar faction developed a plan to satisfy some objections, but Mexican merchants remained convinced that the total absence of the streetcars was necessary to reduce El Paso's traditional stronghold over the purchasing power of *juarenses*. Thus, because of lobbying efforts by the Juárez Chamber of Commerce, former President Luis Echeverría Alvarez reportedly "categorically refused renewal" of this transportation system. Even then, prominent El Pasoans remained determined to overcome the resistance of the Juárez merchants. Their efforts were in vain, however, and by the late 1970s hope vanished that the streetcars would ever return to the two cities.[27]

Seeing an opportunity to meet an obvious need for inexpensive mass transportation between El Paso and Juárez, a maverick Juárez businessman in 1974 started operating a fleet of aged, battered "red" buses along the old streetcar route, much to the delight of El Paso retailers and the dismay of Juárez merchants. Officials from the state of Chihuahua, under pressure from influential *juarenses*, stopped the buses temporarily by first fining the drivers and later impounding their vehicles. The troubles of the Mexican bus company were compounded by a series of challenges in El Paso to the routes used by the buses and to alleged infractions of U.S. transportation regulations. The "red" bus company, however, overcame the opposition and continued to operate in both cities.

A related local issue that contributed to the strained relations of the 1970s was the confrontation over taxi service. The El Paso City Council, in part retaliating for the lack of cooperation in Juárez over mass transportation, at one point required taxi liability insurance that few Juárez *taxistas* could afford. Mexican municipal leaders responded by passing an anti–El Paso taxi ordinance that required U.S. drivers to obtain Mexican insurance as a condition for driving in Juárez—practically an impossible condition, since Mexican insurance companies did not insure American cabs.[28] Eventually the two cities reached an agreement over the insurance matter, but the taxi controversy left a trail of negative feelings behind.

Throughout the duration of the conflict over the streetcars and taxis, truces were declared, with each side backing off just enough to permit limited binational transportation. By 1987, the situation was only slightly improved. Even though the cities still desperately needed a modern, efficient international mass transit system, the prospects for bringing that about appeared very dim.

Another issue that has caused considerable problems at the border has been drug smuggling.[29] On two occasions the United States has taken major steps to disrupt the flow of traffic in its effort to ameliorate the problem. For nearly a month in 1969, U.S. authorities sustained a campaign known as "Operation Intercept" to curtail the entry of drugs onto American soil. Tight inspections at many crossing points from Brownsville-Matamoros to Tijuana–San Ysidro caused tempers to flare and business on both sides to decline drastically. Federal officials in

Washington, D.C., received much criticism for their handling of the issue. Many border residents felt the resulting negative economic and diplomatic effects, especially in the frontier communities, far outweighed the seizure of limited amounts of drugs.[30]

In February 1985, the drug problem once again prompted the U.S. government to institute rigid inspections at the border for several weeks, predictably causing havoc in the border communities. The kidnapping and murder of an American drug agent and numerous assaults on American tourists in Mexico ostensibly served as the motive for taking that drastic action. U.S. officials apparently hoped that the interruption of trade and tourism at the border as well as in the interior of Mexico would put pressure on the Mexican government to become more aggressive in the fight against drugs. It also appears that the Reagan administration used the tightening of the border to accomplish broader policy objectives toward Mexico, that is, to pressure Mexicans to modify their position on Central America and on other foreign policy questions where significant differences existed between the two nations.

As traffic from Mexico to the United States slowed to a crawl and as trade transactions plummeted, a coalition of business, labor, and political organizations in Juárez implemented "Operación Respeto" ("Operation Respect"), which exhorted *juarenses* to boycott El Paso. Brigades of volunteers handed out flyers at the international bridges, which carried the message: "*Juarense*: defend your dignity, don't go to El Paso; you do not deserve to be treated like a delinquent by North American officials."[31]

Over time, political demonstrations at the border stations have also caused interruptions in the transboundary flow. Immigration issues have been a major source of such demonstrations, often bringing together protesters from both sides of the border to show binational solidarity. In recent years activists from student, labor, and radical political groups on the Mexican side have repeatedly disrupted the border traffic as a pressure tactic to realize demands made on local or federal officials. On numerous occasions student demonstrators in Juárez have blocked traffic to El Paso with parked buses or burning tires. Disputes over Mexican election results have also produced tension at the international bridges, as illustrated by violence in Piedras Negras in 1984 and repeated demonstrations in Juárez in 1984, 1985, and 1986.[32]

Thus economic rivalry, drugs, and political demonstrations have damaged the normal interchange that takes place between one side of the border and the other. Yet the impact of such phenomena extends far beyond the border. Frontier tensions receive front-page coverage in the national media of both countries, frightening prospective

tourists to the area into changing or canceling their plans. A drastic
drop in tourism, which brings devastation to the border communities
as well as to tourist centers and coastal resorts throughout Mexico, has
often resulted. Such a pattern was evident during 1985, a year made
even worse by the tragic earthquake in Mexico City, and in 1986, a year
marked by political turmoil in northern Mexico.

SUMMARY AND CONCLUSION

Population expansion in the borderlands has taxed the carrying capac-
ity of a resource-scarce region, challenging the United States and
Mexico to find effective means of preventing possible ecological disas-
ters. The potential for serious conflict over ecological and environmental issues is most evident at the border, where "twin" urban clusters
struggle to secure sufficient quantities of water to sustain their populations and to keep their environment clean in the face of ever-growing
pollution problems. As in previous eras, the immigration issue continues to strain binational relations, with the cities adjacent to the border suffering the greatest consequences of policies calculated to stop
or slow down the movement of migrants. Fronterizos have also had to
contend with a variety of disruptions and incidents, the effects of which
have been to interrupt the normal flow across the border.

Despite the instability inherent along the border, the area continues
to grow and even prosper. That growth is explained by the opportunities that prevail in the region and the commitment that exists at
the local level on both sides to manage conflict effectively. The efforts
of fronterizos to maintain good neighborly relations have spanned a
wide variety of arrangements, including the creation of a binational
Border Cities Association and the maintenance of international relations committees by municipal governments, chambers of commerce,
and service clubs on both sides of the boundary. Additionally, health
organizations, churches, and cultural, sports, and youth groups have
maintained less-formal but very significant contact. Finally, the daily
transborder contact stemming from the extensive routine movement
of workers, businessmen, students, shoppers, and tourists has fostered
a wide network of positive relationships.

Efforts at the state levels have also helped to promote positive cross-
border relationships. For example, Texas has long had a Good Neighbor Commission that has worked to smooth out problems between
Texas and its bordering Mexican states. Similarly, California and Baja
California have established commissions to coordinate matters of

mutual concern. The governors of Arizona and Sonora have had frequent meetings to promote trade, cultural exchange, and friendship across the political line. In recent years the governors of the border states in both countries have met regularly to promote good relations and to discuss ways of influencing federal policy making.[33] Although these state and local initiatives have certainly not solved major problems, they have helped considerably to maintain calm, order, and a semblance of security along the border.

Afterword

The historical record reveals a turbulent border relationship between Mexico and the United States during the nineteenth and early twentieth centuries. Serious conflict erupted repeatedly over issues such as the delimitation and maintenance of the boundary, filibustering, Indian raids, banditry, revolutionary activities, and ethnic strife. Continuous clashes led to a full-scale war between the two nations and frequently verged on an outbreak of hostilities on other occasions. This pattern did not change until after the Mexican Revolution, when a region weary of violence and destruction began to experience stability. Border problems continued to trouble binational relations, but after 1920 the two sides sought solutions within a framework of peaceful negotiation and diplomacy, thus keeping tension levels well in check. Even though issues such as undocumented migration today continue to engender controversy, disagreements are unlikely to lead to violent confrontation, as they did a few generations ago.

The recent stability along the U.S.-Mexico border contrasts sharply with conflicts in certain other border zones in the world. In the Middle East, for example, the difficulties involved in fixing boundaries recognized by all nations in the region has embroiled Jews and Arabs in continuous bloodshed and interethnic struggles. India faces enormous difficulties in its efforts to achieve true national integration, owing to religious, linguistic, and cultural fragmentation in many areas. Countless African nations continue to struggle with the problem of ethnic populations partitioned by artificial boundaries. In the Western Hemisphere, unresolved territorial disputes periodically disrupt peaceful relations between a number of neighboring nations. Thus, when viewed in a global context, the troubles faced by the United States and Mexico along their common border appear to be much less threatening and well within the range of resolution—or at least to approach acceptable accommodation.

To their credit, therefore, the United States and Mexico have made significant progress in managing border conflict. On the other hand, they have fallen short of the accomplishments of a number of Western European nations, whose border zones have become focal points for meaningful interchange and cooperation.[1] Increased binational integration has spurred Europeans to enter into pacts to facilitate joint planning and to promote economic development along frontiers. Old fears pertaining to territorial security have given way to concerns over solving transborder problems, especially those of a social and environmental character. A prime example of transborder cooperation is found in the Basel area, a trinational region that overlaps France, Germany, and Switzerland. Through a unique body known as the Regio Basiliensis, the frontier cantons of Switzerland, the German *Land* of Baden-Wurttemberg, and the French Region of Alsace coordinate regional planning and smooth out border problems.[2]

Unfortunately the United States and Mexico seem distantly removed from negotiating an agreement that would establish a binational commission modeled after the Regio Basiliensis. Nationalistic feelings and mutual suspicions remain strong enough to block such an eventuality. Of the many border issues that continue to stir nationalism among Americans, immigration is the most compelling. Many Americans perceive the heavy influx of Mexicans across the border as a security threat. The strong support for federal legislation to restrict immigration has been based to a significant extent on the fear that if the country does not "regain control" of the southern border, Mexicans and other Latin Americans will continue to pour across the line and eventually become a political force in the United States, a situation that could lead to the destabilization of American society. This notion is based on the perception that Mexican Americans, Puerto Ricans, Cuban Americans, and others of Latin American extraction tend not to assimilate into the U.S. mainstream but to maintain close ties and loyalties to their countries of origin, which often are at odds with U.S. foreign policy.

The belief that U.S. Hispanics lack commitment to the American way of life rests largely on lack of information and misunderstanding in Anglo society. That Hispanics wish to preserve at least some of their culture, language, and traditions is a well-established fact. Yet it does not follow that they reject American culture. The outspoken objection of many Mexican Americans to what they believe are discriminatory immigration policies does not mean that they wish to have an open border with Mexico. For Mexican Americans, the major issue in the immigration debate has been the protection of basic rights of immigrants as well as those of long-term U.S. residents of Hispanic heritage.

The heated controversies generated in recent years over immigration and the related issue of bilingual education is to some extent a product of the large-scale internal movement of people from the U.S. Anglo-dominated "snow belt" to the heavily Hispanic "sun belt." Many Anglo newcomers unacquainted with the Spanish-Mexican antecedents in the Southwest resent the imposing Hispanic presence in the area. They believe the large Hispanic population stems from unwise, lenient immigration policies of the past, and they deeply dislike expenditure of public funds for social and educational programs that benefit a "foreign" group. The widespread use of the Spanish language in the area is a constant irritant to these Anglos, not only because they feel left out when they cannot understand what is being said but more fundamentally because they deem it "un-American" for anyone to speak a language other than English on U.S. soil.[3] With the emergence of the "English-only" movement, which promotes the primacy of English, and U.S. Secretary of Education William Bennett's recent public statement that bilingual education is a failure, the debate will deepen and ethnic divisiveness will become more pronounced.[4]

If confrontations between Hispanics and non-Hispanics are to be avoided, Anglos who live in the Southwest, especially those along the border, will need to become more fully informed about the peoples, cultures, and history of the region. They will need to recognize that the Spanish language and Mexican culture in the area go back several centuries and that the human interaction across the border is long standing and a contemporary fact of life.

With regard to perceptions in Mexico about the border, the view of many Mexicans that their northern frontier is "drifting away" from the rest of the nation is also in need of modification. Concern over the pronounced American economic presence in the region is understandable, but such is the nature of remote zones in close proximity to wealthier neighbors. Despite their ties to the American side, there is no evidence to suggest that the people of the North wish to be something other than loyal Mexicans. The current political revolt against the ruling party is a product of dissatisfaction with government inefficiency, corruption, and policies harmful to the region's economy, rather than a reflection of foreign influences present in the polity of the North. Existing misconceptions and stereotypes about fronterizos and their unique relationship with the United States serve only to promote internal divisiveness and retard needed solutions to pressing border problems.

Thus, both nations need to rethink their perceptions of what the border zone is, how it functions, and how it relates to national interests. The prevailing notion that each country ends at the boundary is certainly accurate from a political point of view, but it is incorrect in many other respects. Demographically, economically, linguistically, and culturally the U.S. border area is functionally an extension of Mexico, and in a similar fashion, the Mexican border zone is an extension of economic, social, and cultural influences from the United States. The massive movement of people and products across the border and the sharing of resources, jobs, and space make clear that the sharp division implied by the line of demarcation does not mirror reality. It is more meaningful to visualize the border as a zone of "overlapping territoriality," as Professor Ellwyn R. Stoddard has observed. "This concept of overlapping territoriality reflects the functional interrelationship which exists along both sides of the binational border and seeks to replace the erroneous structural model which characterizes the international boundary line as a point at which two distinct nations touch."[5] Recognition of the "overlap" concept necessitates putting aside nationalistic considerations that cause people to see the border as an untouchable and impenetrable barrier.

Stoddard's suggestion that both countries adopt a "doctrine of mutual necessity"[6] as a framework for tackling border problems is worthy of serious consideration. Under such a policy, both countries would allow problem-solving mechanisms and institutions to function on both sides of the boundary with minimum restrictions. For example, in addressing the air pollution problem, the two parties would be prepared to create a binational body that would utilize resources from both nations and would implement measures to improve the environment on *both* U.S. and Mexican soil. The recent experience of El Paso and Ciudad Juárez demonstrates that it is absurd to attempt to clean up the air of one city without doing the same on the opposite side of the Rio Grande. "Twin city" complexes along the boundary need to be treated as unified metropolitan areas sharing single airsheds.

On the question of undocumented migration, the United States, as the initiator and implementer of major policy initiatives, should accept the issue as a bilateral matter that requires transboundary coordinated planning and mutually determined courses of action. The 1986 Simpson-Rodino law resulted from a process that in essence ignored Mexico's views and ideas for lasting solutions. As with air contamination, policies to curb migration that are formulated unilaterally and directed at only one side of the border are doomed to fail. Short of sealing the border with troops from the Gulf to the Pacific, nothing will stop economically desperate Mexicans from crossing into the United States in search of job opportunities. Besides, the labor provided by these migrants is badly needed by the American economy; thus anything done in Washington to interrupt the flow of workers damages U.S. interests, particularly along the border.

As we near the end of a century marked by enormous scientific breakthroughs and great improvements in people's material well-being, it is disturbing to realize that the progress achieved in international relations has been relatively unimpressive. The current condition of the world, including the state of the relationship between the United States and the countries south of the Rio Grande, suggests that many lessons from the past have not been learned and that much remains to be done to achieve an acceptable international climate. Certainly the U.S.-Mexico border has advanced from a once-violence-ridden zone to one of manageable conflict. But that progress has come about largely through an evolutionary process and through the efforts of the people of the region rather than as a product of deliberate planning and action on the part of high-level policy makers. A decision to try new approaches for conducting U.S.-Mexico transboundary relations is essential if pressing issues are to be addressed successfully. It is in the best interest of both nations as well as of the borderlands population to make that commitment.

NOTES TO CHAPTERS

PREFACE

1. See Fernandez, *United States–Mexico Border*; House, *Frontier on the Rio Grande*; and Weber, *Mexican Frontier*.

INTRODUCTION

1. Myers, *Border Wardens*, 3.

2. The portrayal in the novel *Warday* of an independent Mexican American country known as "Aztlán" emerging in the southwestern United States in the aftermath of a nuclear war illustrates the fears about the alleged separatist tendencies at the border. El Paso, the largest U.S. city directly on the border, appropriately becomes the capital of Aztlán, a socialist nation unfriendly to Americans. Strieber and Kunetka, *Warday*.

3. *Newsweek*, June 25, 1984, 18.

4. In Ciudad Juárez, the Comité de Defensa Popular, a grass-roots organization with a Marxist ideology, has led many mass demonstrations. Residents of poor neighborhoods have protested increases in the cost of living, student groups have repeatedly demanded improvements in the educational system, and teachers have pressed aggressively for salary increases. Many of the demonstrations have resulted in stoppage of traffic in downtown Juárez and at times interruption of movement at the international bridges. Violence has often broken out. Recent disturbances are covered in the *Diario de Juárez*, April 7, 1984, 1; May 28, 1984, 1; May 30, 1984, 1; and June 9, 1984, 1.

5. Mexican political leaders are well aware of resistance to national policies present in the northern frontier in past eras. Norteños, for example, led the Revolution of 1910–20 that deposed a dictatorial regime and restructured Mexican society.

6. See Kristof, "Nature of Frontiers and Boundaries," 271–273; and Lattimore, "Frontier in History," 374.

7. Neuberger, "Natural and Artificial Borders," 99; Jones, "Boundary Concepts," 251.

8. For views on the arbitrary division of ethnic groups in Africa, see Asiwaju, *Partitioned Africans*; Saadia, *Boundary Politics of Independent Africa*; and Widstrand, *African Boundary Problems*. The Soviet Union, China, India, and the

United States are among the many countries that have experienced problems as a result of the absorption of ethnic groups against their will.

9. Leonard, "Southwestern Boundaries," 40, 42.

CHAPTER 1

1. Nasatir, "Shifting Borderlands," 4–5, 7.

2. *American Museum*, III (1786), 434–435. Quoted in Fidler, *Acquisition of All Mexico*, 12–13.

3. Fidler, *Acquisition of All Mexico*, 7–13.

4. The most thorough study of the Louisiana-Texas border question was conducted by Father José Antonio Richardo, who completed an authoritative treatise of over five thousand sheets in 1812. His findings supported the Spanish position and appear to have been influential in subsequent negotiations with the United States. See Hackett, *Richardo's Treatise*.

5. Nasatir, "Shifting Borderlands," 14–15.

6. Binkley, *Expansionist Movement in Texas*, 8. On the Adams-Onís treaty, see Brooks, *Diplomacy and the Borderlands*.

7. Weber, *Mexican Frontier*.

8. García Cantú, *Invasiones norteamericanas en México*, 17–18.

9. Quotes from Rippy, *United States and Mexico*, 2.

10. Medina Castro, *Gran despojo*, 12, 17, 20; Binkley, *Expansionist Movement in Texas*, 13; Zorrilla, *Historia de las relaciones* 1: 67.

11. Historian Justin H. Smith, who wrote the classic defense of the United States's role in the outbreak of the Mexican War, used the following terms in his devastating characterization of Butler: "a national disgrace," "bully," "swashbuckler," "ignorant," "shamefully careless," "scandalous in conduct," "a cantankerous, incompetent rascal." *War with Mexico* 1: 62–63.

12. Because it was bankrupt, Mexico had defaulted on payments, and Polk made this a major grievance. The sum outstanding was $3,250,000, which was small compared to the contemporary default of American states and corporations on bonds in British possession, amounting to $220,000,000. Merk, "Dissent in the Mexican War," 36.

13. For guides to the literature on the U.S.-Mexico War, see Benjamin, "Origins of the Mexican War"; Tutorow, *Mexican American War*; Vásquez de Knauth, *Mexicanos y Norteamericanos*; Zavala, "Historiografía americana." See also the annotated bibliography in Connor and Faulk, *North America Divided*.

14. The legality of the Treaty of Velasco, the document signed by Santa Anna with the Texans, is discussed in Escoto Ochoa, *Nuestra frontera norte*, 77–84.

15. Binkley, *Expansionist Movement in Texas*, 9; Cox, "Southwest Boundary of Texas," 97–98; Merk, *Monroe Doctrine*, 147–48.

16. Even Justin F. Smith, who blamed Mexico for the war, rejected Polk's claim that the Rio Grande was the Texas boundary. However, Smith buried that opinion in a footnote after giving the impression in the text of his *The War with Mexico* that he agreed with Polk (see 138–39, 448–49).

17. Only a few historians have defended Polk's policies that led to the war with Mexico. Smith's *The War with Mexico* holds that Polk acted aggressively only as a last resort, after Mexico had insulted the United States and refused to negotiate. A modern variation of Smith's interpretation is found in the following works: Connor and Faulk, *North America Divided*; and Faulk and Stout, *Mexican War*.

18. Merk, "Dissent in the Mexican War," 38–40, 43, 46, 48; Ruíz, "American Imperialism," 221.

19. Texas, of course, had been acquired through annexation in 1845.

20. Miller, *Treaties and Other Acts* 5: 263, 288, 325.

21. On the "all Mexico" movement, see Fuller, *Acquisition of All Mexico*.

22. Merk, "Dissent in the Mexican War," 51–52.

23. Billington, *Westward Expansion*, 586–87; Fuller, *Acquisition of All Mexico*, 81; Weisberg, *Manifest Destiny*, 160. Paul F. Lambert disagrees on the inevitability of the annexation of all Mexico had the treaty not been negotiated by Trist or had it been rejected by Polk. Lambert points out that a strong peace movement had developed to counter the "all Mexico" drive. See Lambert's "'All-Mexico' Movement," 171–72.

24. For the story of the surveying and marking of the boundary, as well as the negotiations that led to the signing of the Gadsden Treaty, see Faulk, *Too Far North*; Garber, *Gadsden Treaty*; Goetzmann, "United States-Mexican Boundary Survey"; Schmidt, "Manifest Opportunity."

25. Washington deemed Tehuántepec of great importance for a railroad route that would connect the Atlantic with the Pacific and would be readily accessible to Americans. The proposal to acquire U.S. rights became complicated when American private interests clashed with the Mexican government over claims they had obtained in the area.

26. Zorrilla, *Historia de las relaciones* 1: 343–44. For a detailed record of the Gadsden Treaty negotiations, see Miller, *Treaties and Other Acts* 6: 342–91.

27. Garber, *Gadsden Treaty*, 91–93.

28. Rippy, *United States and Mexico*, 141–42.

29. Garber, *Gadsden Treaty*, 103–4.

30. The United States retained rights in Tehuántepec until 1937, when Mexico convinced the American government to do away with that anachronistic and burdensome part of the Gadsden Treaty. Miller, *Treaties and Other Acts* 6: 432–33; Sepulveda, *Frontera norte de México*, 78.

31. Zorrilla, *Historia de las relaciones* 1: 377, 379–80; Forsyth's "we will take it" statement is found in Rippy, *United States and Mexico*, 216.

32. Rippy, *United States and Mexico*, 217–19, 223; Webb, *Texas Rangers*, 197–215. Houston's amendment is found in U.S. Congress, S. Misc. Doc. 241.

33. Schmitt, *Mexico and the United States*, 83–85.

34. Rippy, *United States and Mexico*, chap. 13. Quote on p. 231.

35. The story of the Chamizal dispute is told in Liss, *Century of Disagreement*.

36. Pre-treaty discussions established that jurisdiction over Morteritos rightfully belonged to the United States. Mueller, *Restless River*, 40–42.

37. In 1944 the commission was renamed the International Boundary and

Water Commission to indicate the added responsibility of finding solutions to water problems along the border.

38. Zorrilla, *Historia de las relaciones* 2: 139–41.

39. Ibid., 145–46; Mueller, *Restless River*, 53–57.

40. Zorrilla, *Historia de las relaciones* 2: 147; Friedkin, "International Boundary and Water Commission," 3.

41. U.S. State Department, *Chamizal Settlement*, 2.

42. Ibid; Mueller, *Restless River*, 69–73.

43. Friedkin, "International Boundary and Water Commission," 5; Mueller, *Restless River*, 75, 86–90.

44. Discussions of the 1970 treaty appear in Sepulveda, *Frontera norte de México*, 145–53; and Mueller, *Restless River*, 105–20.

45. The standard source on this subject is Hundley, *Dividing the Waters*.

46. The Colorado River water dispute is discussed in Sepulveda, *Frontera norte de México*, 129–44.

CHAPTER 2

1. Pike's edited journals and correspondence appear in Jackson, *Zebulon Montgomery Pike*.

2. Warren, *Sword Was Their Passport*, chaps. 1–3; Zorrilla, *Historia de las relaciones* 1:39.

3. Warren, *Sword Was Their Passport*, chap. 11. Other significant filibustering ventures prior to 1820 include the following:

1806 Aaron Burr plans an invasion of Florida, Texas, and other Spanish territories with the intention of combining them with Louisiana and Mississippi to form a new nation. Abandoned by fellow plotters, Burr is arrested by U.S. authorities and tried for treason but is acquitted.

1810 Following the seizure of the Spanish fort at Baton Rouge, Louisiana, American settlers in West Florida seek and receive annexation to the United States during the James Madison administration. A detachment of U.S. troops from Mississippi then occupies the area. At the time the United States claimed a portion of West Florida as part of the Louisiana Territory.

1812 Backed by the James Madison administration, expansionist George Matthews leads two hundred American volunteers in a temporary occupation of East Florida.

1818 Proclaiming their sympathies with Mexican independence fighters, French and British sailors attack Monterey, California. They encounter strong resistance in other coastal cities.

1818 General Andrew Jackson, who has a notorious ambition to seize the Floridas from Spain, claims approval of the James Monroe administration as he invades West Florida with a force of three thousand men. Jackson destroys Indian settlements, captures Pensecola, and metes out frontier justice during his raid.

4. Ibid., 255–56.

5. Horgan, *Great River*, 559–69.

6. Kendall, *Texas Santa Fe Expedition*; Loomis, *Texas–Santa Fe Pioneers*.

7. Price, *War with Mexico*.

8. Ibid., chap. 3.

9. See Stenberg, "Polk and Fremont;" Tays, "Fremont Had No Secret Instructions;" Hawgood, "John Charles Fremont."

10. Rippy, *United States and Mexico*, 85.

11. Stout, *Liberators*, chap. 1.

12. Wyllys, *French in Sonora*, 8. See also Stevens, "Forsaken Frontier."

13. Odie B. Faulk, "Colonization Plan," 300.

14. Ibid., 295.

15. Stout, *Liberators*, 29.

16. Comisión Pesquisadora, *Reports of the Committee*, 182–214.

17. See, for example, U.S. Congress, S. Rept. 39, and U.S. Congress, H. Rept. 343.

18. Carbajal later became an important government official in Tamaulipas when the Liberals assumed political power in that state. He also distinguished himself against the French during the occupation of Mexico in the 1860s. Zorrilla, *Historia de las relaciones* 1: 298, 301, 302; Rippy, *United States and Mexico*, 89–90; Utley, *International Boundary*, 64.

19. Wyllys, *French in Sonora*, chap. 3.

20. Ibid.; Stout, *Liberators*, chaps. 4–5. Other significant contemporary French expeditions into Mexico:

1851–52   Charles de Pindray leads over 150 Frenchmen in colonization effort in Sonora, which initially has the permission of Mexican officials. Suspicious of Pindray's motives, however, the government subsequently withholds support, leading to the disintegration of the colony.

1855   Apparently intending to revolutionize Mexico's northwestern frontier, Admiral Jean Napoleon Zerman leads a band of Frenchmen and Americans to Baja California but is unsuccessful.

21. Walker managed to get elected president of Nicaragua in 1856, and backed by American southerners who wished to see Nicaragua become another U.S. slave state, he stayed in power until 1857. He returned to the United States and in 1860 made two other attempts to invade Central America. He was executed in Honduras that same year. See Green, *Filibuster*; and Brown, *Agents of Manifest Destiny*, chaps. 8–19.

22. Forbes, *Crabb's Filibustering Expeditions*.

23. *U.S. Statutes at Large*, sec. 6.

24. Zorrilla, *Historia de las relaciones* 1:310–13.

25. Rippy, *United States and Mexico*, 96, 102, 171–72.

26. Rippy, "Anglo–American Filibusters," 180.

27. Webb, *Texas Rangers*, chap. 10.

28. McPherson, "William McKendree Gwin."

29. Rippy, *United States and Mexico*, 249–51; Ellison, "Anglo-American Plan," 51–52.

30. Webster, "Intrigue on the Rio Grande."

31. Rolle, "Futile Filibustering," 160.

32. Ibid.

33. Fremont's statement appears in the *San Diego Union*, May 26, 1890. Cited in Rolle, "Futile Filibustering," 165.

34. Martínez, *Border Boom Town*, 19–21.

35. Blaisdell, *Desert Revolution*, 21–37; Chamberlain, "Mexican Colonization," 44.

36. Gerhard, "Socialist Invasion," 295, 302.

37. Cited in Blaisdell, "Revolution or Filibustering?" 150. Seeing the prospect of a rebel victory, two Imperial Valley newspapers urged U.S. acquisition of Baja California.

38. *San Diego Sun*, June 23, 1911. Cited in Blaisdell, *Desert Revolution*, 181.

39. Ibid., 199, 202.

40. Ibid., 148, 203–4.

41. Works that present the filibustering thesis include Gerhard, "Socialist Revolution"; González and Figueroa Domenech, *Revolución y sus heroes*; and Ponce de Leon, *Interinato presidencial de 1911*. Revisionist works that look favorably on the Liberal Party include Blaisdell, "Revolution or Filibustering?"; Blaisdell, *Desert Revolution*; and Martínez, *Historia de Baja California*.

42. Blaisdell, "Harry Chandler," 388.

43. Ibid., 386–93. In *Historia de Baja California* (p. 531), Martínez flatly accuses Chandler of initiating the attempted coup with the intention of detaching Baja California from Mexico in the tradition of earlier filibusters.

44. Chamberlain, "Mexican Colonization," 46–49; Price, *Tijuana*, 52–56.

45. Chamberlain, "Mexican Colonization," 51–53. Quotation appears on p. 52.

46. Ibid., 53–55.

47. See Piñera Ramírez, *Panorama histórico*, chap. 11.

CHAPTER 3

1. Spicer, *Cycles of Conquest*, 12–16.

2. Bannon, *Spanish Borderlands Frontier*, 76–77, 167–89.

3. Spicer, *Cycles of Conquest*, 239–40.

4. Newcomb, *Indians of Texas*, 349.

5. Comisión Pesquisadora de la Frontera del Norte, *Reports of the Committee*, 245–50.

6. Dale, *Indians of the Southwest*, 21.

7. Rippy, *United States and Mexico*, 68–69.

8. Zorrilla, *Historia de las relaciones* 1: 276.

9. Rippy, *United States and Mexico*, 69–70.

10. Comisión Pesquisadora, *Reports of the Committee*, 253–56; Zorrilla, *Historia de las relaciones* 1:290.

11. Bailey, *Indian Slave Trade*, 41–42; Zorrilla, *Historia de las relaciones* 1:284.

12. Rippy, *United States and Mexico*, 76. See also Bancroft, *Arizona and New Mexico*, chap. 26.

13. Webb, *Texas Rangers*, 127–28.

14. Zorrilla, *Historia de las relaciones* 1: 285; Rippy, *United States and Mexico*, 72.

15. Zorrilla, *Historia de las relaciones* 1: 284, 286; Rippy, *United States and Mexico*, 74–75.

16. Garber, *Gadsden Treaty*, 36–38; Rippy, *United States and Mexico*, 76.

17. Zorrilla, *Historia de las relaciones* 1: 283, 279–80; Rippy, *United States and Mexico*, 79–80.

18. Zorrilla, *Historia de las relaciones* 1: 288–89; Garber, *Gadsden Treaty*, 35–40.

19. The detailed record of the Gadsden Treaty negotiations is found in Miller, *Treaties and Other Acts* 6: 293–437. Rippy, *United States and Mexico*, 148, 152–53.

20. Rippy, *United States and Mexico*, 192, 279–80, 282.

21. Congress, S. Rept. 39.

22. Comisión Pesquisadora, *Informe de la Comisión*.

23. Comisión Pesquisadora, *Reports of the Committee*.

24. Cosío Villegas, *Porfiriato*, 271–74.

25. Rippy, "Pershing Expedition," 313–15; Zorrilla, *Historia de las relaciones* 2:75.

26. If a sense of "mission" existed in the Anglo-American approach, it is detected in the desire to make farmers out of the Indians and to improve their lives through technology, yet those policies developed slowly and did not have much impact until the latter nineteenth century. Spicer, *Cycles of Conquest*, 343–44.

27. Garner, "Treaty of Guadalupe Hidalgo," 10–13.

28. Dale, *Indians of the Southwest*, 83, 89.

29. Comisión Pesquisadora, *Reports of the Committee*, 406–16; Rippy, "Border Troubles," 100; Porter, "Seminole in Mexico."

30. Webb, *Texas Rangers*, 135–36.

31. Newcomb, *Indians of Texas*, 341–42.

32. Webb, *Texas Rangers*, 55.

33. Newcomb, *Indians of Texas*, 350–53.

34. Webb, *Texas Rangers*, 161–72; Comisión Pesquisadora, *Reports of the Committee*, 309.

35. Beck and Haase, *Historical Atlas of New Mexico*, 22; Walker and Bufkin, *Historical Atlas of Arizona*, 22; Richardson and Rister, *Greater Southwest*, 276–77.

36. For a detailed narrative of events connected with "The Long Walk" see Bailey, *Long Walk*.

37. Lamar, *Far Southwest*, 438, 446–49.

38. Walker and Bufkin, *Historical Atlas of Arizona*, 42–43; Lamar, *Far Southwest*, 449.

39. The Navajo Reservation had been established in 1868. Hollon, *South-*

west: Old and New, 304; Beck and Haase, *Historical Atlas of New Mexico,* 38; Walker and Bufkin, *Historical Atlas of Arizona,* 42–45.

40. Richardson and Rister, *Greater Southwest,* 323–24; Dale, *Indians of the Southwest,* 111; Spicer, *Cycles of Conquest,* 255–56.

41. Bailey, *Indian Slave Trade,* 59–69.

42. Garner, "Treaty of Guadalupe Hidalgo," 12–13.

43. Dale, *Indians of the Southwest,* 82–89.

44. Dana and Krueger, *California Lands;* 52–53.

45. For surveys of Kickapoo and Yaqui history see Gibson, *Kickapoos;* Latorre and Latorre, *Mexican Kickapoo Indians;* Hu-DeHart, *Missionaries, Miners, and Indians;* and Spicer, *Yaquis.*

46. Latorre and Latorre, *Mexican Kickapoo Indians,* 9, 11–12, 24; U.S. Congress, Rept. 97–684, 13.

47. Latorre and Latorre, *Mexican Kickapoo Indians,* 17–18.

48. Ibid. 24–28.

49. Ibid., 12, 22.

50. Ibid., 24–25.

51. Ibid., 13–14, 25.

52. Jamail, "Indians on the Border," 34–37; Miller, *On the Border,* chap. 6.

53. Public Law 97–429 (H.R. 4496, January 8, 1983), *U.S. Code.*

54. Hu-DeHart, *Missionaries, Miners, and Indians,* 28; Spicer, *Yaquis,* 236.

55. Spicer, *Yaquis,* 236.

56. In 1917, eight Yaquis from Tucson attempted to cross into Mexico intent on fighting the Sonora government, but on the way U.S. cavalry troops intercepted them. Accused of violating American neutrality laws, they were tried in court but were released on condition that they not repeat the action. Spicer, *Pascua,* 21–22.

57. Spicer, *Cycles of Conquest,* 83; Spicer, *Yaquis,* 236.

58. Spicer, *Yaquis,* 235, Spicer, *Pascua,* 18–20.

59. Hu-DeHart, "Resistance and Survival," iii; Hu-DeHart, *Missionaries, Miners, and Indians,* 2.

60. Spicer, "Highlights of Yaqui History," 2–9, 53.

61. Hu-DeHart, *Missionaries, Miners, and Indians,* 2.

62. Ibid. Aside from the Yaquis, many other indigenous groups in the U.S.-Mexico borderlands have successfully resisted assimilation into the white man's world, but of course none have remained culturally intact. Groups like the Mayos, Ópatas, Seris, Pimas, Tarahumaras, Mescaleros, Pueblos, Navajos, Hopis, and the Tohono O'odham have a relatively autonomous existence, although they are perennially afflicted by economic marginalization, poverty, and other social problems.

63. Spicer, "Highlights of Yaqui History," 2; Spicer, *Yaquis,* 329.

64. U.S. Commission on Civil Rights, *Profile of American Indians, 1–2.*

65. *El Paso Herald Post,* May 5, 1983, 1.

66. U.S. Commission on Civil Rights, *Southwest Indian Report,* 2, 53.

67. Ibid., 2–3.

68. *El Paso Herald Post,* May 5, 1983, 1; *Diario de Juárez,* June 2, 1983, 1, 8.

CHAPTER 4

1. U.S. Congress, House, *El Paso Troubles*, 51, 78.

2. See statement of Paso del Norte priest Ramón Ortíz, *Ibid.*, 68–69.

3. Bowden, "Magoffin Salt War"; U.S. Congress, House, *El Paso Troubles*, 68; Sonnichsen, *El Paso Salt War*, 7–8.

4. U.S. Congress, House, *El Paso Troubles*, 14–15.

5. Ibid., 14, 132–34, 137. Determining the citizenship of people who lived in the U.S. border communities often presented problems, as indicated by Captain Thomas Blair of the Fifteenth Infantry: "The Citizenship of some of the [participants in the disturbance] seems to be rather uncertain, as they sometimes live in one side of the border, sometimes on the other, and had resided for some time previous to the riot in Texas and in New Mexico" (Ibid., 58).

Recognition of the strong bonds that linked Mexicans across the border is underscored by the following statements: "The people of one [side of the Rio Grande] are bound to those of the other by more than the ordinary obligation of race and hospitality. They have married and intermarried; their interests are in many respects indentical; their wants and fears spring from the same source and hold them in sympathy; for time out of mind they have reciprocally enjoyed the same feasts and festivities; they are invited by the same religion, and have all the passions and prejudices common to an ignorant [*sic*] people" (Statement of J.P. Hague, Ibid., 50). "Having lived here over 25 years, ever since I have been here, the Mexicans have claimed this country [the El Paso area] as belonging to the Republic of Mexico. I have never been able to prevent or keep the Mexicans of El Paso, Mexico, from herding my lands" (Statement of Joseph Schutz, Ibid., 54).

6. Ibid., 143.

7. Ibid., 153.

8. Ibid., 115.

9. Ibid., 120, 137, 140–141, 146.

10. Ibid., 152.

11. Sonnichsen, *El Paso Salt War*, 4.

12. Martínez, *Fragments of the Mexican Revolution*, 137–40, 145–48.

13. Crisp, "Anglo-Texan Attitudes," 90–92, 96.

14. Ibid., 325–26.

15. Ibid., 340, 392, 396; Tijerina, "Tejanos and Texas," 319–20.

16. Tijerina, "Tejanos and Texas," 318.

17. *Morning Star* (Houston), May 28, 1942. Cited in Crisp, "Anglo-Texan Attitudes," 387–88.

18. *Personal Memoirs of Seguín*, 1.

19. Ibid., 1, 8, 10–11.

20. Ibid.; Crisp, "Anglo-Texan Attitudes," 368–69, 399–403.

21. The unique characteristics of the Lower Rio Grande Valley as a closely integrated and independent-minded region are discussed in Rosenbaum, *Mexican Resistance*, 35–39.

22. Goldfinch, "Juan N. Cortina," 23–24, 37; Webb, *Texas Rangers*, 193.

23. Acuña, *Occupied America*, 34.

24. Goldfinch, "Juan N. Cortina," 25; Canales, *New Trial*, 6; U.S. Congress, House, *Southwestern Frontier*, 72.

25. U.S. Congress, House, *Southwestern Frontier*, 82.

26. Ibid., 71–72.

27. Goldfinch, "Juan N. Cortina," 62–63; Acuña, *Occupied America*, 37.

28. The defamation of the Mexican character by American fiction writers as well as the print and visual media has been well documented. See Paredes, "Mexican in American Literature"; De León, *They Called Them Greasers*; Pettit, *Images of the Mexican American*; Robinson, *Ears of Strangers*; Robinson, *Hispanic Southwest in American Literature*; and Martínez, "Advertising and Racism."

29. Additional terms used by Mexican Americans to refer to themselves have included "Spanish American," "Latin American," "Hispano," and "Latino." Some regional variants are "Tejano," "Nuevo Mexicano," and "Californio."

30. *New York Times*, May 4, 1969, 78; Saxbe v. Bustos, 419 U.S. 65 (1974).

31. *El Paso Herald Post*, Nov. 22, 1974, sec. A, 1.

32. The following incident is an example of Chicano contempt for Mexican currency. As I prepared to pay the donation at a community fundraiser in El Paso in mid-1983, a prominent Chicano elected official boasted that the event was raising lots of money, that among the bills stuffed in the collection box there was even *"uno de cien bolas"* (one one-hundred-denomination bill). He then asked the person in charge of taking the money to show me the big bill. She dug into the box and produced a one-hundred-peso note and they both smiled wryly.

33. Mexico's problems, of course, are a product of complex forces frequently not understood or deliberately ignored by many people. Just as Americans in general fail to appreciate the worldwide drop in oil prices, the recurring recessions in the global economy, and other external factors that account largely for Mexico's misfortune, so do many Chicanos. Critics fall back instead on negative stereotypes to explain conditions in the neighboring country.

34. One example is Ruben Bonilla, Chairman of the Texas Mexican American Democrats and ex–LULAC National President, who called on the Mexican government to annul the 1986 Chihuahua elections.

35. The feelings of Chicanos toward Mexico are explored in De la Garza, "Chicano Perspective of Mexico."

36. De la Garza, "Chicanos and U.S. Foreign Policy." See also Juan N. Vásquez, "Mexico-Chicano Political Dialogue Fades," *Los Angeles Times*, Aug. 12, 1983.

CHAPTER 5

1. The literature on northern Mexico is vast, but few efforts have been made to seriously examine the history of the region and its relationship to the rest of Mexico. The recent outpouring of works on border problems by Mexican writers clearly illustrates Mexico's preoccupation with conditions in the

border states. Helpful sources for the understanding of the North include Bannon, *Spanish Borderlands Frontier*; Escoto Ochoa, *Nuestra frontera norte*; Flores Caballero, *Evolución de la frontrea norte*; Gonzáles Salazar, *Frontera del norte*; León-Portilla, "Norteño Variety of Mexican Culture"; Martínez, *Border Boom Town*; Martínez, *Fragments of the Mexican Revolution*; Martínez, *Historia de Baja California*; Ojeda, *Desarrollo de la frontera norte*; Sepulveda, *Frontera norte de México*; Weber, *Mexican Frontier*.

2. Details of how the PRI rigged the elections in Sonora are given in the *Financial Times of London*, July 16, 1985, 34.

3. The strategy formulated by the PRI to recapture Chihuahua is detailed in *Proceso*, July 7, 1986, 6–10. Interestingly, this article was published a few days *before* the elections (held on July 6), which gave voters advance notice of what the ruling party would do to "win." The widespread evidence of fraud gathered by civic groups during the elections is contained in Comité de Lucha por la Democracia, *Chihuahua '86.*

4. *Diario de Juárez*, July 14, 1986, 2, and Aug. 10, 1986, 1.

5. For reports on the demonstrations and the bridge takeovers, see the *El Paso Herald Post*, July 12, 1986, sec. A, 1; *El Paso Times*, Aug. 4, 1986, sec. A, 1; *Diario de Juárez*, Aug. 10, 1986, 1, and Aug. 18, 1986, sec. A, 2.

6. Their stay in El Paso lasted two weeks, after which they returned to Parral upon being assured that they would not be arrested. *El Paso Herald Post*, Aug. 21, 1986, sec. A, 1; *Diario de Juárez*, Aug. 31, 1986, 1.

7. *Diario de Juárez*, Aug. 10, 1986, sec. A, 1.

8. Meyer and Sherman, *Course of Mexican History*, 446–47.

9. Martínez, *Border Boom Town*, 10–13. The historical background of the border communities presented in this section is based largely on *Border Boom Town*.

10. *Programa Nacional Fronterizo*; Secretaría de Industria y Comercio, *Estudio del Desarrollo Comercial.*

11. *Proceso*, Oct. 11, 1982; Alm, "Economic Crisis Shows Links across the Border," *Dallas Morning News*, Feb. 27, 1983, sec. A.

12. Martínez, *Border Boom Town*, 29–31.

13. *Kansas City Star*, July 21, 1930.

14. The role of the Mexican border cities in providing cheap labor for the American borderlands is explained in Martínez, "Chicanos and the Border Cities."

15. *Washington Post*, April 20, 1986.

16. El Paso Chamber of Commerce, *El Paso Area Fact Book*, 12: 1.

17. The history of Mexican migration to the United States is treated in the following works: Cardoso, *Mexican Emigration*; Corwin, *Immigrants and Immigrants*; Cross and Sandos, *Across the Border*; Reisler, *Sweat of Their Brow*; Samora, *Los Mojados.*

18. Cited in Weber, *Mexican Frontier*, 207.

19. *Revista Novedades*, Feb. 14, 1948.

20. *A Toda Máquina*, March 1954.

21. *Norte*, Aug. 31, 1957.

22. On North American cultural influences in the Mexican border region and suggested strategies for dealing with the "problem," see Castellanos

Guerrero y López y Rivas, "Influencia norteamericana"; Mendoza Berrueto, "Algunos aspectos socioeconómicos," especially pp. 58–67.

23. Hidalgo, *Language Attitudes*, 8–9.

24. Ibid. An interesting project at the state level is former Chihuahua Governor Manuel Ornelas's creation of a Centro de Estudios Musicales (Center for the Study of Music) in Chihuahua City to facilitate the learning of Mexican classical music. By elevating the taste of youth for national forms, the governor hoped to counteract the constant onslaught of rock music from the United States. *Diario de Juárez*, June 8, 1984.

25. Bustamante, "Identidad nacional."

26. *Wall Street Journal*, May 27, 1986.

CHAPTER 6

1. Rice and Bernard, *Sunbelt Cities*, 11–15.

2. Ibid., 16–20.

3. I thank Larry McConville, Research Associate at the Center for Inter-American and Border Studies, University of Texas at El Paso, for his contributions to this section.

4. To provide the energy for the enormous consumption of electricity for air conditioners in the Phoenix area, large parts of Arizona and New Mexico have been mined for coal. The extraction of coal from the Four Corners area and the Colorado Plateau has had considerable impact upon the landscape.

5. Hundley, *Water and the West*.

6. The El Paso–New Mexico dispute has received extensive coverage in the El Paso and Albuquerque newspapers. See, for example, *El Paso Times*, June 4, 1983, sec. A, and Dec. 31, 1984, sec. A; *El Paso Herald Post*, Aug. 4, 1984, sec. A; *Albuquerque Journal*, Dec. 11, 1983, sec. B.

7. Hundley, *Dividing the Waters*; Sepulveda, *Frontera norte de México*, Chaps. 12–14.

8. *Symposium on U.S.-Mexican Transboundary Resources*; Ross, *Ecology and Development*, Chap. 4.

9. Day, "International Aquifer Management"; *El Paso Herald Post*, Dec. 5, 1983, sec. A; Jamail and Mumme, "Disputing Hidden Waters."

10. The seriousness of the water problem in Juárez is reflected in the following headlines from the *Diario de Juárez*: "Grave Escasés de Agua Amenaza a 42 Colonias" ("Grave Scarcity of Water Threatens 42 Neighborhoods"), April 15, 1985; "Crece la Tensión Social por Falta de Agua" ("Social Tension Rises as a Result of Lack of Water"), June 8, 1985; "Mueren Deshidratados dos Niños cada Día" ("Two Children Die from Dehydration Daily"), June 9, 1985; "Sin Gota de Agua las Partes Altas" ("The High Areas Are without a Drop of Water"), June 11, 1985.

11. Undated article from the *Washington Post*, reprinted in *Estudios Fronterizos*, 83–84.

12. *Los Angeles Times*, Sept. 26, 1983, Feb. 22, 1987.

13. Call, "Survey of Environmental Problems."

14. Martínez, *Border Boom Town*, 80–82. The Institute of Oral History at the University of Texas at El Paso has an extensive collection of tape-recorded interviews that document many problems encountered by Mexicans crossing the international border.

15. Kristein, "Anglo over Bracero," 145–49.

16. The "Tortilla Curtain" incident is discussed in Stoddard, Martínez, and Martínez Lasso, *El Paso–Ciudad Juárez Relations*.

17. Martínez, "Frontera vista por Mascareñas Miranda," 287–88.

18. The latter argument has been articulated by Dr. Arthur F. Corwin in an unpublished manuscript (June 1985) sent to then–U.S. Secretary of State Henry Kissinger. Corwin warned that one very possible consequence of continued large-scale Mexican immigration into the United States would be the emergence of a "Chicano Quebec" in the area bordering with Mexico. Corwin, "America's Immigration Dilemma," 19–22.

19. Cornelius, *Mexican Migration*; Villalpando et al., *Socioeconomic Impact of Illegal Aliens*; Community Research Associates, *Undocumented Immigrants*; Weintraub and Cardenas, *Use of Public Services*.

20. Stoddard, *Patterns of Poverty*, 2.

21. Ibid.

22. *Los Angeles Times*, June 9, 1975. Hidalgo county in the Texas Lower Rio Grande Valley reported the highest incidences of the diseases named.

23. Martínez, "Chicanos and the Border Cities," 105.

24. Bell and Smallwood, *Zona Libre*.

25. Martínez, *Border Boom Town*.

26. Ibid., 66, 78–82.

27. Ibid., 124–25.

28. Ibid.

29. For an analysis of the effect of drug trafficking on U.S.-Mexico relations, see Lupsha and Schlegel, "Drug Trafficking."

30. Cruz Soto, "Operación Interceptación."

31. *El Diario de Juárez*, Feb. 21, 1985.

32. *El Diario de Juárez*, Jan. 15, 1984, and May 30, 1984; *El Paso Herald Post*, Dec. 31, 1984; *El Paso Times*, July 15, 1985, and July 26, 1986.

33. For a survey of commissions that have functioned along the border over the years, see Reeves, *U.S.-Mexico Border Commission*.

AFTERWORD

1. Hansen, "Comparative Perspective," 9.

2. Briner, "Regio Basiliensis."

3. Such sentiments emerged in a report issued by the San Diego, California, grand jury in April 1984 that called bilingual education "impractical, expensive and in a sense un-American." Claiming that bilingual education programs waste millions of dollars that could be better spent for other purposes, the

grand jury urged the San Diego County Board of Supervisors to seek a constitutional amendment that would establish English as the official language of the United States. The report drew an immediate strong rebuttal from Mexican American organizations, with the result that ethnic frictions were once again rekindled unnecessarily. *Hispanic Monitor*, July 1984, 4–5.

4. See the *El Paso Times*, Oct. 13, 1985, sec. F, for the text of Bennett's statement, along with a rebuttal from Raul Izaguirre, president of the National Council for La Raza.

5. Stoddard, "Northern Mexican Migration," 64.

6. Ibid.

BIBLIOGRAPHY

PRIMARY SOURCES

Bartlett, John Russell. *Personal Narrative of Explorations and Incidents in Texas, New Mexico, California, Sonora, and Chihuahua.* 2 vols. New York and London: D. Appleton and Co., 1854.

Comisión Pesquisadora de la Frontera del Norte. *Reports of the Committee of Investigation Sent in 1873 by the Mexican Government to the Frontier of Texas.* New York: Baker and Goodwin, 1875. (Translation of original report: *Informe de la Comisión Pesquisadora de la Frontera del Norte al Ejecutivo de la Unión.* México, D.F.: 1874.)

El Paso Chamber of Commerce. *El Paso Area Fact Book, 1981–1982.* El Paso, 1982.

Los Angeles Times. Poll No. 65 (Latinos). February 1983.

Personal Memoirs of John N. Seguín, from the Year 1834 to the Retreat of General Woll from the City of San Antonio, 1842. San Antonio, Tex.: The Ledger Book and Job Office, 1852. Typescript in Barker Library, University of Texas at Austin.

Programa Nacional Fronterizo. México, D.F., 1961.

Secretaría de Industria y Comercio, *Estudio del desarrollo comercial de la frontera norte.* México, D.F., 1972.

U.S. Bureau of the Census. *Census of Population: General Social and Economic Characteristics,* United States Summary and State Reports, 1980.

U.S. Code Congressional and Administrative News, 9th Cong., 2d sess. Vol. 2, St. Paul: West Publishing Co., 1982.

U.S. Commission on Civil Rights. *Socio-economic Profile of American Indians in Arizona and New Mexico.* Washington, D.C., 1972.

———. *The Southwest Indian Report.* Washington, D.C., 1973.

U.S. Congress. House. *Difficulties on the Southwestern Frontier.* 36th Cong., 1st sess., 1860. H. Exec. Doc. 52.

———. *Troubles on the Texas Frontier.* 36th Cong., 1st sess., 1860. H. Exec. Doc. 81.

———. *El Paso Troubles in Texas.* 45th Cong., 2d sess., 1878. H. Exec. Doc. 93.

———. H. Rept. 343. Serial 1709. 44th Cong., 1st sess., 1876.

U.S. Congress. Senate. S. Misc. Doc. 241. 35th Cong., 1st sess., 1858.

———. S. Rept. 39. Serial 1565. 42d Cong., 3d sess., 1872.

———. S. Rept. 97–684. 97th Cong., 2d sess., 1982.

U.S. National Archives. Selected correspondence and documents.

U.S. State Department. *The Chamizal Settlement.* Washington, D.C., 1963.

NEWSPAPERS AND MAGAZINES

Albuquerque Journal: December 11, 1983.
A Toda Máquina (Ciudad Juárez, México): March 1954.
Dallas Morning News: February 27, 1983.
Diario de Juárez (Ciudad Juárez, México): 1983–86.
El Fronterizo (Ciudad Juárez, México): June 9, 1983.
El Paso Herald Post: January 2, 1936; November 22, 1974; 1983–86.
El Paso Times: April 15, 1937; 1983–86.
Financial Times of London: July 16, 1985.
Hispanic Monitor:: July 1984.
Kansas City Star: July 21, 1930.
Los Angeles Times: June 9, 1975; August 12, 1983; September 26, 1983.
The Monitor (McAllen, Texas): April 21, 1983.
New York Times: May 4, 1969.
Norte (Ciudad Juárez, México): August 31, 1957.
Proceso (México): October 11, 1982; July 7, 1986.
Revista Novedades (Ciudad Juárez, México): February 14, 1948.
Wall Street Journal: May 27, 1986.
Washington Post: April 20, 1986.

SECONDARY SOURCES

Unpublished Sources

Bustamante, Jorge. "Identidad nacional en la frontera norte de México: Hallazgos preliminares." Centro de Estudios Fronterizos del Norte de México, Tijuana, México, 1983.

Corwin, Arthur F. "America's Immigration Dilemma; With Special Reference to Mexico." June 1975.

Crisp, James Ernest. "Anglo-Texan Attitudes toward the Mexican, 1821–1845." Ph.D. diss., Yale University, 1976.

Cruz Soto, Gustavo. "Efectos económicos de la Operación Interceptación en Ciudad Juárez." Tesis, Universidad Nacional Autónoma de México, 1972.

De la Garza, Rodolfo O. "A Chicano Perspective of Mexico." Author's files, n.d.

———. "Texas Land Grants and U.S.-Mexican-Chicano Relations: A study in Linkage Politics." Paper presented at the meeting of the Latin American Studies Association, Mexico City, October 1, 1983.

Friedkin, J. F. "The International Boundary and Water Commission, United States and Mexico." Paper presented at the UCLA Chicano Studies Center Symposium on U.S.-Mexico Border Relations, Santa Monica, California, April 24, 1981.

Griswold del Castillo, Richard. "La Frontera and the Border: Mexican and American Historical Views of the Mexican American Frontier." Paper presented at the Border Governors' Conference, Tijuana, Mexico, September 20–21, 1982.

Hu-DeHart, Evelyn. "Resistance and Survival: A History of the Yaqui People's Struggle for Autonomy, 1533–1910." Ph.D. diss., University of Texas at Austin, 1976.

Kristein, Peter N. "Anglo over Bracero: A History of the Mexican Worker in the United States from Roosevelt to Nixon." Ph.D. diss., St. Louis University, 1973.

Lupsha, Peter A., and Kip Schlegel. "Drug Trafficking in the Borderlands: Its Impact on North/South Relations." Paper presented at the meeting of the Latin American Studies Association, Pittsburgh, April 5–9, 1979.

Martínez, Oscar J. "La frontera vista por René Mascareñas Miranda: Entrevista de historia oral." Institute of Oral History, University of Texas at El Paso.

Paredes, Raymund. "The Image of the Mexican in American Literature." Ph.D. diss., University of Texas at Austin, 1974.

Salazar, Robert J., et al. *Asociación de Reclamantes v. The United Mexican States: Texas Land Grants Heirs Seek Justice.* 1981.

Stevens, Robert C. "Forsaken Frontier: A History of Sonora, Mexico, 1821–1851." Ph.D. diss., University of California, Berkeley, 1963.

Tijerina, Andrew Anthony. "Tejanos and Texas: The Native Mexicans of Texas, 1820–1850." Ph.D. diss., University of Texas at Austin, 1977.

U.S. Immigration and Naturalization Service. Unpublished statistical reports. Author's files.

Webster, Michael G. "Texas Manifest Destiny and the Mexican Border Conflict, 1865–1880." Ph.D. diss., Indiana University, 1972.

Books, Articles, and Reports

Acuña, Rodolfo. *Occupied America: A History of Chicanos.* 2d ed. New York: Harper and Row, 1981.

Alisky, Marvin. "Mexican Border Conflicts and Compromises." *Southeastern Latin Americanist* 17, No. 2 (1973): 1–5.

Asiwaju, Anthony I., ed. *Partitioned Africans: Studies in Ethnic Relations across Africa's International Boundaries, 1884–1984.* London: C. Hurst and Company, 1984.

Bailey, Lynn R. *Indian Slave Trade in the Southwest.* Los Angeles: Westernlore Press, 1966.

———. *The Long Walk: A History of the Navajo Wars, 1846–1868.* Pasadena, Calif.: Socio-Technical Books, 1970.

Bancroft, Hubert Howe. *Works.* Vol. 27, *History of Arizona and New Mexico, 1530–1888.* San Francisco: The History Company, 1889.

Bannon, John Francis. *The Spanish Borderlands Frontier, 1513–1821.* New York: Holt, Rinehart, and Winston, 1970.

Beck, Warren A., and Ynez D. Haase. *Historical Atlas of New Mexico.* Norman: University of Oklahoma Press, 1969.

164   *Bibliography*

Bell, Samuel E., and James M. Smallwood. *The Zona Libre, 1858–1905: A Problem in American Diplomacy.* Southwestern Studies Monograph no. 69, El Paso: Texas Western Press, 1982.

Benjamin, Thomas. "Recent Historiography of the Origins of the Mexican War." *New Mexico Historical Review* 54, no. 3 (1979): 169–81.

Benjamin, Thomas, and William McNellie, eds. *Other Mexicos: Essays on Regional Mexican History, 1876–1911.* Albuquerque: University of New Mexico Press, 1984.

Billington, Ray Allen. *Westward Expansion: A History of the American Frontier.* New York: Macmillan, 1960.

Binkley, William C. *The Expansionist Movement in Texas.* Berkeley: University of California Press, 1925.

Blaisdell, Lowell J. *The Desert Revolution: Baja California, 1911.* Madison: University of Wisconsin Press, 1962.

———. "Harry Chandler and Mexican Border Intrigue." *Pacific Historical Review* 35, no. 4 (November 1966): 385–93.

———. "Was It Revolution or Filibustering? The Mystery of the Flores Magón Revolt in Baja California." *Pacific Historical Review* 23, no. 2 (May 1954): 147–64.

Bowden, J. J. "The Magoffin Salt War." *Password* (El Paso County Historical Society) 8, no. 3 (Summer 1963): 95–121.

———. *Spanish and Mexican Land Grants in the Chihuahuan Acquisition.* El Paso: Texas Western Press, 1971.

Briner, Hans. "The Regio Basiliensis: A Model of Transfrontier Cooperation." In *Across Boundaries: Transborder Interaction in Perspective*, edited by Oscar J. Martínez, 45–53. El Paso: Texas Western Press, 1986.

Brooks, Philip C. *Diplomacy and the Borderlands: The Adams-Onis Treaty, 1819.* Berkeley: University of California Press, 1939.

Brown, Charles H. *Agents of Manifest Destiny: The Lives and Times of the Filibusters.* Chapel Hill: University of North Carolina Press, 1979.

Call, Frank J. "A Survey of Environmental Problems along the U.S.-Mexico Border." In *Air Quality Issues in El Paso–Cd. Juarez Border Region*, edited by Willard P. Gingerich, 1–3. Center for Inter-American and Border Studies, Occasional Paper No. 5, El Paso: University of Texas at El Paso, 1980.

Canales, José T. *Juan N. Cortina Presents His Motion for a New Trial.* San Antonio: Artes Gráficas, 1951; New York: Arno Press, 1974.

Cardoso, Lawrence A. *Mexican Emigration to the United States, 1877–1931.* Tucson: University of Arizona Press, 1980.

Castellanos Guerrero, Alicia, and Gilberto López y Rivas. "La influencia norteamericana en la cultura de la frontera norte de México." In *La frontera del norte: Integración y desarrollo*, edited by Roque González Salazar, 68–84. México, D. F.: El Colegio de México, 1981.

Chamberlain, Eugene Keith. "Mexican Colonization versus American Interests in Lower California." *Pacific Historical Review* 20, no. 1 (February 1951): 43–55.

Clendenen, Clarence C. *Blood on the Border: The United States Army and the Mexican Irregulars.* New York: MacMillan, 1969.

Coerver, Don M. "From Morteritos to Chamizal: The U.S.-Mexican Boundary Treaty of 1884." *Red River Valley Historical Review* 2, no. 4 (1975): 531–38.

Comité de la Lucha por la Democracia. *Chihuahua '86. ¿Vencedores del desierto o asesinos de la democracia?* 1986.

Community Research Associates. *Undocumented Immigrants: Their Impact on the County of San Diego.* San Diego, Calif.: Community Research Associates, 1980.

Connor, Seymour V., and Odie B. Faulk. *North America Divided: The Mexican War, 1846–1848.* New York: Oxford University Press, 1971.

Cornelius, Wayne A. *Mexican Migration to the United States: Causes, Consequences, and U.S. Responses.* Cambridge: Massachusetts Institute of Technology Center for International Studies, 1978.

Corwin, Arthur F., ed. *Immigrants and Immigrants: Perspectives on Mexican Labor Migration to the United States.* Westport, Conn.: Greenwood Press, 1978.

Cosío Villegas, Daniel. *Historia moderna de México. Vol. 6, El Porfiriato: La vida política exterior.* México, D.F.: Editorial Hermes, 1955–70.

Cox, I. J. "The Southwest Boundary of Texas." *Quarterly of the Texas State Historical Association (Southwestern Historical Quarterly)* 6, no. 2 (October 1902): 81–102.

Cross, Harry E., and James E. Sandos. *Across the Border: Rural Development in Mexico and Recent Migration to the United States.* Berkeley: Institute of Government Studies, U.C. Berkeley, 1981.

Cue Canovas, Agustín. *Los Estados Unidos y el México olvidado.* México, D.F.: B. Costa-Amic, 1970; New York: Arno Press, 1976.

Dale, Edward E. *The Indians of the Southwest: A Century of Development under the United States.* Norman: University of Oklahoma Press, 1949.

Dana, Samuel Trach, and Myron Krueger. *California Lands: Ownership, Use, and Management.* Washington, D.C.: The American Forestry Association, 1958.

Day, J. C. "International Aquifer Management: The Hueco Bolson and the Rio Grande River." *Natural Resources Journal* 18 (January 1978): 168–69.

De la Garza, Rodolfo O. "Chicanos and U.S. Foreign Policy: The Future of Chicano-Mexican Relations." *The Western Political Quarterly* 33, no. 4 (December 1980): 571–82.

De la Garza, Rudolph O., Z. Anthony Kruszewski, and Tomás A. Arciniega. *Chicanos and Native Americans: The Territorial Minorities.* Englewood Cliffs, N.J.: Prentice-Hall, 1973.

De León, Arnoldo. *The Tejano Community, 1836–1900.* Albuquerque: University of New Mexico Press, 1982.

———. *They Called Them Greasers: Anglo Attitudes toward Mexicans in Texas, 1821–1900.* Austin: University of Texas Press, 1983.

Demaris, Ovid. *Poso del Mundo.* New York: Pocket Books, 1971.

Ellison, Simon J. "An Anglo-American Plan for the Colonization of Mexico." *Southwestern Social Science Quarterly* 16, no. 2 (1935–36): 42–52.

Escoto Ochoa, Humberto. *Integración y desintegración de nuestra frontera norte.* México, D.F.: Universidad Nacional Autónoma de México, 1949.

Estudios Fronterizos. México, D.F.: ANUIES, 1981.

Faulk, Odie B. "A Colonization Plan for Northern Sonora, 1850." *New Mexico Historical Review* 44, no. 4 (October 1969): 293–314.

Faulk, Odie B. *Too Far North, Too Far South.* Los Angeles: Westernlore Press, 1967.

Faulk, Odie B., and Joseph A. Stout, Jr., eds. *The Mexican War: Changing Interpretations.* Chicago: Sage Books, 1973.

Fernández, Raúl A. *The United States–Mexico Border: A Politico-Economic Profile.* Notre Dame, Ind.: University of Notre Dame Press, 1977.

Fidler, John D. *The Movement for the Acquisition of All Mexico, 1846–1848.* Baltimore, Md.: Johns Hopkins University Press, 1936.

Flores Caballero, Romeo. *Evolución de la frontera norte.* Monterrey, México: Universidad Autónoma de Nuevo León, 1982.

Forbes, Robert H. *Crabbs's Filibustering Expeditions into Sonora, 1857: A Historical Account.* Tucson: Arizona Silhouettes, 1952.

Fuller, John D. P. *The Movement for the Acquisition of All Mexico.* Baltimore, Md.: Johns Hopkins University Press, 1936.

Garber, Paul Neff. *The Gadsden Treaty.* Philadelphia: University of Pennsylvania Press, 1923.

García Cantú, Gastón. *Las invasiones norteamericanas en México.* México, D.F.: Ediciones Era, 1971.

Garner, Van Hastings. "The Treaty of Guadalupe Hidalgo and the California Indians." *The Indian Historian* 9, no. 1 (Winter 1976): 10–13.

Gerhard, Peter. "The Socialist Invasion of Baja California, 1911." *Pacific Historical Review* 15, no. 3 (September 1946): 295–304.

Gibson, Arrell M. *The Kickapoos: Lords of the Middle Border.* Norman: University of Oklahoma Press, 1963.

Gibson, Lay James, and Alfonso Corona Rentería, eds. *The U.S. and Mexico: Borderland Development and the National Economies.* Boulder, Colo.: Westview Press, 1985.

Goetzmann, W. H. "The United States–Mexican Boundary Survey, 1848–1853." *Southwestern Historical Quarterly* 62 (1958–59): 164–90.

Goldfinch, Charles W. "Juan N. Cortina, 1824–1892: A Re-Appraisal." Master's thesis, University of Chicago, 1949; New York: Arno Press, 1974.

González, Antonio P., and J. Figueroa Domenech. *La Revolución y sus héroes.* México, D.F.: 1911.

González Salazar, Roque, ed. *La frontera del norte: Integración y desarrollo.* México: El Colegio de México, 1981.

Gregg, Robert D. *The Influence of Border Troubles on Relations between the United States and Mexico, 1876–1910.* Baltimore, Md.: Johns Hopkins Press, 1937.

Green, Lawrence. *The Filibuster: The Career of William Walker.* Indianapolis: Bobbs-Merrill Co., 1937.

Hackett, Charles W., ed. *Richardo's Treatise on the Limits of Louisiana and Texas.* 3 vols. Austin: University of Texas Press, 1931–34.

Hansen, Niles. "Comparative Perspective on Border Region Development in Western Europe and in the U.S.-Mexico Borderlands." In *Across Boundaries: Transborder Interaction in Perspective,* edited by Oscar J. Martínez, 31–44. El Paso: Texas Western Press, 1985.

Hawgood, J. A. "John Charles Fremont and the Bear Flag Revolution: A Reappraisal." *Southern California Quarterly* 44, nos. 1–4 (1962): 67–96.

Hidalgo, Margarita. *Language Attitudes and Language Use in Ciudad Juárez, México.* Center for Inter-American and Border Studies, Border Issues and Public Policy Reports, no. 17, El Paso: University of Texas, October 1984.

Hinojosa, Gilberto Miguel. *A Borderlands Town in Transition: Laredo, 1755–1810.* College Station: Texas A & M Press, 1983.

Hollon, William Eugene. *The Southwest: Old and New.* New York: Knopf, 1961.

Horgan, Paul. *Great River: The Rio Grande in North American History.* 2 vols. New York: Rinehart, 1954.

House, John W. *Frontier on the Rio Grande: A Political Geography of Development and Social Deprivation.* New York: Oxford University Press, 1982.

Hu-DeHart, Evelyn. *Missionaries, Miners, and Indians: Spanish Contact with the Yaqui Nation of Northwestern New Spain, 1533–1820.* Tucson: University of Arizona Press, 1981.

Hundley, Norris, Jr. *Dividing the Waters: A Century of Controversy between the United States and Mexico.* Berkeley: University of California Press, 1966.

———. *Water and the West: The Colorado River Compact and the Politics of Water in the American West.* Berkeley: University of California Press, 1976.

Jackson, Donald, ed. *Zebulon Montgomery Pike, 1779–1813. Journals, with Letters and Related Documents.* Norman: University of Oklahoma Press, 1966.

Jamail, Milton H. "Indians on the Border." *Indian Historian* 10, no. 3 (1977): 34–37.

Jamail, Milton H., and Stephen H. Mumme. "Disputing Hidden Waters: Groundwater along the U.S.-Mexico Border." *The New Scholar* 9 (1984): 215–30.

Jones, Stephen B. "Boundary Concepts in the Setting of Place and Time." *Annals* (of the Association of American Geographers) 46, no. 3 (September 1959): 241–55.

Kendall, George W. *Narrative of the Texas Santa Fe Expedition.* 2 vols. Edited by Milo M. Quaife. London: 1848; Chicago: University of Chicago Press, 1929; Austin: University of Texas Press, 1935.

Kristof, K. D. "The Nature of Frontiers and Boundaries." *Annals* (of the Association of American Geographers) 49 (September 1959): 269–82.

Lamar, Howard Roberts. *The Far Southwest, 1846–1912.* New York: Norton, 1970.

Lambert, Paul F. "The 'All-Mexico' Movement." In *The Mexican War: Changing Interpretations,* edited by Odie B. Faulk and Joseph A. Stout, Jr., 163–72. Chicago: Sage Books, 1973.

Lattimore, Owen D. "The Frontier in History." In *Theory in Anthropology: A Sourcebook,* edited by Robert A. Manners and David Kaplaw, 374–86. Chicago: Aldine, 1968.

Latorre, Dolores L., and Felipe A. Latorre. *The Mexican Kickapoo Indians.* Austin: University of Texas Press, 1976.

León-Portilla, Miguel. "The Norteño Variety of Mexican Culture: An Ethnohistorical Approach." In *Plural Society in the Southwest,* edited by Edward H.

Spicer and Raymond H. Thompson, 77–114. New York: Weatherhead Foundation, 1972.

Leonard, Glen M. "Southwestern Boundaries and the Principles of Statemaking." *The Western Historical Quarterly* 8 (January 1977): 39–53.

Liss, Sheldon. *A Century of Disagreement: The Chamizal Conflict, 1864–1964.* Washington, D.C.: University Press, 1965.

Loomis, Noel M. *The Texas-Santa Fe Pioneers.* Norman: University of Oklahoma Press, 1958.

McPherson, Hallie M. "The Plan of William McKendree Gwin for a Colony in North Mexico, 1863–1865." *Pacific Historical Review* 2, no. 2 (December 1933): 357–86.

McWilliams, Carey. *North from Mexico.* New York: Greenwood Press, 1968.

Martínez, Orlando. *The Great Landgrab: The Mexican-American War, 1846–1848.* London: Quartet Books, 1975.

Martínez, Oscar J. *Border Boom Town: Ciudad Juárez since 1848.* Austin: University of Texas Press, 1978.

———. "Chicanos and the Border Cities: An Interpretive Essay." *Pacific Historical Review* 46 (February 1977): 85–106.

———, ed. *Across Boundaries: Transborder Interaction in Perspective.* El Paso: Texas Western Press, 1986.

———, ed. *Fragments of the Mexican Revolution: Personal Accounts from the Border.* Albuquerque: University of New Mexico Press, 1983.

Martínez, Pablo L. *Historia de Baja California.* México: Editorial Baja California, 1956.

Martínez, Tomás M. "Advertising and Racism: The Case of the Mexican American." In *Voices,* edited by Octavio L. Romano-V., 48–58. Berkeley, Calif.: Quinto Sol, 1971.

Medina Castro, Manuel. *El gran despojo (Texas, Nuevo Mexico, California).* México, D.F.: Editorial Diógenes, 1971.

Meinig, Donald W. *Southwest: Three Peoples in Geographical Change, 1600–1970.* New York: Oxford University Press, 1971.

Mendoza Berrueto, Eliseo. "Algunos aspectos socioeconómicos de la frontera norte de la República Mexicana." In *La frontera del norte: Integración y desarrollo,* edited by Roque González Salazar, 46–67. México, D.F.: El Colegio de México, 1981.

Merk, Frederick. "Dissent in the Mexican War." In *Dissent in Three American Wars,* edited by Samuel Eliot Morrison, Frederick Merk, and Frank Freidel, 35–63. Cambridge: Harvard University Press, 1970.

———. *The Monroe Doctrine and American Expansionism, 1843–1849.* New York: Knopf, 1967.

Meyer, Michael, and L. Sherman. *The Course of Mexican History.* New York: Oxford University Press, 1979.

Miller, Hunter, ed. *Treaties and Other Acts of the United States of America.* Vols. 5 and 6. Washington, D.C.: U.S. Department of State, 1937, 1942.

Miller, Tom. *On the Border: Portraits of America's Southwestern Frontier.* New York: Harper and Row, 1981.

Miranda, Mario, and James W. Wilkie, eds. *Reglas del juego y juego sin reglas en la vida fronteriza.* México, D.F.: ANUIES/PROFMEX, 1985.

Mueller, Jerry E. *Restless River: International Law and the Behavior of the Rio Grande.* El Paso: Texas Western Press, 1975.

Myers, John. *The Border Wardens.* Englewood Cliffs, N.J.: Prentice-Hall, 1971.

Nance, Joseph Milton. *After San Jacinto: The Texas-Mexican Frontier, 1836–1841.* Austin: University of Texas Press, 1963.

Nasatir, Abraham P. *Borderland in Retreat: From Spanish Louisiana to the Far Southwest.* Albuquerque: University of New Mexico Press, 1976.

———. "The Shifting Borderlands." *Pacific Historical Review* 34:1 (February 1965): 1–20.

Neuberger, Benjamin. "Natural and Artificial Borders: The African View." *International Problems* (Israel) 17; no. 1 (1978): 95–102.

Newcomb, W. W., Jr. *The Indians of Texas, from Prehistoric to Modern Times.* Austin: University of Texas Press, 1961.

Nostrand, Richard L. *Los Chicanos: Geografía Histórica Regional.* México, D.F.: SepSetentas, 1976.

Ojeda, Mario, ed. *Administración del desarrollo de la frontera norte.* México, D.F.: El Colegio de México, 1982.

Park, Joseph F. "The Apaches in Mexican-American Relations, 1848–1861: A Footnote to the Gadsden Treaty." *Arizona and the West* 3, no. 2 (Summer 1961): 129–46.

Perrigo, Lynn Irwin. *The American Southwest: Its People and Cultures.* New York: Holt, Rinehart and Winston, 1971.

Peters, Donald W. "The Rio Grande Boundary Dispute in American Diplomacy." *Southwestern Historical Quarterly* 54, no. 4 (April 1951): 412–29.

Pettit, Arthur G. *Images of the Mexican American in Fiction and Film.* College Station: Texas A & M University Press, 1980.

Piñera Ramírez, David, ed. *Panorama histórico de Baja California.* Tijuana: Centro de Investigaciones Históricas UNAM-UABC, 1983.

Pletcher, David M. *The Diplomacy of Annexation: Texas, Oregon, and the Mexican War.* Columbia: University of Missouri Press, 1973.

Ponce de León, Gregorio. *El interinato presidencial de 1911.* México, n.d.

Porter, Kenneth W. "The Seminole in Mexico, 1850–1861." *Hispanic American Historical Review* 31, no. 1 (February 1951): 1–36.

Prescott, John R. V. *Boundaries and Frontiers.* Totowa, N.J.: Rowman and Littlefield, 1978.

Price, Glenn W. *Origins of the War with Mexico: The Polk-Stockton Intrigue.* Austin: University of Texas Press, 1967.

Price, John A. *Tijuana: Urbanization in a Border Culture.* Notre Dame, Ind.: University of Notre Dame Press, 1973.

Reeves, T. Zane. *The U.S.-Mexico Border Commissions: An Overview and Agenda for Further Research.* Center for Inter-American and Border Studies, Border Issues and Public Policy Reports, no. 13, El Paso: University of Texas at El Paso, March 1984.

Reich, Peter L., ed. *Statistical Abstract of the United States–Mexico Borderlands.* Los

Angeles: University of California, Los Angeles, Latin American Center Publications, 1984.

Reisler, Mark. "Always the Laborer, Never the Citizen: Anglo Perceptions of the Mexican Immigrant during the 1920's." *Pacific Historical Review* 45 (May 1976): 231–54.

————. *By the Sweat of Their Brow: Mexican Immigrant Labor in the United States, 1900–1940*. Westport, Conn.: Greenwood Press, 1976.

Rice, Bradley R., and Richard M. Bernard, eds. *Sunbelt Cities: Politics and Growth since World War II*. Austin: University of Texas Press, 1983.

Richardson, Rupert Norval, and Carl Coke Rister. *The Greater Southwest*. Glendale, Calif.: Arthur H. Clark Co., 1934.

Rippy, J. Fred. "Anglo-American Filibusters and the Gadsden Treaty." *Hispanic American Historical Review* 2 (May 1922): 155–80.

————. "Border Troubles along the Rio Grande, 1848–1860." *Southwestern Historical Quarterly* 23 (October 1919): 91–111.

————. "The Indians of the Southwest in the Diplomacy of the United States and Mexico, 1848–1853." *Hispanic American Historical Review* 2 (August 1919): 363–96.

————. "Some Precedents of the Pershing Expedition into Mexico." *Southwestern Historical Quarterly* 24, no. 2 (April 1921): 292–316.

————. *The United States and Mexico*. New York: Knopf, 1926.

Rister, Carl Coke. *The Southwestern Frontier, 1865–1881*. Cleveland, Ohio: Arthur H. Clark Co., 1928.

Ritzenthaler, Robert E., and Frederick A. Peterson. *The Mexican Kickapoo Indians*. Westport, Conn.: Greenwood Press, 1970.

Robinson, Cecil. *Mexico and the Hispanic Southwest in American Literature*. Tucson: University of Arizona Press, 1977.

————. *With the Ears of Strangers: The Mexican in American Literature*. Tucson: University of Arizona Press, 1963.

Rolle, Andrew F. "Futile Filibustering in Baja California, 1888–1890." *Pacific Historical Review* 20, no. 2 (May 1951): 159–66.

Rosenbaum, Robert J. *Mexican Resistance in the Southwest: The Sacred Right of Self-Preservation*. Austin: University of Texas Press, 1981.

Ross, Stanley R., ed. *Ecology and Development of the Border Region*. Mexico, D.F.: ANUIES/PROFMEX, 1983.

Ruiz, Ramón Eduardo. "American Imperialism and the Mexican War." In *American Vistas, 1607–1877*, edited by Leonard Dinnestein and Kenneth T. Jackson, 217–28. 3d ed. New York: Oxford University Press, 1979.

Saadia, Touval. *The Boundary Politics of Independent Africa*. Cambridge: Harvard University Press, 1972.

Samora, Julián. *Los Mojados: The Wetback Story*. Notre Dame, Ind.: University of Notre Dame, 1971.

Schmidt, Louis Bernard. "Manifest Opportunity and the Gadsden Purchase." *Arizona and the West* 3, no. 3 (Autumn 1961): 245–64.

Schmitt, Karl M. *Mexico and the United States, 1821–1973: Conflict and Coexistence*. New York: Wiley, 1974.

Sepulveda, César. *La frontera norte de México: Historia, conflictos, 1762–1975.* México, D.F.: Editorial Porrúa, 1976.
————. "Historia y problemas de los límites de México." *Historia Mexicana* 8 (1958): 1–34, 145–74.
————. *Tres ensayos sobre la frontera septentrional de la Nueva España.* México, D.F.: Editorial Porrúa, 1977.
Sierra, Carlos J. *Los indios de la frontera.* México: Ediciones de la Muralla, 1980.
Smith, Justin H. *The War with Mexico.* 2 vols. New York: MacMillan, 1919.
Smith, Ralph A. "Indians in American-Mexican Relations before the War of 1846." *Hispanic American Historical Review* 43, no. 1 (February 1963): 34–64.
Sonnichsen, C. L. *The El Paso Salt War (1877).* El Paso: Carl Hertzog and The Texas Western Press, 1961.
Spicer, Edward H. *Cycles of Conquest: The Impact of Spain, Mexico, and the United States on the Indians of the Southwest, 1533–1960.* Tucson: University of Arizona Press, 1962.
————. "Highlights of Yaqui History." *Indian Historian* 7, no. 2 (1974): 2–9, 53.
————. *Pascua: A Yaqui Village.* Chicago: University of Chicago Press, 1940.
————. *The Yaquis: A Cultural History.* Tucson: University of Arizona Press, 1980.
Stenberg, R. R. "Polk and Fremont, 1845–1846." *Pacific Historical Review* 7 (September 1938): 211–27.
Stoddard, Ellwyn R. "The Adjustment of Mexican American Barrio Families to Forced Housing Relocation." *Social Science Quarterly* 58, no. 4 (March 1973): 749–59.
————. "Northern Mexican Migration and the United States-Mexican Border Region." *New Scholar* 9 (1984): 51–72.
————. *Patterns of Poverty along the U.S.-Mexico Border.* Center for Inter-American and Border Studies, University of Texas at El Paso, 1978.
Stoddard, Ellwyn R., Oscar J. Martínez, and Miguel Angel Martínez Lasso. *El Paso–Ciudad Juárez Relations and the Tortilla Curtain: A Study of Local Adaptation to Federal Border Policies.* El Paso, Tex.: Council on the Arts and Humanities, 1979.
Stout, Joseph Allen, Jr. *The Liberators: Filibustering Expeditions into Mexico, 1848–1862, and the Last Thrust of Manifest Destiny.* Los Angeles: Westernlore Press, 1973.
Strieber, Whitley, and James W. Kunetka. *Warday.* New York: Holt, Rhinehart and Winston, 1984.
Symposium on U.S.-Mexican Transboundary Resources. Special issues, *Natural Resources Journal* 17, no. 4 (October 1977): 543–634; and 18, no. 1 (January 1978): 1–212.
Tays, George. "Fremont Had No Secret Instructions." *Pacific Historical Review* 9 (June 1940): 157–71.
Timmons, W. H. "The El Paso Area in the Mexican Period, 1821–1848." *Southwestern Historical Quarterly* 84, no. 1 (July 1980): 1–28.
Tutorow, Norman E., comp. *The Mexican-American War: An Annotated Bibliography.* Westport, Conn.: Greenwood Press, 1981.
Utley, Robert. *The International Boundary, United States and Mexico: A History of*

Frontier Dispute and Cooperation, 1848–1963. Santa Fe, N.M.: U.S. Department of the Interior, National Park Service, 1964.

Vásquez de Knauth, Josefina. *Mexicanos y norteamericanos ante la guerra del 47.* México, D.F.: Secretaría de Educación Pública, 1972.

Velázquez, María del Carmen. *Establecimiento y pérdida del Septentrión de Nueva España.* México, D.F.: El Colegio de México, 1974.

Villalpando, M. Vic, et al. *A Study of the Socioeconomic Impact of Illegal Aliens on the County of San Diego.* San Diego, Calif.: County of San Diego Human Resources Agency, 1977.

Voss, Stuart F. *On the Periphery of Nineteenth-Century Mexico: Sonora and Sinaloa, 1810–1877.* Tucson: University of Arizona Press, 1982.

Walker, Henry P., and Don Bufkin. *Historical Atlas of Arizona.* Norman: University of Oklahoma Press, 1979.

Warren, Harris Gaylor. *The Sword Was Their Passport: A History of American Filibustering in the Mexican Revolution.* Baton Rouge: Louisiana University Press, 1943.

Wasserman, Mark. *Capitalists, Caciques, and Revolution: The Native Elite and Foreign Enterprise in Chihuahua, Mexico, 1854–1911.* Chapel Hill: University of North Carolina Press, 1984.

Webb, Walter Prescott. *The Texas Rangers: A Century of Frontier Defense.* Austin: University of Texas Press, 1965.

Weber, David J. *The Mexican Frontier, 1821–1846. The American Southwest under Mexico.* Albuquerque: University of New Mexico Press, 1982.

Webster, Michael G. "Intrigue on the Rio Grande: The *Rio Bravo* Affair, 1875." *Southwestern Historical Quarterly* 74, no. 2 (October 1970): 149–64.

Weintraub, Sidney, and Gilberto Cárdenas. *Use of Public Services by Undocumented Aliens in Texas.* Austin: Lyndon B. Johnson School of Public Affairs, 1983.

Weisberg, Albert K. *Manifest Destiny.* Baltimore, Md.: Johns Hopkins University Press, 1935.

Widstrand, Carl Gosta, ed. *African Boundary Problems.* Uppsala, Sweden: Scandanavian Institute of African Studies, 1969.

Wyllys, Rufus Kay. *The French in Sonora (1850–1854): The Story of French Adventurers from California into Mexico.* Berkeley: University of California Press, 1932.

Xirau Icaza, Joaquín. *Nuestra dependencia fronteriza.* México, D.F.: Fondo de Cultura Económica, 1976.

Zavala, Silvio. "La historiografía americana sobre la guerra del '47." *Cuadernos Americanos* 38, no. 2 (March-April 1948): 190–206.

Zorrilla, Luis G. *Historia de las relaciones entre México y los Estados Unidos de América, 1800–1958.* 2 vols. México, D.F.: Editorial Porrúa, 1977.

INDEX

ABOUT THE AUTHOR

OSCAR J. MARTÍNEZ, Professor of History at the University of Texas at El Paso, has also served as Director of the Center for Inter-American and Border Studies and Director of the Institute of Oral History at that institution. His research has focused on the social and economic history of the U.S.-Mexico border region, including the Chicano population in the American Southwest. He has published four other books, as well as numerous articles. He is a former President of the Association of Borderlands Scholars and has held leadership positions in the Latin American Studies Association and the National Association for Chicano Studies.